F*Words

My Life of Film, Food, Feminism, Fun Family, Friends, Flaws, Fabric, and the Far-Out Future

Jeanne Field

Cover Design by Cindy & Steve Vance

Thank you to Adyashanti for permission to use his quotes at the beginning and the end of the book

Thank you to Bob Dylan for permission to use lines from his book, "Tarantula".

Excerpt from THE WATERWORDS by E.L. Doctorow, copyright ©1994 by E.L. Doctorow. Used by permission of Random House, an imprint and division of PenguinRandom House LLC. All rights reserved.

ISBN-10: 0692577262
ISBN-13: 978-0692577264 (Custom Universal)

F*Words

Years ago, when people would ask "What are you into?", an easy answer was, "Things that start with "F"....film, food, fabric....etc. wink wink."

I am a voice of my generation, beginning in the 1940s and continuing until the present. I have lived in remarkable times and have met and befriended remarkable people.

I didn't make these connections out of ambition. I'm adventurous but I'm also practical. Usually, I was just looking for a job and ended up with amazing people with great work ethics. I spent much of my time behind the scenes with people of substance, even genius.

Practicality can lead you to magic.

I am convinced that each person has an amazing story, whether told through a novel like Carol Shields' "The Stone Diaries" or described in terrifying detail in "Anne Frank's Diary".

I was young in the time of extraordinary change in America, post-war and into the '60s and lo and behold, things have been changing rapidly ever since. I'm telling this story because I feel proud and grateful to have witnessed, and even taken part in, many moments of change and beauty.

I hope I'm talking to young women who will see that your life's journey doesn't have to be planned, that you can stay open and resilient and let nothing bring you down.

This book is dedicated to John, cooler than average,
who put glue on the chair.

CONTENTS

Chapter 1

Roving

"Just watch your mind.
You'll hear the story of the myth that you live by.
The nice thing is that it can be rewritten."

It started snowing around three. I'd picked up the kids, Heidi from school and Jimmy from ski school, and was at home on Durant Avenue in Aspen, Colorado, 1/2 block from the Little Nell ski lift in the center of town. The phone rang. It was Bill Harris in from New York for a few days of skiing with some friends. Would I like to join them in the early morning to catch some powder? Absolutely. Lift Number One at 8am.

I'd been in Aspen since November '66 having escaped New York City because of a failed romance and a muddled mind. I left a job in Advertising and Public Relations for The Rover Motor Company of North America, Ltd. in the Chrysler Building and, although my bosses were terrific people, I kept thinking this was not what I was destined to do.

Jimmy McWilliams, an English woman, was an advertising genius working with Howard Gossage who was known as the "Socrates of San Francisco". They came up with such lines as "At 60 miles an hour the Loudest noise in this new Land Rover comes from the roar of the engine" which referenced a Rolls Royce ad that said the loudest thing in their car was the clock. Or, "The Land Rover is built to withstand the full charge of a bull rhinoceros." Through Howard, Jimmy made friends with John Steinbeck and I delivered a Land Rover to him at his apartment on the upper eastside on 3rd and 68th so he could test the vehicle and write some promo material for the company. He wrote that a Land Rover had "a will toward immortality". I lived around the corner from him and we compared our favorite haunts none of which would have insured our own personal immortality.

Working with us were Hoda, young, serious, married, and Maria who had been in NYC PR for years and was good friends with the columnist, Liz Smith. She took me under her wing and introduced me to restaurants like Pearl's, a midtown Chinese restaurant meeting place for writers who knew everyone and everyone knew.

Bruce McWilliams, president of the company, had met Jimmy in London during WWII when he worked for the OSS, the precursor to the CIA. They lived in Pound Ridge with their two sons who attended boarding school. Jimmy, wearing Saks Fifth Avenue suits and alligator pumps, and Bruce, impeccable in Brooks Bros., either drove to work in a Rover 2000 or took the train from Stamford. Bruce's secretary, Ruth, was a Bronx no-nonsense unmarried woman who's highest moment came from Broadway plays. She was ecstatic one morning having just seen "Rosenkrantz and Guildenstern Are Dead". She danced on air in the Chrysler Building.

This was a quintessential New York group of people and I felt lucky to have my job but complicating my rather straight-laced life were the current events in New York City, the social tumult created by the civil rights movement and the growing involvement our country had in Viet Nam.

New York had always had a high level political nature and Greenwich Village embraced angry young men and women activists who were intent on creating upheaval and discontent. I had recently moved from the Upper Eastside to the center of this, St. Mark's Place between 2nd and 3rd, across from the wild discotheque, the Electric Circus and below it, the Dom where Lou Reed and The

Velvet Underground with Nico played, a few doors down from the Five Spot, a great jazz club, and one door away from Abby Hoffman's apartment building.

In the early '60s, my generation had gone through the assassination of our President and the purported lies surrounding this catastrophic event. This fed the already angry feelings we had about the compulsory military draft, racial segregation everywhere, not just the South, and the entrenched poverty across the land. Change was in the air and I wanted to find my place in it individually and collectively. My college major at the University of Wisconsin, Political Science, had heightened my awareness of my times just as growing up in progressive Madison did and now I was challenged to either get on the bus or get off.

That April I had met a man, Peter Desmond, much older than I at thirty-eight. He was a committed revolutionary, working at Mobilization for Youth which tutored the low 3%ers - the bad boys on the Lower East Side who had rap sheets which even included murder. I'd also heard he ran guns to Puerto Rico aiding their independence movement, something he didn't discuss. We met because we were both interested in taking a share in a house at the eastern end of Fire Island. What does a rabid communist agitator do on the beach? Like everyone, even he needed downtime off the bus and Bayberry Dunes, a small collection of homes built on the sand between the Atlantic Ocean and Long Island Sound, provided a perfect shelter. It was primitive with gaslights and a propane-fueled kitchen, the perfect antidote to the loud, congested streets of the city, offering relaxation or great conversations and romance.

I'd visited another house on the Island the year before, my first summer in New York City, when college friend Susan Scarnecchia and I shared an apartment on Lex and 71st St. We'd had fun living on our very small secretarial salaries and were also featured in a Look Magazine article about the Single Girl in the City.

Susan Scarnecchia and Jeanne with Two Swedes

At a party on 72nd St., we met a woman editor of the magazine and she asked if we'd be the centerpieces of the spread. We went to mixers, clubs, meeting other young adults looking for connections. Finally, they put us on a boat that plied the waters of the East River, brought in two Scandinavians and made it seem we did this all the time.

In real life, we'd gone to an event at the National Arts Club on Gramercy Square and met a charming banker, Steve Friedman. He insisted we come to his house on Fire Island that weekend and we both loved it and made it a habit.

It was easy to get there on the Long Island Railroad, getting off at Patchogue and catching the ferry to Davis Park or a crash boat to Ocean Ridge, walking a short way east along the wooden sidewalks that were laid on top of the sand, to the houses, simple clapboard structures with a deck, a main room and four bedrooms. A more exciting way to get there was in the Land Rover 88 I borrowed one night. One of my housemates, Miles Donis, a writer who worked at Columbia Pictures, and I were at a party wishing we were at the beach and I said, "Let's go." We went to the garage where the Company kept their PR cars, picked up the keys and we were on our way, out the LIE, past Patchogue to a Parkway that crossed the Great South Bay to Fire Island. We tooled down the beach after midnight, staying on the hardpack nearest the water, and surprised our friends. On Monday, Jimmy asked how the sand got in the hubcaps of our demo vehicle and I had to admit I'd hijacked the thing on a lark, Miles and I pretending we were in the foreign legion sent out on a dangerous mission.

Peter and I spent a wonderful summer together, swimming in the ocean, walking along the beach, plucking mussels from their grip on the shore of the Long Island Sound and cooking them in wine and herbs. And making love – for me the first time because I lost my virginity to Peter.

I'd waited a long time, as I'd actually bought into the notion that a woman should save herself for marriage. But, that wasn't on the horizon and I couldn't hold out for the ring and ceremony any longer.

Besides our tranquil weekends on Fire Island, we shared a passion for the anti-war and civil rights demonstrations that stalled the city during that summer. Peter and friends were united in their hatred of President Johnson and his illegal war and went to great lengths to show it. This included carrying signs, making obscene gestures, shouting arguments and was capped off by throwing large-headed short nails into the paths of motorcycle policemen whose bikes would slowly come to a stop as the air leaked out of the tires. I was both shocked and energized by this street action, more drawn to the older people chanting "Hey, hey, ho, ho, LBJ has got to go. Hey, hey, ho, ho, Ho Chi Minh is gonna win.", but I ran alongside Peter and his radical friends. We had also seen the newsreels of Selma, Alabama, been sickened by the many murders of Goodman, Schwerner and Cheney, Viola Liuzzo, Medgar Evers, which followed a century of lynching in the south. As CORE, SNCC, SCLC marches gained momentum, these grievances were added to the anti-war sentiment.

Peter's dedication to radical change also extended to the teenage boys he taught auto mechanics and English at Mobilization for Youth. There was a core group of guys, white, black & latino, who orbited around him, looking for the attention they didn't get from their families. He proposed that we take a few of them out to Fire Island, get them off the mean streets of the Lower Eastside and into the clean ocean air of the beach. We checked with our friends Bernie and Penny who owned the house and were also involved in social work and activism. They thought it was a great idea and suggested we do it during the week when Bayberry Dunes was quiet.

Peter was able to score a van thru MFY which we drove to Patchogue and parked in the Ferryboat lot. On the ferry the boys were ecstatic that they were out of the city and exclaimed they wouldn't be bad if they lived out here.

We walked down the beach carrying their gear and they couldn't wait to get to the water. They threw their stuff into the house, changed and ran over the dunes to the shore. It was a strong surf that day and this was not a patrolled beach, no lifeguards, you were on your own. Fish, the leader of the group, ran into the waves, screaming happily. Quickly, he was caught in a rip tide and carried out beyond the waves. Peter dove in to try to rescue him and he too, was pulled out to sea. The two of them floundered together but luckily, another wave caught them and brought them closer to shore. I ran out with another kid and we were able to pull Fish ashore. He was a keeper. I asked if this was how he got his name.

No, he said, he was always the decoy in their schemes and crimes, that's why he was called Fish.

We walked over to the Sound side of the island where they could swim in calmer water. It was hot that day and standing knee deep in the water refreshed all of us. We pulled up mussels that clung to the sandy bank, filling a large pot with them still wrapped in the weeds. We took them back to the house and spent a lot of time cleaning them, talking, Fish reliving his near-drowning, crowing about his good fortune. When his friends complained about cleaning their dinner, he said, he was happy to be sitting on the beautiful deck with his hands on a dinner he was making. We put the clean mussels back in the pot with herbs, white wine and tomatoes and cooked them up, served them with French bread and a salad, scooping up every last drop.

On the way back to Davis Park to catch the boat at the end of the next day, we walked by a large house owned by a man we called "The Tomato King". The guy was a farmer on Long Island and indeed was one of the biggest suppliers of tomatoes to grocery stores and restaurants around the state. Peter got into one of his rants about rich people and how they treat their workers, the pickers in the fields in the hot sun, paid a few dollars a day. Fish and the boys wanted to go over and discuss this with the Tomato King and Peter encouraged it. I'm shaking my head, saying "No, this is not how you deal with this with these kids", but now they were on his property, climbing up the wood supports of his deck up to the second floor. We knew he was home because his Tomato King flag was flying, his invitation for people to drop by. "See, Jeanne, he wants to talk to us."

No one was around, probably at the beach, so the kids climbed down, but I was very upset that an embarrassing argument might have happened. I agreed that the Tomato King was a capitalist pig but that wasn't my way to deal with him, if at all. I was still a very straight person.

Peter and I took the kids to the New Jersey Pine Barrens in September, to the Batsto River for a canoe trip. It's a wild part in the southern part of the state, rural, boglike and I hoped there wouldn't be a target for their revolutionary class war taunts. We rented four canoes, loaded up all their sleeping bags and gear and the kids took off, not waiting for instruction or for Peter to lead them down the river. It was an amazingly beautiful fall day, maples beginning to turn color and as they were in a flooded area, their yellow and red reflections played on the river. We came to a cranberry farm and as far as we could see, red berries floated on the sun-spotted blue water. All this came alive as the kids played in the canoes, standing up, rocking them, then falling in, turning over the boats, dumping all their belongings into the water. We paddled up to them, grabbing as many things as possible before the sleeping bags got too soaked and sunk. We'd only traveled a mile or so and there was a beach area where we could pull in and get everything dry. That was it for the canoe trip and maybe it was just okay, no reason to try to paddle all the way to the Atlantic Ocean. I'd bought a cast iron pot from a roadside stand we had passed. We built a fire and cooked up a stew and thought how nice it was to be out of the city. I still have that pot and remember this day every time I use it.

My job with Rover was still holding my interest but it was just about selling cars. It wasn't addressing my agitation about the world around us. The failure of some of my co-workers to see what I thought was squarely in front of us, upset me. I tried to quell the hotheadedness but that would eat at me too. This was only 3 years following the assassination of JFK and I was one of many who had a hard time believing the Warren Commission's report, plus the Viet Nam War really heating up, plus the poverty I was surrounded with in NYC. Maybe, I wasn't ready to be an adult, dealing with the huge problems I wasn't aware of in Madison, Wisconsin. On St. Mark's Place, it was all right there, the Bowery with the drunks living on the street, the growing tension in the business world - we women didn't intend to stay in the background, the underlying racism and patriarchal attitudes in even left-leaning friends. It was confusing and I was feeling powerless to do anything about it.

Chapter 2

Rocky Mountain High

In the late fall, I realized I had a rival, another woman Peter had met trekking the canyon lands of Utah and I was beyond sad. I felt betrayed and abandoned, my virginity gone with the wind. I was living alone on St. Marks Place in a fourth floor walk-up, "grooving on poverty", caught in a job that paid me $95 a week and it felt like a dead end. My boss was very considerate and tried to help but nothing seemed to be working. At twenty-four, Destiny was keenly on my mind. It was now or never that I had to plot my career, make the big moves.

I reached out to old friends around the country for a check in. One of them, Dave Gernon, was in Aspen bartending, sharing an apartment with other Madison friends. He said "Come on out. You can stay with us until you get settled."

I'd been to Aspen on a ski trip during college and it was the Nirvana for skiers. As a New Yorker, I'd gone to Vermont with Susan and her boyfriend Hubie who had a farmhouse near Mad River Glen. We'd drive up Friday night, a six-hour journey, ski Saturday and Sunday, then back to the city. It was exhilarating and exhausting. The idea that I could be in a place like Aspen, getting that mountain energy which I knew was a source of power for me, all made sense. A clean break from an encumbered path was the answer, even though I was aware that I was abandoning The Cause of the '60s radicals. Within a few weeks, I had quit my job, told Peter good-bye, sublet my apartment and I was on my way to Aspen.

After a week in the thin air, I was a mess. What was I doing?? Dave was a good friend but the other guys he roomed with were the crazy, chauvinistic boys I'd avoided even in high school. They were rude, crude, messy, and certainly not sympathetic that I couldn't help crying a lot. Their answer to everything was "get drunk." The restaurants and hotels were holding off hiring winter help because the snowfall was light and they were hedging their bets. I'd made the rounds and left my name and contact number, but nothing had come of it.

At Thanksgiving another friend from NYC came out for a visit and when we got together I told him I had to find another place to live and get a job. He said he'd just met the Director of the Ski Schools and his wife. They were looking to hire an au pair girl for their three-year-old son and five-year-old daughter. Their name was Chase. Curt and Betsy Chase.

A few days later I was walking through town with a new friend telling him about this prospect and he said, pointing, "They're they are. That's Curt Chase." Two people who looked very much at home on the snowy streets were walking toward us. I stopped them, introduced myself and told them I'd heard they were looking for a nanny. I wanted to apply for the job. We set a time for me to visit them at home, that afternoon, 4pm.

I found their custom-built house easily, a cozy and simple three bedroom home with a patio that looked up on Ajax Mountain. There was an upstairs unit that was rented out to an older couple and Curt had a tool shop next door which had a very small bedroom above it. Curt had actually built his own home with the help of some friends during a summer. He was a sardonic New Hampshirite and a 10th Mountain Vet, as were so many of the men who settled in Aspen's Roaring Fork Valley following WWII. They'd all trained at near-by Camp Hale, had gone to Italy to fight, then bought property in Aspen upon their return home. Curt had worked as a ski instructor during the winter and a carpenter during

Curt, Jimmy, Heidi, Jeanne (bg)

the summer. He was quiet, self-contained and handsome. Betsy was the daughter of a CU/Boulder Professor and had lived in Colorado most of her life except for when she'd won a Fulbright scholarship and spent a few years abroad in Austria studying Folk Lore and Music. I was told her German was flawless.

We quickly took to each other and they made an offer: room (shared with three-year-old Jimmy) and board, $100 per month, free ski pass and free ski lessons whenever I could join a class, and the use of a family car. I leapt at it and was ready to move in the next day. Betsy said she was taking a trip to Denver in two days and I should come then. It would give the children and me a chance to get to know each other without her presence. I'd be jumping in with both feet and taking charge. Trial by fire but I was ready, so ready to get out of the apartment I was sharing with the four Madison guys.

I was embraced by the Chases and their friends, many of them working in the ski school or ski patrol, motel and restaurant workers and owners. Every Thursday there would be a big ski school party for all the vacationers who had enrolled at one of the mountains for ski lessons. There was an Oompah band and since quite a few of the instructors were originally from the mountains of Europe, the polka reigned. I was usually asked to dance by one of the German or Swiss guys and we whirled around laughing and hooting, enjoying ourselves so much that the tourists quickly joined in.

My job was so easy. Betsy and Curt would go off to breakfast at 7am followed by their daily jobs at the ski school. I'd get the kids up and fed then would drop Heidi off at kindergarten and Jimmy at ski school at Buttermilk Mt. Then I was on my own to ski or take in the beauty of the valley which was formed by the Roaring Fork River as it cascaded down from Independence Pass high above us.

I met Bill Harris and friends at #1 Lift the next morning as it was the first one that got rolling each day. The ski patrol would go up for their early sweep to check for any bulge on a slope that could become an avalanche, then any hardy soul could follow. It was a single chair lift and at that hour, very cold. It had a piece of canvas on each side of the chair that you could fold over yourself so that the wind didn't tear into you. We each lined up and slid into our chairs. It was still snowing and it promised to be a great powder day.

But, as we neared the top, I could see there was a problem. Actually, I couldn't see the problem because I couldn't see anything at all. We were being delivered into a total white-out. The thick snow clouds draped the mountains with an impenetrable fog and as I slipped off the chair lift, I had to trust my skis and follow them off the ramp. It's curious how the gift of sight and confidence are connected. It was cold out but that didn't account for the shaking that began to grip me. I side-slipped down the hill a bit to make sure I was out of the way of the other skiers coming off the lift. I called out to Bill and heard his voice. His friends joined us, actually collided with us. Sometimes there isn't safety in numbers.

There was no way we were skiing that day. A ski patrol member came up and told us to either stay there or get off the mountain. In fact, they were closing the lifts. The only two restaurants on the mountain were above us and we didn't want to stand around. I proposed that I lead them down the roads that the snow cats used to get up the mountain for the nightly grooming of the slopes. They agreed and we set out to find the road down. It was very slow going but I had the map of the mountain in my head and could recognize certain signposts as we got up close and knew that we were on the right course. The road was built into the side of the mountain so that we could hug the safe side and ski slowly, snowplowing much of the way. It made us all feel like beginners which in a way we were. None of us had ever been blinded by lack of visibility like this.

In time, thirty minutes, two hours, it was hard to say, we got to the middle of Little Nell, the bunny slope that led to the ski chalet, and we could begin to see the town below us. It gave us some of that spirit that a good ski run can provide and we pushed on, even making some turns. The mountain flattened out and we skied up to the wood frames where we parked our skis.

We blew into the bar at the bottom of the run. Even though it was early morning we needed something to calm the shakes we all had. Bill was very kind, congratulating me on bringing them down safely. In fact, there were a number of double diamond runs which, had they stumbled on, would have challenged them fiercely.

When we were warmed and comfortable again, Bill mentioned that he'd just invested in a small film company in New

York. They were planning an expansion and he promised that if I came back to the city, I would have a job. It was payback for being cool under pressure. Films? What did I know about that? Not much, except that like any city dweller I went to a few. He suggested that my last job in PR would be my calling card. Okay, we'd see.

Meanwhile, I was living a long-held dream of being in the mountains, skiing a lot, breathing that alpine air, enjoying people who felt the same way. Skiing and mountains were in my blood, Norwegian on my mother's side and Swiss on my dad's. Mom's father, Earling Landvick, had immigrated from Norway in 1909, leaving behind two brothers who were on Norway's Olympic Ski team. Earling had big ideas and saw them come to fruition when he built Wisconsin's first ski jump in Stoughton, Wisconsin. He hosted many jumping tournaments bringing in his brothers to compete against the local boys, crying out, "Yump, you Norskis." One of my neighbors in Madison when I was growing up was a kid my age, Dave Norby, whose father was a skier. When we were 5, he taught us how to go off the small ski jump in the village of Shorewood Hills where we lived. We could also ski on the golf course, a few hills around Madison and as we grew older, trips way up to Telemark on the south shore of Lake Superior. Dave Norby went on to become an Olympic jumper by the time he was eighteen.

On the Aspen mountains, preferring Ajax to Buttermilk, my skiing was getting strong. I took advantage of two great ski instructors, Curt and Betsy, and learned the American Technique which the Aspen Ski School designed and embraced. Sometimes, I joined a class on the hill, having gotten to know some of the teachers who had smaller classes that took on the steeper slopes or the mogul runs. Or, I'd see friends at Gretl's Restaurant, grab some lunch then bomb down the mountain with them. It certainly was one version of paradise.

In January, Curt broke his leg. It was a clean break, boot-top but really laid him up. He was a stay-at-home guy anyhow but now he really had no desire to go out at night. His daytime job of running the ski schools and overseeing his supervisors who had to fill in for him was tiring enough. Betsy, on the other hand, was beginning to enjoy herself. Perhaps it was our growing friendship which included outings on the town and girl talk or it was the beginning of the carefree '60s, but she was in favor of letting Curt stay home with the kids so that she and her nanny could party. This became a running joke that has carried through all these years. The year the babysitter turned her employer into a babysitter and changed the Chase family for good and for bad.

Aspen in 1966-67 was still a little old ex-mining town with mom and pop businesses, unpaved dirt streets, and a community in which ski bums and trust fund babies partied at the local bars and restaurants with no concern of bank accounts or the size of a house. Everyone knew that the town catered to tourist dollars so few conversations dealt with politically controversial subjects like anti-war or civil rights. Aspen = Escape. They were on Vacation. Was I on a permanent one?

A favorite night-out was at the Hotel Jerome where Vince Guaraldi frequently played in a barroom off the lobby. This was nice jazzy music which attracted an older crowd and Betsy loved it. During this time, she began to think that her solid marriage with Curt was more of a friendship. And she also realized that as a woman in her mid-thirties, she still had a lot of life in her when it came to other men. I can't say that I encouraged this but I certainly fueled a change in their relationship. They continued to live together for years but developed an understanding that allowed each of them to live their own lives.

Places like Aspen collect interesting, attractive people. Outdoor, sporty types who, like me, were trying to find themselves and once that was accomplished, move on to do whatever it was they'd figured out. A few people I met back then are still there but most moved on as Aspen became very expensive. One young man I met at the Hotel Jerome bar was Les, who was serious-looking, blond and spoke with a European accent. Typical bar talk was describing an incredible run you had on the mountain or a joke you'd heard on the lift. And Les and I did all of that but as we got to know one another, it took another turn. We were attracted but abrasive with one another. We had such different takes on just about everything. He always ran down Aspen, saying Mammoth Mountain was a better place. I've always had a hard time with people who think some place else is better than where they are and I challenged him on this. Then he told me his story.

He was from Hungary and when the Revolution began in 1956, the Soviet tanks rolling into the country, Les made the decision of a much older person. He was fourteen and knew he had a chance to get out so, along with a few friends, he took off for the border. His family stayed behind, not wanting to give up their homeland or as adults, risk execution or imprisonment if they were caught. As Les and his friends neared the border, they were seen by the guards. The whole country was in a lock-down mode and the guards shouted for them to stop. Les began to run, outdistancing himself from his friends. Then he heard the shots and bobbing and weaving, he ran on, not looking back, not knowing how close the guards were coming. He ran for a long time and came to a town. He was in Austria. Through the Catholic Church, he was brought to America and taken into a foster home. He learned English, studied hard, went to college and became a biology teacher. All this on his own and he was now exhausted from ten years of proving himself. Aspen was his moment to take some time off and figure out what was next. But, it also was a mirror of his unsettled yet determined self that now could look for other things.

One night our conversation was particularly agitated about Viet Nam. We were really not getting along and he made some comment about the Jews. It was a real racist statement and it caught me the wrong way, as broad characterizations usually did. I looked him in the eye and called him on it. His response was that Jews were like that. I asked if I was like that. He said no. I said well, I'm jewish. He couldn't believe it. I stood by it and lied, oh yes I am.

My identification with other cultures was instilled early when I was growing up and I was always curious about different people. Shorewood Hills was adjacent to the University of Wisconsin and many of the homes were owned by professors, doctors and other university personnel. Nearby was a housing development owned by the university and used by the married students who were getting advanced degrees. Our neighbors were intellectual and prosperous and from all walks of life. I continued my schooling at the University prep school, a lab school for college students majoring in Education. One of my teachers even taught a Russian History class, showing Eisenstein's films, "Potemkin" and the Ivan films.

In 1954 when I was twelve, my father bought our first television set. The programming for the four channels we got (ABC, NBC, CBS, NET) was the national shows that came on for a few hours in the evening. The other hours were filled with local stuff and a lot of wartime footage like "Victory At Sea". One night the UW's NET station, a forerunner to PBS, broadcast some Army footage that had the most horrifying pictures I had ever seen – the arrival of the allied troops at the concentration camps run by the Nazis. The survivors, the corpses, the camps were shocking, disturbing my daydreams and causing nightmares. The thought that people did this to other people was beyond my comprehension. Conversations with my parents didn't result in any further acceptance or understanding. How does something like this go on for years and nobody knows? Or say they never knew, that it wasn't about them, or their fault? Nothing Mom or Dad could say or did say helped me get past this horrible crime.

Then, the realization that most of these victims were there because of their religion put me over the edge. I slowly got the picture that Jews, collaborators, priests, homosexuals, gypsies, had been rounded up by the Nazis. They were the "outsiders", social poison, condemned to ethnic cleansing. Susan Sontag talked about the Holocaust years later saying that in a population, 10% are cruel, 10% are merciful and the other 80% can be pulled in either direction.

18

Can we all learn that no matter how desperate we may become, mass killing doesn't alleviate suffering? Yet it continues today, with no end in sight.

First they came for the Socialists, and I did not speak out —
Because I was not a Socialist.
Then they came for the Trade Unionists, and I did not speak out —
Because I was not a Trade Unionist. Then they came for the Jews, and I did
not speak out — Because I was not a Jew.
Then they came for me — and there was no one left to speak for me.
(Martin Neimoller)

This was one of the defining moments of my life and perhaps defined my generation. There would never be justice for the Holocaust. We were the War Babies and the war was our early history. When we were three and four, we would see Life Magazine and pictures of the war, know that a family on the block was sad. I wouldn't know the details but would overhear that a neighbor's brother had died or one of my dad's friends didn't come home or he wasn't "quite right" if he did. These lasting memories and images and their long term affects have fueled the changes that my generation began to urge on the world during the '60s. The fights for racial and gender equality, the willingness to say "no" to a country drafting my friends for a war we didn't support, the "change the world" attitudes that were perpetuated by even the squarest and most obedient, most middle-class among us.

So to be sitting in a bar, supposedly having fun, and have these torrents of memories come back to me because of this man who I thought was smart, was too much. I got up, walked out and never talked to him again. These were the things I needed to know about myself. What is it that truly defines us as we mature? Decisions for our own position of what's right and what's not. What will you tolerate and what makes you say "enough"?

Jeanne with Peter Desmond

Peter came to visit, me as much as Aspen, the adventurer that he was. Curt gave Peter a ski pass and some equipment and he floundered around on the slope until his innate grace and strength balanced out and he was a natural. Timmy Carter, a friend who liked to ski on ice, took us to the Roaring Fork for fly fishing. It was fun but I was wary. I'd been burned so I took it a day at a time and he left on good terms. One day, I'd see him again. This was another big step for me. Not to feel the jealousy that can consume your every thought. I could let it go and not be threatened. I came to realize some time later, that not being jealous, feeling comfortable in your own skin, is a sign of maturity, living your own life, not wishing for or lusting after something out of reach and probably something that ultimately doesn't make a difference anyway.

In March, the weather began to warm and Betsy, our friend Diana and I would put on our bikinis and catch some rays on their protected patio, blaring the Mamas and the Papas so loud skiers coming down Little Nell heard it. Diana was married to a German mountain climber/skier, Fritzy Stamberger, who worked at the Aspen Times and was a master printer. They were the epitome of Aspen glamour, she with her svelte model looks and he with his strong physique and adventuresome spirit. Diana was from Canada and not close to her family so Aspen was her life. Fritzy had climbed peaks all over the world but his reputation was sullied by the rumors that he had left a fellow climber behind in order to reach a summit and that climber hadn't survived. He, allegedly, had broken the golden rule of the mountain but he denied this was the case.

The lifts would be shutting down in the first week of April and I was facing a decision. I had been embraced by many of the locals who encouraged me to stay on, get my own place, become an Aspenite. And it was tempting. It was and still is, despite the sprawl both down valley and the sizes of the homes being built, one of nature's best efforts. But, I still felt a need to make a difference in the changing world, still be political, be an activist, so I knew I would go back to New York.

A lot of my acquaintances were making plans to head for Mexico. The skiers became surfers once the weather changed. Mazatlan was the destination and that sounded fun to me. At the UW, I'd studied a lot of Spanish for my minor in Latin American Studies and I'd never been to Mexico. I could convince myself and my parents that this was an opportunity I couldn't pass up. A friend, Phil Miller, was planning to fly to Los Angeles, buy a car and travel all over the country and invited me to go with him. I'd met Phil at Stromberg's, a very cool restaurant. I'd gone to meet a friend there and as we were having a wet snow, had taken an umbrella to stay dry. I was dressed in a skirt and jacket with tights and boots and a long colorful scarf around my neck. As I descended the stairs with my umbrella, my friend called out, "Here comes the nanny."

Al Stromberg immediately yelled out "Mary Poppins" and this name stuck.

Before I left Aspen, one of Betsy's friends, Patty, came up from Denver for a week of spring skiing. In tow were her kids, one of them a drop-dead gorgeous guy named Kevin who was going to CU in Boulder. We really liked each other, had fun skiing and dancing, and he suggested that I visit him after my trip to Mexico.

I finished up the season skiing the last day, enjoying the wild parties that marked it. Skiers would tear down Little Nell, take off from a small jump and land in a huge puddle of water that had accumulated from the snow run-off. April winds began to kick up clouds of dust from the unpaved streets and I learned why everyone who could left town. Most of them headed to someplace in Mexico, others off to the other warm resort areas to the southeast. I made a plan to leave my winter things with the Chases which would also allow me come back and say good-bye to all of them.

Maroon Bells - Aspen

Chapter Three

Hasta La Wasta

I travelled more than 5,000 miles through Mexico. Phil was a mild-mannered man, very sweet and dependable, not like a lot of ski bums I'd met. He was planning on returning to Aspen to live, work in real estate and was happy he'd found his home. We were good buddies and that made for a relaxed journey.

But things are never that simple. He started out driving the VW 1500 station wagon he'd bought and after a day, suggested I take over. He crawled in back and napped. Somehow I missed a turn-off and we ended up on a truck route through the Sonoran Desert which seemed absolutely unpopulated and worse than that, there were no gas stations. The engine began to sputter and I checked the gas gauge. We were on empty. I slowed to a stop on the side of the road. It was a humiliating moment for me as I have always prided myself on being a good driver, not the typical female version who dithers about anything automotive. My first and only car had been a TR-3 when I was in college and I'd tried to be "one of the guys" racing through the countryside surrounding Madison.

We both stood by the road waving at the diesel-powered trucks that sped by us. No one stopped. It was hot and dusty and we were incredibly vulnerable out there with no real food and little to drink. Finally, a car slowed, then pulled over. We looked at them and agreed these were the last people we would ask for help. The three men stepped out of their car. They were the toughest looking guys I'd seen in a long time, but then, I'd been in the paradise of Aspen. They'd rolled their shirt sleeves over their pack of cigarettes and their jeans were slung low and tucked into boots. They looked like banditos, pachucos, our worst nightmare.

My Spanish was fairly good as I'd studied in school and had also spent some time in Spain in 1964. I did my best to be friendly, off-hand, but when they understood that we were out of gas they just looked at us. They walked back to the car. I was almost relieved that they were leaving. No, they weren't. One of them took a jack from the car and put it under it's frame. He jacked his car up high enough, then his friend took a gas can and handed it to the third man who slid under their car and drained some of their gas into the can. They brought the can to Phil's car and poured the gasoline in. We offered them money but they refused. They got in their car and sped off, waving out the window.

A palm reader once told me that I had a lucky star in my left palm. What does that mean, I asked. It means what it says – you have a lucky star. When you could be in danger, things will work out for you. Something is looking out for you so danger passes you by. These tough angels in the Sonoran Desert were part of that luck.

The next night, we were in Topolobampo, south of Guaymas, north of Culiacan. Both of us were doing this trip on a budget so we would ask about campsites along the way. We'd buy food that we could cook on the hibachi we carried. This also took us off the main roads and into areas that were used by the locals. Topolobampo was a prime fishing spot on the Pacific Ocean. There was a large bay with many inlets and our campsite was on a low hill overlooking it. The fish we cooked that night was delicious and we were enjoying the moonrise over the water when we heard very loud breathing noises. We couldn't imagine that what we were hearing was human but it sounded like it. We walked to the edge of the bay and the water in all directions was alive. Dolphins had come in to feed and their prey were swimming into the shallow parts to escape their fate. The dolphins arced out of the water in their chase and when they did, they expelled air from their blow holes. This is what we had heard. There were thousands of them and thousands of smaller fish trying to stay alive, splashing on the edge of the bay, swimming for their lives in the shallow water.

Mazatlan was a gringos paradise. Great surf, cheap restaurants and hotels, beautiful warm weather. We popped for a really inexpensive hotel in town, ate at the market place where tacos, enchiladas and huachinango (red snapper) could be had for less than a dollar. And I got too much sun. After the northern exposure to the sun in the mountains, Mexico was like a huge sun lamp and my fair skin defied protection and Phil was a redhead so we decided to leave the beach community and head inland for Guadalajara, Guanajuato, San Miguel de Allende. A day later, in Guadalajara, I fainted on the Cathedral steps and people thought I was a "borracha", drunk from too much tequila and not just sick from the sun.

These 17th century cities really personified old Mexico. The War of Independence from France and Napoleon began in these parts and they are a serious tourist's mecca, surrounded by mountains, ranches, farms and quaint villages. About 4 hours south of Guanajuato is Mexico City which has the pyramids, the floating islands, fabulous homes and museums, plazas and parks and millions and millions of people. It was also expensive for us so we stayed only a few days.

My parents had an acquaintance who lived in the city. He was attached to the American Embassy and invited us to dinner. I later learned that Eldon Rudd was CIA. We had a gracious dinner at a restaurant and when we told him of our travels he became furious. What would my parents say? I kept thinking it was because he probably thought Phil and I were a couple. But, no. It turned out that statistically, our mode of travel, camping, cooking out, etc. was incredibly dangerous. What were we thinking? We had planned to leave that night to head for Acapulco, but he said No Way were we going to be on that road in the middle of the night. I learned later that the states we would go through were the major marijuana growing areas and that the campesinos didn't trust anyone.

In Acapulco, we met Nancy, a friend from Aspen. The three of us split a hotel room, simple but clean, which was near the local market. While hanging out on the beach, we met a local hustler, Carlos, who thought we might be tourists with money. When he understood that we weren't, he took us to the market to introduce us to his aunt and uncle who had a food stand there. They fed us good home-cooking for $1.00 and a beer was $.50. Carlos fronted for a beach business that took people out water skiing or paragliding. A Navy ship was in port and lots of American sailors were in town looking for good times. Carlos asked Nancy and me if we wanted to go water skiing with the sailors and of course we did. I had grown up water skiing and my time in Aspen had made my legs very strong so we were Carlos's calling card with the sailors.

Our plans were to stay in Acapulco then head north to Zihuatanejo, about a half-days' drive. When we told Carlos good-bye, he quickly wrote a note which he said would help us in Z-town, as it was called. He instructed me to go the barbershop – the only one in town – and see his uncle.

The trip north took a long time because it was mostly a dirt road through the jungle, full of pot holes and ruts, sometimes narrowing to one lane. We finally arrived in the afternoon and no one was around. Siesta time, we figured. Our hope was to sleep on the beach in one of the grass huts called palapas that were there. I went off to find the barbershop.

It wasn't hard to locate – Zihuatanejo had one main road, also unpaved, with a few restaurants, some tourist traps and the barbershop. When I walked in, a large man emerged from the back through a curtain that split the room in two. He looked menacing but when I said that Carlos had sent me and I had a letter of introduction, he invited me to sit down at a table in the back. He motioned me to a chair and I sat. He then reached into the front pocket of his large baggy pants and pulled out a large revolver which he put on the table between us. He was the barber, the cop, the mayor; he ran the town. He took the time to read the letter I handed him and then he launched into a tirade about how American drug dealers and Timothy Leary had brought the wrong element to his town. Were we looking to buy drugs? I assured him we were three tourists who wanted to stay on the town beach, swim, eat, but cause no trouble. We wanted his permission otherwise we would go back to Acapulco. We really didn't want any trouble. He walked down to the beach with me and met Phil and Nancy and then pointed out the palapas we could use and rented us some hammocks.

The next morning I awoke to a strange noise. As I came out of the slumber state, I sat up and looked around the surrounding beach. There were dozens of turtles there, on their back, struggling. Z-town was a fishing village, built on a beautiful bay which had a natural reef between it and the Pacific. Larger predators couldn't come into the bay, so it teemed of fish and turtles. The locals had fished very early that morning and had brought their catch into town. They threw the turtles onto the beach and let them suffocate to death.

I hated to see this but it was their way of life and I was an honored guest of the Jefe. That night, we went to one of the local restaurants, and of course, there were lots of turtle meat dishes on the menu. I learned that there are seven different cuts of turtle and they are quite different from each other, as thigh and breast meat are on poultry.

Our last day there we took a boat across the bay to a beautiful beach. A man had a grill set up and bar-b-qued red snapper, (huachinanga), corn, onions and along with a tortilla, it was a delicious lunch. Afterwards, we took a walk away from the beach into the adjacent jungle and came upon a small roofless house made out of concrete blocks. Looking in, we could see writing, small script in English, covering the interior walls. It was the saga of some

Americans who had been rousted for drugs, arrested and beaten up. It was a warning that these people here are not to be crossed. Don't even think about trying to buy or sell drugs because that's the main source of income for all of these locals.

On our way out of town, I stopped at one of the shops and picked up a shirt I'd had made. Blue denim with embroidery that cost about $6. I wore that shirt for years and it always made me think of this strange town. Years later, Z-town grew and joined a near-by town, Ixtapa, and became one of the largest Mexican resorts on the west coast. I'm sure that bay is no longer the quiet turtle-fishing spot we got to know.

I was now anxious to get back home. Nancy left us and Phil and I began the drive north. In Culiacan, the trusty Volkswagen broke down and it was going to be several days before it was ready for the road. I asked Phil if he would mind if I went on and he agreed it would be okay. We had been good traveling buddies, but both admitted we'd like a separate peace. I boarded a train for the border, one that would put me in Nogales. An older man, a conductor on the train, drove me from the Mexican side to the American side and I realized years later, that it was a real act of kindness as at the time Nogales was a very rough border town and if I had made my own way, there was a good chance I'd have been robbed, etc.

After buying my ticket at the bus station on the US side of the border, I called Kevin in Boulder, using my last ten cents. I know that sounds almost unbelievable but the rest is too. I had traveled 5,000 miles, spending a month in Mexico on $75.

When Kevin picked me up, we drove to his small cabin near the Flat Irons, the upright sheets of rock that are an oft-photographed site in Boulder. I called my dad and he was pleased I'd come back whole and was also glad to wire me some money. Kevin took me to the movie "A Man and A Woman", the incredibly romantic French movie and as we drove back to his house, Kevin hummed the theme from the movie and I realized he was a real musician, getting the nuance of the song. It was easy to pretend we were the couple in the car, Anouke Aimee and Jean-Louis Trintignant, meant for each other but held apart by real life considerations. We were captured by each other and spent a week enjoying spring in the mountains. Then it was time to go to Aspen to collect my belongings and head back east through Madison. We vowed to be in touch.

I arrived at Betsy and Curt's house and we had a good reunion. I was tanned and skinny, the result of eating once a day on my tight budget. We went up to the Maroon Bells for picnics, hiked up the mountain I'd learned to ski and hit the bars at night. As we said our good-byes, we were sad, but I promised I'd be back. And, they could visit. All of that came true with Betsy coming to see me in New York and Aspen remained a place that I continued to go to throughout the years.

On the Road in Mexico

Chapter Four

Damaged Goods

I arrived in Madison and my family, even my brother, Charles, was relieved that I was back home. They had hopes that I would call it quits in New York and return to make Madison my home, but I was now filled with the dreams that I was going to get a job in the film business.

I have always said that Madison was a good place to be from. When I was seven it hit me that I would leave my hometown and go off to ......where, who knew. But something told me that I would not stay there. As a college student at the UW, I was one of the large number of respectable, privileged kids who saw that changes were happening. I went to college from 1960-64 and the whole country was going through the same changes. Civil rights, anti-war movements were strong and beginning to cut through racial and social lines. Like a lot young people, I was having huge arguments with my parents and their friends about politics. Kennedy had been killed and our minds had been blown. If that could happen, what else could happen? No one was prepared for all that did. Not even our parents.

I wanted change and I wanted it now. There had been several demonstrations on the university campus that spring protesting the presence of Dow Chemical and other large corporations which were recruiting students for employment. The demonstrations had gotten violent, with arrests being made, students and professors alike being hauled off to jail. Once the students finished on campus they marched down State Street toward the capitol building in the center of Madison's downtown.

My father was part of a large hardware business in town and he managed one of the company's stores which happened to be on State Street. As the students streamed up the street, they broke windows in the buildings to show their contempt for "the pig". My dad was furious about this. He didn't care for the war but he would never have gone into the streets to protest. And for them to defile property was not acceptable in his book. I knew that if I stayed in Madison, I would probably embarrass Mom and Dad and their friends. So, I stuck to my plans to return to New York.

Another important thing was happening however. While in Madison, I did not get my period. When Kevin and I had made love, neither of us had used protection. Quite honestly, I'm not sure it occurred to us. I was in a quandary about this. I wished that I could talk to my mother about it, but she had always been judgmental about sexual promiscuity and I feared her response. I was already questionable because of my political stance and to now also tell her that I might be pregnant was more than I could bear, let alone her. I knew I needed to get a pregnancy test and I didn't want to do this in Madison.

Back in NYC, Peter was very happy to see me. I couldn't figure this out – he'd basically dumped me for another woman, had come to Aspen to see me, now was really glad I was back. I moved back in to 16 St. Marks Place and made an appointment at the Margaret Sanger Clinic. My test came back negative and I was incredibly relieved, even though I still had not gotten my period. Peter and I saw each other a lot, sleeping at his place most of the time.

I called Bill Harris at Janus Films and he set up an appointment. I went in and met with him and his partners, Saul Turrell and Bill Becker. They questioned my business background with my job at Rover Motors, but Bill really wanted me to get a job there, so I was hired. My title was Director of Advertising and Public Relations/Non-Theatrical. I would spearhead a new campaign directed at schools, film societies, libraries; all the places that rented films that weren't movie theaters. That department was run by Bill Pence, who several years later, co-founded the Telluride Film Festival.

Janus was a small company with offices on 58th St., across from the back door of the Plaza Hotel. One of the employees who was my age was Gene Stavis who handled rentals to the theaters across the country that played classic and foreign films, which were in the Janus catalogue. Gene was a large man with a heart of gold and a memory for the thousands of movies he had seen. This became my film school – watching the Janus collection with Gene, going to screenings of new available films, talking everyday about the greatest movies ever made.

The one film that totally captured my heart and imagination was Truffaut's "Jules and Jim". It is a romance with mystery and feminine wiles and Jeanne Moreau was entrancing in it. The catalogue also included "400 Blows", 19 Bergman films, Antonioni, Fellini, Kurosawa. It was a great beginning of a love affair. A friend of Gene's worked at Pathe Contemporary, a small company similar to Janus. His name was Jonathan Demme and he had a similar job to mine. So the three of us spent a lot of time together seeing and talking films.

Meanwhile, I knew I was pregnant. I went back to the Sanger Clinic and this time the test was positive. I went to Peter and told him we'd gotten pregnant, which I really believed as the other earlier test had been negative. This was 1967 and abortion in the United States was illegal. Peter had been through this before and said I had two choices that he could recommend. Go to Puerto Rico for a few days or to New Jersey where he knew of a doctor who performed abortions. Puerto Rico scared me. Having just been through Mexico, I thought I would take my chances in New Jersey.

I was relieved to see that the clinic was actually nice and clean with doctors and nurses. I was examined and when they asked when I got pregnant, I told them we thought it was in June.

They wanted to perform the abortion between the eight-week point and the twelve-week point so my appointment was to be a few weeks in the future. But by the time I was in the doctor's office undergoing the procedure, I was three months pregnant. Although I was given a drug to relax me, I could tell that the doctor and his nurses were concerned as they realized the fetus was older than they had figured. They knocked me out as they proceeded.

Peter was furious with me when I came out. I was woozy and needed help to the car but I couldn't really blame him as he had just paid half the fee. The nurse had told him how far along I had been and it was now obvious that he wasn't the father. He dropped me at my apartment and left me alone.

I had made plans to stay the weekend with my good friend Susan and her boyfriend, Hugh. When he came to pick me up, I fainted as I made my way to the car. I was bleeding heavily and was barely conscious when we got to their place on the upper west side. I slept from the middle of the afternoon until Susan woke me up for dinner. I couldn't touch food and went back to sleep again, after attending to the heavy bleeding. The Kotex wasn't enough, so Susan gave me some towels. By Monday morning, I was able to get into a cab and head home. Susan and Hugh had gone to work, she at Putnam where she was assistant to the Editor-in-Chief, Bill Targ, and Hugh to IP, International Paper, where he was an executive.

I called in sick at Janus, promising I'd be back at work soon. In retrospect, I could have died. I continued to bleed for weeks and, although I was unaware of it at the time, am now sure that I also contracted pelvic inflammatory disease. I weighed about hundred pounds and had a grey pallor even months later. Could I blame the Sanger Clinic for their erroneous test and their refusal to help me find a solution and then again, following the abortion? The abortion doctor who set my appointment too far in the future? I can only look to myself and accept that I was the one who should have been better informed and better able to deal with the consequences.

One year later, I was again pregnant. Stupid? Yes. I was seeing someone and it turned sexual and I learned the hard way that a diaphragm doesn't always protect you. Ray was a wealthy ad man, turning out high-end commercials for television. He looked like an Italian thug but had great spirit and taste. He loved music and we hung with famous jazz musicians. One night, it happened and 6 weeks later, when we were no longer hanging out, I sent him a formal announcement: "Jeanne Field regrets to announce the forthcoming birth of our child. RSVP immediately to determine the next course of action."

He called, laughing at my chutzpah, but concerned that we deal with this immediately. This time was comparatively easy. Almost too much so. We met a man at the Hudson Hotel on 33rd and 8th Avenue, near Madison Square Garden. Several other couples were there too and we were instructed to get separate cabs and follow the man who was in his car, caravanning to Brooklyn. We women were taken upstairs to an apartment and the men waited on the sidewalk below. We were each put in a room to wait.

When it was my turn, I was led to the kitchen. Dr. Adams was waiting there and helped me lie down on a table. My god, the kitchen table abortion. I couldn't believe it. He was a nice older man and talked to me soothingly so that I would relax. He learned that I was from Madison and said his son was going to the university there, my alma mater. This really bothered him. What was I doing in his kitchen? Didn't I know better? He carried on with the D&C.

As he finished, he asked, "Have you ever seen a fetus?"
"No," I answered.
"Well take a good look," as he held it in front of my face. "And I never want to see you back here again."

The bloody tissue I was looking at didn't resemble anything human but it also didn't make me feel better about what choice I had made.

He helped me off of the table and walked me back to my room. "Lie here for thirty minutes then you can go."

There was a radio on a side table next to the bed. It played on a low volume but I could hear that it was a talk show and the subject was, strangely, abortion. Women were calling in and talking to the host about their opinions and experiences. Once again, I had given up a chance to have a baby. My mistake and my choice. An illegal choice, one that made me an outlaw. Both Dr. Adams and I could have faced a jail sentence in 1968.

Ray was waiting for me on the sidewalk. Two hours had passed. He was sweet and helped me into the cab that had waited at the curb. He was really hungry and, surprisingly, so was I. He bought me a steak dinner at the restaurant across the street from my place on St. Marks then we said good night.

Now in the 21st century, the abortion, or as I prefer to call it, a woman's right to choose, is still a political football. And no surprise that it's conservative men who want to make it illegal. Do I want women now to face what I did? No way. How I went through this, I'm not sure, but I wouldn't wish it on anyone. Eventually, I went into the mountains and said prayers for my unborn children and it relieved the guilt I felt.

•<•>•<•>•<•>•<•>•

Back at Janus Films, I had a big meeting. The famous Hollywood comic actor, Harold Lloyd, was coming to town to help us put together promotional material for "The Funny Side of Life", a Janus "hard ticket" evening of his films. This included "Safety Last!", a favorite silent film which has Harold as the Boy, trying to make his way in the big city. He gets into trouble and scales the facade of a building up to a large clock, from which he dangles. This had become an iconic image for Harold and silent films. Also part of the program was a series of bits from other films. We booked this into large, up-scale auditoriums which touted the night as a special event and charged a much higher price than the usual movie theater ticket. Harold held forth at the meeting, giving us great ideas and we put our thoughts on the table as well.

Later, he came into my office and asked if I could join him for the rest of the day. A date with the famous Harold Lloyd! My bosses said of course I should go and help Harold find a stand somewhere down Broadway that made the best non-alcoholic Pina Coladas. I thought, who better to stroll down Broadway with than Harold Lloyd on a mission as whimsical as one of his movies, looking for Pina Coladas? So, we set out, wandering down the famous street. He was positive it was on one corner but it wasn't so we journeyed on. Perhaps, we found the one he had remembered – God knows how old that memory might have been, as he was 74 at the time – but we did find one place and it seemed to satisfy him as the drinks were refreshing and we had fun with the counterman who asked if he was the famous Harold Lloyd.

Then he asked if I'd seen "The Dirty Dozen". I hadn't, so that was the next stop, at one of the big movie palaces on Broadway where the film was playing. Of course, the movie is a real crowd pleaser, but so different than the movies – or should I say "films" - that Janus collected and I sold.

After that, of course, we were hungry. Where to go for dinner? Of all the places in NYC, he went for PJ Clarks on 3rd, the hamburger joint. Good burgers, but really casual with it's aluminum front room and the darker backroom with tables. We had a blast. He walked in and it was like being with the Mayor. We took a table in the bar and everyone came to pay homage to him. He couldn't pay for a drink, let alone a burger. We were there until 1am when he led me outside into a waiting limo. As we cruised toward my apartment, he kept commenting on how far downtown we were getting. As the car turned on St. Marks Place which was, as usual, a zoo teeming with all sorts of people looking for fun, he couldn't believe I actually lived there. Gentleman that he was, he dropped me off at the door, made sure I got in okay, then was off.

38

Some time later, when I realized where he lived, I was chagrined. Harold owned 105 acres in Beverly Hills and had a magnificent estate and here I was in a fourth floor walk-up in the East Village.

5am, I woke up and my eyes are on fire. I couldn't open them to see. I barely made it to my neighbor's door and asked him to call a cab for me. He helped me down to the street and into the car. I was rushed to an emergency ward of the nearest hospital where corneal abrasions were diagnosed and attended to. I wore contact lenses which back then were glass and the hours spent partying with Harold Lloyd has been too much in the smoky environment. I'd never experienced this injury to my eyes and was frightened, patched up and blind. Who could I call to get me home? I decided to call a friend from work, Craig, who was a salesman for Janus. He came to the hospital and we took a cab back to my apartment. He was being so nice that all my panic went away. Then he hugged me and started to kiss me and led me to my bed. What was happening? I told him I needed to sleep and he forced himself onto me. Having sex with a blind helpless girl was outside my understanding but I let him do it. I was stunned that he took advantage of me like that. I should have had some of my radical friends take revenge on him for me. But I survived it, so I let it pass. The joy of going to work did diminish after that.

The summer of 1967 had so many high tension power lines running through it: Anti-war, Be-Ins, Civil rights, Drugs, Women's Lib. If you needed a cause, just pick one. Or, if you wanted to escape, go into your head, marijuana, LSD, DMT, speed, downers were all readily available and so was meditation and yoga. Rents were cheap, jobs easy to get, positive and negative energy surged together, against each other like a throbbing eternal rock 'n roll lightshow. Marches in Washington and New York thronged down the streets gathering hippies, commies, activists of all ages, returning Viet Nam vets, politicians, wannabes, chanting "Hell No, We Won't Go, Hey Hey LBJ, How Many Kids Did You Kill Today." Central Park came alive on weekends as huge crowds gathered in Sheep Meadow to bliss out, Be Here Now, Love Everyone, Dance To

The Music, Turn On, Tune In, Drop Out. You could be a rabid anti-war Peacenik one weekend, the next, a zoned-out hippie Buddhist chanting along with Allen Ginsberg. The External vs. the Internal, we were being challenged within and without. Was War the Answer? Do we give Peace a Chance? The volatility of the culture of politics was confusing, a revolving conundrum that asked the basic questions of what will you do for yourself, your street, city, state, country? Uptight business types grew their hair long, threw away their neckties, bought a pair of bell bottoms. They wore military surplus jackets and hats and surged into the lines of cops who patrolled the street marches.

We women bought scarves, long flowing skirts and put flowers in our hair. We wore jeans and turtlenecks, burned our bras and said no to makeup. You could sleep with anyone you wanted to and not expect love, marriage or devotion. Superficially, at least, there were changes. Going a step further, Women's Lib was also Men's Lib, although most of the men didn't want to consider this. The point was, that if women became part of the workforce because they wanted in, men could also opt out of the obligation to be the sole support of the family. They could become house husbands, let their wife be the money-earner. Today, this is almost a non-issue. In 1967, it was huge, and our parents were quaking in their boots. Everything they'd worked for was being questioned by their privileged progeny.

Down in the Village, St. Mark's Place was a tireless party grooving with the times. Kids from Long Island came in droves on the week-end turning the street into a gridlocked paradise. The Fillmore East around the corner on 2nd Ave. rocked every night. Blue Cheer, the loudest band on earth, the San Francisco imports, good fusion jazz, all played at Bill Graham's palace. I got to know the doorman through my friend Valerie Gold, a kewpie doll girlfriend from Fire Island. Jerry Pompili, who manned the door, would always let me in and continued to do so as he rose up in the ranks of Graham's empire.

But for me it wasn't just play, I had work to do and at Janus it wasn't going as well as I had hoped. My PR background from Rover Motors didn't quite transfer to the film business. I didn't have the rolodex I should have had, filled with newspaper and magazine editors and writers who would plug the Janus films I was sending out across the country. I struggled to find a place there that made sense.

I loved Truffaut, Fellini, Bergman, Kurosawa and the other filmmakers. I felt so fortunate to be learning from their stories and their artistry. As I mentioned before "Jules and Jim" was a film I could watch over and over, with a woman, Catherine, desired by the two men who were friends but so different. She marries Jules, then the Great War comes and separates them, Jules fighting for Austria, Jim for France. After the war, Catherine is unhappily married and Jim comes to visit. Jules tells Jim to make her happy. Catherine can't hurt Jules more than she already has. She invites Jim to take a ride with her and, telling Jules to watch carefully, she drives them off a bridge to their deaths. All of this is told so lyrically, with a narration and wonderful music that carried the romantic feelings of the three. The film was a hippie dream with a floating camera style and a joie de vivre.

The vibe in the office turned strange and I couldn't put my finger on it. And then it became icily clear – the other woman in the office was spreading tales about me. I was a hippie, I lived in the East Village, did she also know about Craig, had he said something to her? One of the other men in the office was always coming on to me, inviting me to stay late and have a drink or three. He was married but didn't want to take no for an answer. I had one for him. Bill Harris and I started dating. He was wealthy and fun, in a conservative way, and he was an art collector. He loved being around powerful people and had pursued the famous communications philosopher (Hot and Cool mediums), Marshall McLuhan, who was in New York at Fordham University occupying a special chair for a year. "The Medium is the Message" was his mantra and the advertising world was reverberating from it.

The New York Film Festival was held that September and the movie by Pontecorvo, "The Battle of Algiers" was opening it. Bill and I had tickets and joined Marshall for the pre-show cocktail hour. At one point, he took us by the arms and said he wanted to introduce us to an important New York artist, hoping, I'm sure, that Bill would be interested in buying something. There in a corner of the New York State Theater by himself was Andy Warhol, blond hair shock over one eye, who limply shook our hands and spoke so quietly we could barely hear him for the din of the crowd.

We went in to watch the movie and like everyone in that theater, were mesmerized by the film. When it ended, there was a long silence. Then the crowd rose to its feet and roared. The revolutionary spirit of Algeria breaking the chains of French colonialism was in sync with the American leftists who ranted against the war and the blindness of Washington politicians.

A few weeks later, Hubert Humphrey came to town, staying at the Hilton on Avenue of the Americas. I was planning to attend a protest rally there at 6pm. when I got a call from Jonathan Demme. He said it was important that I stop by his office before going to the hotel. When I came in, he didn't look happy. He told me Bill had called him and asked him to relay a message to me that Bill wanted to break up and I should come by his apartment and pick up any clothes or whatever might be there. I couldn't believe it. He couldn't talk to me personally? No, Jonathan said, he couldn't. He could barely talk to Jonathan. I wished I would have let him crash down Aspen Mt. by himself. And, obviously, the job was over too. After this news, I didn't have the heart to go protest Vice President Humphrey so I made my way up to 72nd Street where Bill lived and let myself into the apartment. He was in bed with the covers pulled up over his head. He wouldn't speak but wailed he would talk to me some other time. I grabbed my few belongings and knew that other time would never come and I didn't care less. A week later, I was fired. And they say women are hard to understand.

Hotel Balconies

Chapter Five

Free Lance

For the next year, I worked at several jobs. Jules Maidoff who designed the Janus Catalogue had become a friend and asked me to represent his graphics company, Asterisk Associates. He was a wonderfully expressive painter and some of this work was used on movie posters, record covers and book jackets. Jules' office and studio was on W. 57th Street in a building that had been Stanford White's home. We had the second floor rear which had been a drawing room and gave enough room for the receptionist/bookkeeper, a graphics assistant, Jules' studio/office, and a small desk for me. Stanford White was a famous architect who was killed by the husband of his young lover, Evelyn Nesbit, an actress and model and the whole sordid story was written about in "The Girl in the Red Velvet Swing".

My job at Asterisk was to contact book publishers, record companies, small businesses who might need advertising design. I carried a large portfolio with previous examples of Jules' work to all the meetings I could set up with art directors who worked for the various companies and began to establish a rapport with them.

Jules paid me a salary and a commission on sales but it wasn't enough to cover my New York City lifestyle so I took another job at a high-end ski store in Rockefeller Plaza called Streeter and Quarles. Les Streeter had been a well-known competitive skier who my friend Bill McDonough knew. Bill worked in advertising, lived on 72nd St. and hung out with a successful group of guys like Pier Mapes who would one day be president of NBC. Les hired me on Bill's recommendation and the fact that I'd just spent a winter in

Aspen and was up-to-date on ski wear. The equipment, skis, boots and poles, was the department of real ski experts. I worked nights, showing up at 5pm and closed the store at nine, which still gave me lots of time to hit the clubs with friends. New York is "the city that never sleeps". Why should I?

I still saw the people who I'd met while at Janus and Jonathan Demme was one of them. He'd left Pathe and was working in PR at United Artists. One day he called to say that he had a dream assignment: escorting Francois Truffaut around New York. In fact, he was to meet the director's plane the next day. Before he left for JFK, I went to his office and presented him with one of my favorite possessions, a 5" white "campaign" button that said, "TRUFFAUT". Jonathan wore it to the airport and the director reportedly had a good laugh.

In January, 1968, I returned to Aspen to stay with the Chases, see friends and ski. Betsy returned the favor and came to New York for a visit. Curt had moved to the small cottage on their property and was seeing a blond ski instructor. Betsy had friends as well but she and Curt still met every morning at 7am for breakfast. And, the kids were doing great.

Diana Stamberger, meanwhile, had left her husband Fritz for a New York heir, Doug Burden. They had met in Aspen and the allure of living in New York with the scion of a famous family became a bait she couldn't avoid. They split their time between Aspen and New York where they lived in his mother's apartment at United Nations Plaza. I saw her in Aspen and again in NYC. She was in over her head. Men like Doug are expected to marry women who have family money. Diana didn't and her spending habits soon put the Burdens in the uncomfortable position of cutting her off. She scored a meeting with Oscar de la Renta, hoping to model for him. He insisted she undress in front of him so he could see if she measured up. As beautiful as she was, she didn't meet his standards, or else he could see she might be trouble. Whatever happened, she didn't get the job.

Compared to this, I continued to live a very downtown kind of life. I was a working hippie. I looked into joining Newsreel, a commune of radical filmmakers. If we couldn't make our voices heard in Washington, D.C. perhaps we could make films that could reach out. I went to only one meeting. "The Men" controlled everything, shouting each other down, arguing profanely, fuck that, fuck you, etc. I couldn't believe it. Weren't we all in this together? Wasn't that sort of attitude what we were against? The women were obviously only included as bed partners and considering the level of hygiene, was not something that appealed to me.

The months passed and I was professionally challenged. The right job wasn't in sight, the city was not doing well under Mayor Lindsay, the end of a tumultuous decade was drawing to a close. The assassinations of Martin Luther King in April, then two months later, Robert Kennedy, blew everyone away. Nobody could believe that James Earl Ray or Sirhan Sirhan had acted alone, just as we doubted that JFK's assassination had been done by just one man. Conspiracy was the word of the times. The shadow government was in control. LBJ was not going to run again which paved the way for Richard Nixon to sweep into office. The Yippies - the Youth International Party - Jerry Rubin and my neighbor Abbie Hoffman, had raided Wall Street and the Stock Exchange a few months before, throwing dollar bills down on the traders. Now, they pranked everything and maybe that was the right attitude – don't take the shit seriously and take that to the limit. Most of us felt like outlaws anyway, smoking pot, getting abortions, arrested at marches and demonstrations. But, sadness was the end result, as the idea that corrupt forces could actually be in charge sunk in.

Michael Mann was a close friend from the UW who was living in London attending film school. I had been in touch with Michael as he was making short films and I took them around to American distributors. In college, he'd studied English Lit and read a lot of poetry, Yeats being a favorite. One of his films was shot in India, in the southern state of Kerala, and was visually beautiful, romantic and enticing with sitar music that built like an exotic "Bolero".

In late August, he called with a new project. That spring, in Paris, the students had revolted. They got support from the working class as well and for several long days, held the city in their grip. The Gendarmes, who drank their lunch, would wade into the lines of students protesting and beat them silly. But the students and the workers made a difference, stood strong and all of France listened, a "Les Mis" for the '60s.

When a friend of his, Elio Zarmatti, a Frenchman, called and said he could get a camera crew into the Sorbonne University on an exclusive to follow up on the revolution, Michael asked if I would work with his father-in-law and sell the resulting footage. Michael's wife, Sharon, was from New York and her father was a lawyer for the film industry. With his contacts we were able to get a meeting with an executive at NBC and indeed sold the project. Michael and Elio had their production funds and made a good film but it wasn't explosive or exciting. All of the French zeal of that spring had been spent, and the students only wanted to make up for lost time in their studies.

Michael and I had dated in college and one night went to see a movie at the Student Union Theater. It was a Bergman film which at the time meant nothing to me. Michael was taking a Film History course which had just been added to the university curriculum and had learned about the taciturn Ingmar Bergman who was writing, directing, producing his own films in Sweden. The film was "Wild Strawberries" which tells the story of an elderly man traveling with a young relative to the city to attend a ceremony honoring him. They pick up some young hitchhikers who infuse energy into the trip and their company begin to trigger long-ago memories for the old man. I was knocked out by this movie, thinking, is this what a movie can be? It was thrilling to see it and stayed with me and was instrumental in my move into the film business.

Now, working with Michael, I felt like I was really in the game. Michael, of course, would later go on to very big things, making "Thief", "The Last of the Mohicans", "Ali", "Heat", the list goes on.

One thing I'd figured out at Janus was that I'd rather make movies than sell them. I just had to figure out how to make that transition. I was still going to screenings and one of the people I'd run into was an imposing man, Bob Maurice, who had run an art house theater in Los Angeles and was now employed by two young filmmakers who were shooting documentaries and very low budget features. He asked me several times to come up and talk and maybe join him in a distribution arm of the company. There wouldn't be much money at first, but it was promising. I put him off, needing more money than was being offered.

Another man approached me. He made naugahyde furniture. I was a perfect rep for his line. He even made business cards for me. The money was big, at least for a single woman living in a fourth floor walk-up in the East Village that rented for $67.35. What was it going to be: money vs. art, commerce vs. film?

In December, I heard that the Maysles, two brothers who made ground-breaking documentaries, were looking for someone. I called Porter Bibb who produced for them and got an appointment. We enjoyed the meeting and he offered me a job, starting immediately. Gee, I said, I've made reservations to go to Aspen in January, can I start when I return. His demeanor turned to stone. No, we need you now. Sorry, I said, can't do that. The job went away. I called Bob and told him that if he still had an opening I was there. Now? No, end of January. No problem, he said. Deal, I said.

I was twenty-six years old and still flying student fares that all the airlines offered. I had a bogus ID and could go stand-by but the operative word there was "stand-by". It became a game to zero in on a flight that wouldn't be over-booked and get my tail out to JFK and get on. So, there I was with a large suitcase filled with the absolutely necessary changes of winter clothing befitting an Aspen vacation, my ski boots and skis. Not an easy hump from taxi to shuttle to airport check in. But I made my flight and once again, had a great time in Aspen.

While there, I met a handsome Air Force pilot who had just served in Viet Nam and who was on a well-deserved holiday. Someone was looking out for this guy because he was being feted all over town. Although we were wary of each other, me the anti-war peacenik and he the guy dropping bombs, he invited me to join a group on a snowcat ski excursion into the uncharted reaches of Snowmass, before Snowmass became a resort with condos and ski lifts. We were towed by snowmobiles for a few miles then transferred to three snowcats which took us to the summit. The cat we were in threw a track and we were stuck. My friend had to stay with the driver and asked me to take the lunch backpack down to the rest of the skiers and let them know there was an emergency. I set out, only knowing I had to go down. Snowmass was a huge area. The Burn, a run that is now famous for it's size and difficult status, lay before me. It was untracked, un-groomed snow. I had never been there before and yet here I was, once again, up against the elements, finding my way down a mountain. After scanning the slopes, calling out to the rest of the crew and getting not even a yodel, I managed to make my way to the bottom where I saw the snowmobiles and the other skiers. The weather came in, clouds full of snow filled the valley, and the day was done.

Chapter Six

Paradigm Shift

My return to the city was filled with anticipation of my new job. Bob Maurice was a pretty distinctive-looking man even by New York City, late '60's standards. Usually dressed in skinny jeans and T-shirt, his most distinctive feature was his enormous head with his large glasses, brooding brows and helmet-like long hair. Raised poor, he put himself through college working heavy construction in Los Angeles and his physique and carriage still spoke of those days. He could have a hilarious way of speaking, making up voices and laughing at his own jokes, then he would become absolutely serious. Given his druthers he would have stayed home and read medieval history but here he was trying to carve out a niche in a peculiar and difficult business, art house cinema distribution. He loved to discourse for hours on movies, history, art, drinking and carousing.

Bob worked for Paradigm Films which was a small company owned by John Binder and Michael Wadley who were a documentary team, John taking sound and Mike on camera. They wanted to meet me to give the okay for Bob to bring me into his department. They were both very attractive men, John dark and serious, Mike blond and loquacious. Both were married to modern dancers, Sharon and Renee, who had attended Ohio State University and were now part of Paul Taylor's Company. The four of them had known each other since their early college years. They had a great vibe and I was really excited about my chances. I gave them my pitch about my background in PR and working at Janus Films, finishing with the statement that there was no doubt they'd hire me. Why was that, they asked. Well, you see, when I left Janus I had a copy of their mailing list pulled and I have it. I have the name of every company, cinema, library, school, film society in this country that rents or buys films. They were duly impressed that I'd "liberated" this fantastic resource. Power to the People, I said and I had the job.

Paradigm's offices were on Broadway at 81st Street on the second floor of a nice building with big arched windows. They were there because a year earlier, a large television company, Teletape, had invested in their company. Downstairs, the parent company filmed "Sesame Street" in a large studio. In our offices, there was a large main room for production people; John and Mike each had an office; in-house editor, ex-art history scholar, coolest woman in the room, Thelma Schoonmaker, now Marty Scorsese's long time editor/collaborator, had a cutting room; then along a corridor, offices for Bob, his girlfriend, Joyce, and one for me. We had a small storage room for our distribution prints and a closet in which we could clean and repair those prints before they were sent out again on rental.

The energy in the company really flowed. There were always several productions in different stages and it was the next semester of my film school. I'd learned film history and criticism at Janus, now I could learn the hands-on method of making a movie. I only had to stay cool, do my distribution job, and I was certain that the opportunity would arise.

One of the main reasons Bob had hired me was that Paradigm was making it's own independent films. These included: Martin Scorsese's first feature, "Who's That Knocking at My Door", starring Harvey Keitel, whose day job was selling shoes, and Zina Bethune, a dancer; "David Holzman's Diary" directed by Jimmy McBride starring L.M. Kit Carson which combined documentary and fictional elements; and the latest from Jimmy entitled, "My Girlfriend's Wedding" in which (the title says it all), Jimmy's girlfriend got married to a friend so she could get a green card. Clarissa, the girlfriend, was a voluptuous, gregarious woman from England and she loved all the attention she was getting. Part of the movie included a scene in which she tells about an abortion she chooses to get and it just so happened she went to the same doctor in Brooklyn I had gone to.

This film was not as arresting as the first two and so I viewed it as a real challenge to distribute. "David Holzman's Diary" had captured the imagination of the '60s indie world with it's pseudo-cinema verite style and it's twist at the end. The film had played like a documentary but as the credits rolled you realized that it was totally fictional and the story beat that David's equipment had been stolen brought the film to an abrupt end. In fact, Jimmy had shot an earlier version of this film and then had the entire negative stolen from the trunk of his car. He admitted the second version was far superior to the first and so the theft was a fortuitous event. Of such things greatness is sometimes made. "My Girlfriend's Wedding", the sophomore outing, was almost too personal and Jimmy was coming to that decision as well because he became impossible to deal with. He and Bob had terrible fights, yelling, banging around the office, and finally Jimmy was thrown out and told not to come back. Paradigm had paid for the production so it owned a large part of the film which they wanted to recoup. Bob and I held several "invitation only" screenings for film bookers in New York, the press, groovy film people, but it came a cropper.

This failure scared me. Would I be able to keep my job if I couldn't sell the product? I had to make a difference somehow. Another film that Paradigm had made was "No Vietnamese Ever Called Me Nigger". The awkward title was something Mohammed Ali had uttered and was relevant to the content of the movie. The film was a personal favorite of John Binder's. He had poured himself into it even though another man, David Loeb Weiss, was the director. John and Mike financed it, and shot much of the multi-camera footage, then John edited it. Most of the film was shot during a march from Harlem to the U.N. Plaza where many speakers, including Martin Luther King, held a rally. That day, King connected the civil rights movement to the anti-war movement, saying that black men were not going to wage a white man's war any more. The documentary included in-depth interviews with several young vets who were incredibly verbal – "Say It Loud, I'm Black, I'm Proud" - about their wartime experiences and their current struggle to re-enter American society at a time when black power, civil rights, and anti-war sentiments were foremost in the minds of our generation. They didn't want the same jobs of servitude their parents had settled for but were stymied when they tried to move forward. It was a searing look at the lives facing young black Viet Nam vets who were returning home from Viet Nam to Harlem or the Bronx, ghetto neighborhoods surrounded by white ones where they still faced racism. It also had some very moving and sometimes funny scenes as street people commented on the march and politics of that hideous war. It was, and continues to be, a strong, bold, truth-telling film and is used in many college courses on African-American studies.

I believed in the movie and I sold it. It went out to film societies, college town theaters and the final coup was my selling prints of it to IBM for their company libraries around the country. And what that taught me about myself was that in order to be effective, I have to believe. I wasn't a saleswoman who could sell ice to Eskimos. I had to have a cause, a film that made a difference.

John and Mike had a top assistant, a young man who could do everything on a small film crew: camera, sound, lighting, sound transferring, editing. They called him "Boy Wonder". He was invaluable to the company with his great energy, quick wit, and total dedication. And, he was very attractive. Larry Johnson was an army brat, raised on bases around the world, Japan, Germany, Georgia, Florida. He was twenty-one when we met and I was a five years older. We got to know each other at the office and then dated, and then spent nights at my apartment on St. Marks or his in Boerum Hill in Brooklyn.

I mention the age difference because it was a critical one. I worked – that was good. I wanted to become a filmmaker – also good. There was an acceptance of me as an equal to him that was a new experience. That, combined with Larry's affinity for women, helped make our relationship a different one for me. He saw me as I was not who or what I should be in the pantheon of coupledom.

My war baby generation was the last of something and the beginning of something else. When I graduated from college, many of my girlfriends were pinned or engaged. They would have failed college if they weren't, as wasn't that the one reason women got degrees, but especially their Mrs. There were some of us who knew we had choices. If we wanted the ring and the ceremony to go forth into the world with a significant other, that was possible. But, it was just as possible and acceptable to continue our education or move to a big city and get an interesting job, all before we settled down to a picket fence reality. Of course, the draft was also pushing young couples into marriage as that, at least for a while, kept the guys out of Viet Nam.

I had always been intrigued by the world of business. When I turned sixteen, I got a job at Wolff, Kubly and Hirsig, the hardware store and company my dad worked at. I loved working with the people, waiting on people in the store, manning the gift-wrap concession, whatever department they put me in. I loved talking with my dad about his side of the business in which he worked with architects, builders, contractors on large buildings and custom homes. I met Frank Lloyd Wright when I was a child when he paid a visit to my dad at the store and his democratic architecture made so much sense.

Compared to the homemaking chores my mom did, the outside world was really appealing. I would help her with housework and in the kitchen, but it wasn't my calling. (That actually would come much much later.) I wanted to pursue business in some sense, not sure what, but to see what was out there. When I graduated from college, I again worked at the store, this time in the credit department, but while Fritzy Wolff and Dan Kubly, my contemporaries, were offered positions in the company, I wasn't. Something the bosses held against women in the families coming into the business, per chance? A number of years later, it did occur to me that my dad and men his age weren't necessarily against us working, but they really didn't want us to see how hard the business world was, where they treated each other badly, trading insults, challenging each other in the competition of survival of the fittest.

I had never reached the level in a company where any of this would come into play. And here I was at Paradigm Films, in a job I liked at a company I really liked, and there was an acceptance of me as an employee who could take a path of her own design.

The hours were long. After I did the distribution work, I would stay late and re-wind film, watch Larry or Thelma cut film, absorbing all I could about how to make a movie. There were several in-house productions at that time. Mike had gone to the Hindu Kush in the Himalayas to make a film on an expedition. The climbers could barely make it in the high altitude and here was Wadley filming them as they trekked toward the camera, moving backwards, carrying a twenty-two pound Éclair camera and keeping everything in focus. There were circus commercials for Barnum and Bailey, car commercials for Jam Handy, a big advertising film company in Detroit. But the most exciting were the music specials they were doing for Merv Griffin, road trips with well-known bands or singers that Merv would broadcast on his television show.

Larry stayed so busy that the idea of going to Fire Island to sit on a beach held little interest for him. It was a waste of time when he could be accomplishing so much at the office. He had a great work ethic which continued his whole life and blurred the lines between life and work, it was who and what you were. This matched my long-held desire to be productive in business and what better business could I think of than the film business.

We did take one week-end off and took a friend of mine and his girlfriend out to Bayberry Dunes. Michael Markowitz was one of the co-founders of a commune that lived and worked in the East Village called the Group Image. We had met through Ray Lofaro and had put on a huge party for a group of stockbrokers. The Group Image was a band with groupies that put on happenings. Michael was a wizard at communication, art, music and an all-around "head". He also did a lot of drugs. I had never done acid and Larry had but was interested in taking a trip so we combined all of these elements into a weekend. My friends and Fire Island housemates, Rennie Church and his girlfriend, Valerie Gold, would be our "guides", not partaking in the drugs and making sure we didn't get into trouble.

We dropped the acid at the house then set out for the beach. We walked along a wooden sidewalk into the dunes to the top of the tallest sand mound. As we looked out over the small trees and plants that covered the dunes, everything became ecstatic and alive, nothing like I'd ever seen before. The earth, sea and ski radiated it's incredible energy right into me. It was too much. I had to sit down. We made our way to the beach near the ocean and collapsed. Michael sat in the crossed-legged yoga pose and went straight into his head. His girlfriend decided that she really liked Larry and wanted to make love with him. He was not interested in her and that made her loud and angry. She went crazy and started screaming which caught the attention of a park ranger on his routine beach check. Rennie told Valerie to get me out of there and he went to talk with the ranger.

Val and I walked back to our house. I was zonked. As we walked across the deck to the door, a stranger, an exotic-looking redhead, welcomed me, freaking me out. What's she doing in my house, I asked and then Val reminded me that we'd rented the house to her starting on Monday and that she'd arrived a little early. The weather became cool and some storm clouds blew in from the shore. I pulled on a red and black lumberjack shirt and lay down on the deck by myself, telling Val I'd just hang out alone and she should go back to help Rennie.

Larry

Lying on the wooden deck, smelling the sea and feeling the rainy droplets that were beginning to fall, I went into a vision that I remember to this day. It was the archetypal acid trip, beginning with the void, the blackness of nothing, and the creation of a seed that grows into a life and into the being that was me. I experienced my own birth and thought that I had landed someplace else. Another planet, another reality, another home and it all seemed right.

Larry found me there and we both had entered into that stage of the acid trip where everything is funny. Your sides and face ache from laughing. I looked into a mirror and a duck looked back. My totem. From Duck to Eagle to Phoenix, that would be my path and my challenge. Our shared experience cemented our love and commitment to each other and I was thrilled with my boyfriend.

In early summer, 1969, a rock concert was announced. I was in the East Side Book Store across from my apartment on St. Marks Place and there was a poster with a bird on a guitar and it was called the "Woodstock Festival". Woodstock first came into my consciousness as an art community north of New York City and the home of Bob Dylan where he recuperated from an almost-death experience in a motorcycle crash. As he improved he started playing music with a group called The Band who brought out "Music From Big Pink". The Band was going to be at the festival and maybe Dylan would be too. There were a lot of bands listed on the poster I'd barely heard of but some names stuck out big time: Janis Joplin and the Holding Company, Jefferson Airplane, The Who, Jimi Hendrix, Ravi Shankar, Joan Baez. But who'd heard of Melanie or Jeff something or other. Arlo Guthrie was coming and he was Woodstock incarnate.

Paradigm owned a VW bus, perfect for production and this kind of weekend. I began to lobby Larry to go talk to Mike Wadley about going to the festival in August, camp out, get high, hear music, all near Woodstock. Larry said Wadley was into it, so I bought four tickets for Mike, Renee, Larry and me. Great!

During this time, I was also writing a film column for an underground newspaper, "Culture Hero", run by a Canadian conceptual artist, Les Levine. Following my article on the Puerto Rican cinemas in East Harlem, I did the first-ever print interview with Marty Scorsese. It was conducted in our favorite uptown Italian restaurant, Tony's on 79th St., and covered Marty's insistence that to be a film director you begin by calling yourself a director. He knew from the start that if he filmed the neighborhoods and people he had known all his life, he would be successful. Marty had become a frequent film editor at Paradigm where his dynamic two-fisted editing style earned him the moniker "The Sicilian Butcher". One reason Thelma and Marty became great collaborators, is that Thelma's cutting is smooth as silk.

Bob and I distributed Marty's NYU student films, "It's Not Just You, Murray" and "The Big Shave". Other filmmakers we were setting up relationships with were San Francisco experimentalists, Bruce Baillie, Scott Bartlett and Bruce Connor, indie documentary filmmaker, Les Blank, NYU graduate and director Jeremy Paul Kagan. Then the Woodstock machine began to rumble.

The Promoters of the festival put the word out that they wanted a film made. Leacock/Penebaker, Maysles, Paradigm all made presentations. Michael and John had recently purchased an eight-plate KEM editing machine from Germany with three picture heads and had done an Aretha Franklin film for Merv Griffin. Turning part of the office into a big screening room, we all pitched in to run the resulting multi-screen extravaganza the likes of which had not been seen since Abel Gance's "Napoleon". Aretha hit the high notes of "Respect" in five moving images and you couldn't help but get up and dance.

When David Maysles saw it, he became incredibly angry that Paradigm had gone to all this trouble. He and Mike argued and he ended up punching out Wads, knowing he'd been bested by a junior. Larry jumped in and shoved his fellow soundman down the stairs to Broadway. Paradigm got the gig. Of course, finances played a part in this. The older filmmakers wanted to be paid by the festival organizers to show up. They had demands. Paradigm said they'd cover their own expenses and split the ownership with the producers. They had credit at Kodak and every equipment rental house in New York; they knew all the young, up-and-coming cameramen on both coasts. It was going to happen.

Another media event took place that July in Central Park. As a small lunar landing module settled onto the face of the moon, the CBS, ABC and NBC networks' broadcast of those first steps for mankind were projected onto huge outdoor screens set up in Sheep Meadow. Larry and I spent the night cruising the crowd sharing the amazement at this moment with our friend and fellow space cadet Van Schley. The US was on the moon but it was still in Viet Nam, so overall, we had a guarded opinion of the government's accomplishment.

These days were a big turning point in my life. I had joined Paradigm so I could make movies and "Woodstock" was my chance. I went to Bob, my boss, and told him I wanted to work on the documentary. He said no way. I had to continue covering distribution for him because he was going to be a producer on the film. John and Michael were splitting up. Bob was to be John's replacement. He had his hands full. On top of that, Joyce, had just been diagnosed with a brain tumor. Joyce was a zaftig, pretty, very bright redhead and it was a terrible blow to Bob and all of us, and also to our business. I thought that doing production would be just a few days, then I would be back at my desk concentrating on our film catalogue.

These were difficult times for Bob but it also established a real bond between him and Michael. Wads had gone through three years of medical school at Columbia University and was very astute scientifically. He became a strong ballast for Bob who also wanted to count on me too. And he could, up to a point. My own ambition, my stubbornness prevailed. I begged him to let me do both jobs. He would not work it out with me to do both distribution and production. He said it was all or nothing. Larry was already at the festival site and said I should be there. He talked with Bob and I got a thumbs up. They needed all the help they could get.

On Thursday, the day before the music started, I rode up to Bethel (the new festival site which had been hurriedly found and built when the original Woodstock site was nixed by the near-by neighbors) with Van Schley and Eddie Kramer, music producer for Jimi Hendrix, who the promoters had hired to do the on-site recording. The roads were grid-locked and impassable. Eddie slept through Van's hell-bent driving on the shoulder of the road, and drooled all over my shoulder. Thank god for Eddie Kramer though, as he was the reason we were shepherded over back roads to Yasger's farm. He was also one of the most important people at the festival, since he alone mixed and recorded every moment of music that was played, a truly heroic feat. He did it blind as video taps into a recording truck didn't exist back then. He could not see the musicians as they played. He would say later, there were times when exhaustion made him effectively deaf, too.

We arrived in the middle of the night and the place still looked like a construction site. The stage was barely finished. The movable turntable sections that would have allowed one band to set up while the other played were nowhere near finished and never would be. Wads was on stage in his tall, white western reservation hat with his light meter working with lighting designer Chip Monck to get his readings. Chip was a maestro of lighting for the concert stage. He set the bar for dramatic lighting of live rock and roll shows, but he resisted Michael's request for the additional illumination that film stock of that era required. Some bands at Woodstock don't appear in the film because of it.

Dale Bell, who had given John and Mike their first paying doc job when he worked for Public Television, was the Line Producer working with them. Larry interfaced with the sound and music crew along with Eric Blackstead. The grip truck was parked behind the stage and the camera magazine loading pit was being constructed underneath the stage. The indispensable gaffer, grip, electrician Marty Andrews used his genius to create an electrical patch board out of 2x4's so that all the cameramen could be connected via headsets and their equipment run on AC instead of batteries. This assured that all the cameras ran at identical speed without variance. The place was electric in more ways than one.

The Woodstock Stage - Jeanne with an Éclair magazine

That night was the only one we made it to our motel, The Silver Spur, which we called the Silver Sperm. I have no idea where it was. My sense of geography that is usually akin to Sacagawea was out of whack. They led, I followed. Back again at the stage in the morning, I was assigned to Dick Pearce, a New York documentary cameraman from Kentucky. A calm professional, he in turn was assigned to Stage Left. I pulled cable, kept him in fresh Éclair film magazines, listened on the headset for any directions from Marty Scorsese or Thelma Schoonmaker, who were our assistant directors. I scavenged food, provided Dick a backrest and other novice filmie jobs. We were on the stage or on the film platform four feet just below the front of the stage for the next three days and nights. Endurance was the essential qualifier for this job.

There must have been an opening act that hadn't showed up or beat the traffic, so concert organizer John Morris, a cool man under all the pressure, convinced Richie Havens he had to open the show. They led him over from the performers' area with its tables and chairs covered by a suspended large white silk, across the bridge that connected to the stage that looked out on a sea of hundreds of thousands of people. Dick and I were ready in place, standing on the stage. The crowd roared and Richie struck a chord. It was so exciting and hard to believe it was my first film.

My high was interrupted by a very angry and stressed out Steve Cohen, the stage manager, who came over to me and said, "Who the fuck are you and what are you doing on my stage? You belong down there." pointing at the platform. Dick kept rolling, shooting Richie and I told Steve there was no way we were leaving. You can actually see this event in the movie in a wide shot of the stage during Richie's second song. I'm the small one in the green designer T-shirt.

I have to admit that a lot of these three days were a blur. It's hard to say what I remembered from the experience and what I saw later on film or was told had happened. The music was loud, the hours long, the sleep almost non-existent. The crew slept on the ground under the grip truck and with an evening of music ending early morning, most sleep was caught sometime during a day that was hot, muggy and noisy. And we had it good. You've all seen what the people on the other side of the fence put up with in Max Yasger's cow field.

The music was great but some of it was terrible. The musicians were under stress from the interminable waiting-to-go-on, from the heat and the rainstorms, from the overwhelming crowds and some of them definitely welcomed the offer in post-production to overdub their vocals. High points for me were: Richie H., his passionate singing, his smiling broadly with no teeth; Joe Cocker air-guitaring and delivering "With a Little Help from My Friends"; the Maharishi grinning, addressing the crowd, "The world is a whole"; The Who, with Pete Townsend crowning Abbie Hoffman over the head with his guitar when Abbie rushed the stage and tried to grab Pete's mike, an event unfortunately not captured on film; Arlo, funny and relaxed, talking to the crowd, "The New York State Tollway is closed, man"; Santana, an unknown San Francisco man with a band whose presence was advocated by Bill Graham in his inimitable way; holding AC equipment in the rainstorm, realizing we were all lightening rods; Sly and the Family Stone singing "Higher, Higher" with everyone on their feet screaming with them; CSNY warming the stage when we were all shivering in the wet coldness of 4am Sunday morning; Jimi noodling for an hour before hitting on his stirring war motif "Star Spangled Banner."

Two icons who should have been at Woodstock were Bob Dylan and Joni Mitchell. Joni wrote the anthem "Woodstock" after she watched reports of the festival's success on TV and listened to David Geffen's description. She was scheduled to be on "The Dick Cavett Show" and they didn't think she could perform on stage and then get back to New York in time. Maybe it was more than Dylan could put up with. When The Band came on stage, the film crew was instructed to stay on the shooting platform and if Robbie Robertson had even a glimpse of a camera lens, he was out of there.

What I didn't see at the Festival were all the food and crafts booths, the camps, the lake and nude swimming, the people wandering and wondering. Because of the crowd and my assigned job, I stuck close to home base. Maybe I missed the real deal but this was work and I was making a first film and boy was I serious.

Back in New York, things got into high gear. We celebrated with champagne when a Warner Bros. check in the amount of $100,000 arrived. Thankfully, because the Woodstock filming had been paid for with only $20,000 in cash which Michael and John had in the bank from previous work, and Paradigm's line of credit. The low-key office became a beehive with three shifts synching the hundreds of thousands of feet of film with sounds tracks around the clock. It was a job made impossibly difficult by the fact that most of the footage shot on stage was not "slated", so there were no start

cues and identifiers on the sound track. Shooting under controlled
conditions, the camera pans to a slate or a clapper board which
identifies the number of the shot etc. and the clapper makes a sound
like two hands clapping, so there is a picture of that at the head of
the shot which is matched in the synching process with the clapping
sound on the track. Then picture and sound, film and sprocketed
tape, can be run in synch with each other throughout the editing
process. Woodstock had no controlled conditions, no slate shots, no
start signal on the sound tapes, plus the additional complexity of as
many as eight cameras turning on and off at random during each
performance. Sometimes musicians had to be brought in to
decipher what song a guitarist might be fingering in a camera close-
up with no other visible information. An editor might spend days
trying to synch a guitar solo to the wrong shot.

As the clutch of editors dealt with that synching nightmare,
Sonya Polonsky and Hannah Hempstead ran the office and
production working with Dale. Yeu-Bun Yee, Jerry Huggins, Stan
Warnow and Marty Scorsese edited the synched footage. Phyllis
Smith, Tina Hirsch, Miriam Eger assisted along with several others.
I was dying to join them but Bob prevailed here. I continued my
distribution duties but my heart was elsewhere. Larry was the
Assistant Director and Head of Sound and was working long hours.
I began to work with him after I put in the time for Bob, watching
and learning as he laid in David Crosby's song "Wooden Ships" and
edited the lyrical opening section of the film. Paradigm Films had
now become Wadleigh/Maurice Productions as John had decided to
go off on his own and devote himself to his writing. Wadley
changed the spelling of his name to go with the more dignified
image he was creating for himself. He said his ancestors had spelled
it that way. Whatever the spelling, Wads really needed full-time
allies and in Bob and Associate Producer, Dale Bell, he had them.

One of the perks of being part of the company was attention
from the managers and the musicians who had been in the festival.
Many of them came by the office to see their footage and give
comments on which piece they preferred. CSNY, Joe Cocker, Alvin

Lee came over. Their excitement at the multiple-camera projection of their performances was as great as ours was.

Other perks of being the Woodstock filmmakers were great seats at Steve Paul's Scene for a Jerry Lee Lewis show. Then, a few weeks after the festival, The Rolling Stones came to town, playing several days at Madison Square Garden. Bob Maurice got access-all-area passes for us to see them. I was hanging around the backstage door to collect mine when Al Maysles pulled up all alone in his camera van. I went over to see if I could help him and he gave me his tripod and said to set it up in front of Mick Jagger's microphone. I did that, telling the security guard I had to stay there to make sure it wasn't moved. Al came in, set his trombone-looking camera onto it and still I stayed, Al asking all about my experience on stage at Woodstock. Was he sorry he missed it? Of course, he was, but that's show biz. I saw the concert from this vantage point, staring up at Mick, five feet away, as he sang: "Did you hear about the midnight rambler?" Smack! his belt came down on the stage. "Well, honey, it's no rock 'n roll show." SMACK! as the belt hit the wood. Then the crowd surged forward and Al and I had to be pulled up and across the stage to avoid the crush of screaming fans.

This filming was the beginning of "Gimme Shelter", the antithesis of "Woodstock". Whereas the Woodstock Festival was the last blast of flower power, the free concert at Altamont would be it's last gasp. Woodstock was a coming together, a party where there were a lot of people out there like me, people who wanted to find a way of living that was loose, loving and trusting, others looking for a way to go back to the land. Against that was a murder in the concert crowd and later the Maysles being stomped by some of the Hells Angels viewing their violent footage. The Outlaws ruled rock 'n roll. It was a sobering December, 1969 event which brought the rock 'n roll hippie era of the '60s to an end.

When it was announced that Warner Bros. was moving the crew to LA for the rest of post-production, which meant Larry was going, once again I went to Bob. He would not hear of my going, even though it was obvious to all that distribution could be run from LA as easily or as difficultly from NYC. I was heartbroken. Why couldn't he understand? It seemed to me it was that old guy thing, once again. The man ruled. The woman did what she was bid to do. He wouldn't budge. So, I quit my distribution gig and went to Los Angeles with Larry as his girlfriend, bringing our cat, Woodstock, along. This move pushed me into a realm of tension that began to seep into the production in several areas.

It's not news that when something big is happening, people's egos get warped or bruised and they begin to change. Bob was under immense pressure. He had never produced before, but he was loyal to Michael and he was smart and tough. He wrote me off and I was not usually welcome in the Yucca and Vine office where the production staff and editors worked.

This was okay because Larry was doing most of his work at the brand new Hollywood recording studio on Third Street, The Record Plant, logging tracks, then pre-mixing them down for the final mix and I was able to continue working with him. Eric Blackstead again worked with him and liaised with the bands. We lived at the Orlando Ave. house that Warners had rented with Wads, Dale, editor Yeu-Bun Yee, and Thelma and on occasion I made sure they had dinner waiting and the house in order (this meant cleaning the packing crates that served as furniture once a week). Bob seldom visited there and less after he zoomed into our driveway and ran over Woodstock the cat creating the only death connected to the concert and film that I know of. Bob and I eventually called a truce when he and I agreed that we wouldn't backbite each other in favor of the health of the production and the spirit of the Woodstock Festival.

I don't think any of us loved Los Angeles. The difference between NYC and LA was really extreme in 1970, before Angelenos embraced the idea that they could have a world class city. Driving down many of the major boulevards took us past one story buildings which had no charm, a blur of beige stucco walls.

Wilshire Blvd. in Bev Hills had the big stores – Saks, I. Magnin, etc. and the hotels, but this was an exception. Yes, it was winter and we had a swimming pool that was heated to 90 degrees, a fact which brought out the Gas Company to check if there was a major leak; and yes, there were the mountains which I visited one day to ski some runs. But, it was a hard place to get used to, and in fact, it took me three years to finally get California living. A Cultural Abyss, as we New York transplants called it. Wadleigh went to only two restaurants during all of this post-production, Imperial Gardens on Sunset which had previously been the great director Preston Sturges' private club and the Villa Capri, a favorite of Sinatra and the Rat Pack. He invited a lot of us to join him most nights and picked up the tab to pass on to Warners. This was the only entertainment any of the hard-working filmmakers had during post-production.

Once the mix began at Warner Bros., the mission was almost complete. Everyone knew that this unknown company with an unknown director (a line that circulated was, "Michael has always been famous, just nobody knew it but him") had pulled off something great. But the suits at the studio were still riding the crew hard and it came down to some creative decisions that Wadleigh and team were not willing to give up.

One night we were working late on the Warner lot and Larry told me to go over to the Security Guard and talk to him. I can usually talk to a post so this was not a problem for me. I kept him talking for about twenty minutes and while we chatted, people who will remain nameless sneaked the film's soundtrack original tapes out of the vault and into three car trunks. I said goodnight and we were out of there. A day later, every time we left the lot, our car was searched. But, the plot worked. WB was over a barrel and they had to negotiate. Wads got to keep his vision of the film. We would learn much later that Warners had another editing room in New York, working on a duplicate workprint and track that would result in a film that didn't have all the multiple images Michael, Thelma and Dale were creating. Welcome to Hollywood think.

Larry and Jeanne on Santa Monica Beach

With the film finished, it was on its way to screenings at the Cannes Film Festival, Tokyo, London, etc. Larry and I were invited to join Mike but passed on all of these. We had another job.

Chapter Seven

California Dreamin'

Gary Burden, who is hard to describe in a few words, came to the Warner Bros. studio to meet Larry. He'd been a Marine during the Korean War battling the Chinese at Inchon Reservoir. He'd spent a few years in a Texas prison. He was a bit mystical, too, and a personal friend of some of the spiritually-powerful American Indian leaders. Gary was an art director for the music business who designed album covers for Mama Cass, The Doors, CSNY, Joni Mitchell, and in the process had become good friends with them. He was talking to Warner Records about doing the artwork for the triple album of the "Woodstock" music they were going to release. He was really our first LA friend, taking us to local restaurants, introducing us around. He was very tight with David Crosby and when he told us that CSNY was going to do a cross-country tour and make a documentary film, we were immediately interested. Gary simply said that we were the ones to do it.

Larry and I had both loved the Byrds, David Crosby's earlier band, and Buffalo Springfield which Neil Young and Stephen Stills had been in. They all wrote great songs, sang great, were dynamic guitar players, different from each other but the blended sound killed as they played off of each other. The first CSN album was terrific and now with Neil part of it, what wasn't to love?

First, we went to David's sailboat in Marina del Rey. We smoked a joint and talked. At the time, David was like the mayor of Laurel Canyon music, putting people together, hand on the pulse of the LA sound. David was very bright, talkative and mentioned that he knew a lot about film, in fact, "he was born in a changing bag". This was a reference to his dad, Floyd, who had worked with

Larry, David, Gary, Boat Captain

renowned documentary director, Robert Flaherty, and had also shot "High Noon" and many other movies. This was all good as we hoped it would help shape the film.

Then it was saying hello to Graham Nash, a smart Englishman, who brought the wonderful harmonies to the group and who was Joni Mitchell's boyfriend. They lived in, where else, Laurel Canyon in a small house, perfect in it's simplicity. Graham was also a truly a nice man. Next we met Stephen who had been raised in Tampa and he and Larry had army-brat connections. The last was Neil Young who was living at the top of Topanga with his wife Susan. We sat in his living room as she ironed an elaborately-ruffled shirt which he was going to wear that night when CSNY performed at the Forum in front of 17,000 people. All of Larry's expertise as a tech wizard of Paradigm Films came into play. They had all seen their footage from "Woodstock" and knew that they could trust him to bring the same artistry and tech proficiency to their tour. We were on. Woof, Woof, Woof. (Can't remember where this started but it was major.) What was very clear from these meetings was that these were very smart and talented men who were really aware of the changing times and their place in them.

Larry brought along cameraman David Myers whose Port-a-san man interview remains one of the highlights of the "Woodstock" film. Myers used all his perceptions when he shot, and listening and being aware of what might be just outside his camera lens' perimeter was key to him getting great moments on film. David became an important mentor for me as I continued to learn filmmaking. He trained me to be a real camera assistant, field-stripping the camera to clean it, caring for the lenses, changing film magazines, learning film stock ASA's, what to use, when, speed and apertures, pushing the film stock, lighting, etc. It was everything a doc crew member had to know because we did everything. I also learned to take stills with the Nikon Larry and I bought.

Myers lived in San Francisco and his artist wife, Barbara, had been a model for Imogen Cunningham. Imogen was a member of the prestigious Group f/64 collective of photographers which included Ansel Adams, Edward Weston and Willard Van Dyke, and Dave was influenced by these giants of photography. He was also a conscientious objector as a Quaker during WWII. Some in the government frowned on this and they were going to show the kid how unpatriotic he was being. He was put to work at an abattoir, where they sent him down into a lower room and told him the skins would come through a hole. His job was to straighten them out and pile them up. The place stunk of death but it got worse when the cow skins came flying until he was overwhelmed by hides, bloody and steaming, one after the other. He stayed until noon then went out for lunch and never returned. The job he got next in a mental hospital paled by comparison. Dave also worked on "Gimme

Dave Myers and Larry

Shelter", the Maysles film, shooting the scene when Al and David showed the Hells Angels their footage and were awarded a pummeling by the gang.

Larry contributed to this early education as well by teaching me to run the Nagra tape recorder, a staple of the film business, and he explained the nuances of the different microphones to use in various situations. I never would have been accepted for this job in the male world if Larry hadn't opened the door. It was a great thing he did for me and gave me the confidence and training that still pushes me forward.

Joining us on the road was Fred Underhill who owned the house in Boerum Hill where Larry had rented the third floor apartment. Fred had worked with Dale Bell and Bob on "Woodstock", watching their back, getting equipment and raw stock

Fred Underhill & Gary Burden

into the site, all the things a production manager does. He also shot film at Woodstock.

Fred was one day younger than I was and I never let him forget it. Remember that line about competition in business, well this was it. At first, we were friends. Over the next two years, that would change and it became a battle for Larry's attention. Fred was very bright, a quick study, and if he didn't know something he said he did he'd figure it out within a few hours. We were probably so similar that we couldn't exist in the same space.

We caught up with the CSNY tour in Boston and stayed on through Providence, New York City and Philadelphia, about three weeks. In New York, they were playing the Fillmore East for 6 nights. The tour put us up in the One Fifth Avenue Hotel but, this was my old stomping ground and in fact, I still held the lease on my St. Mark's apartment.

Larry and I walked over to it, hoping to find my renter in. Unfortunately, we did. Linda, who had been my friend Andy Krantz's girlfriend and had sublet my place when I went to Los Angeles, answered the door and it was painfully obvious that she had become a drugged-out junkie. I had called her to say that we were in town and would stop by but I guess she didn't get the message. The apartment was trashed and most of my stuff was gone. Not the furniture which junkies couldn't carry off, but my bike, figure skates, typewriter, good clothes and shoes, all the saleable goods used to buy a fix. What could I say? I bore the responsibility of letting her live in my place, but it was heart-rending to see this friend, also a graduate of the UW, in such a state.

At the Fillmore, in a production meeting for the CSNY filming, there was a never-ending discussion with Bill Graham about cameras on stage, even a film crew anywhere near it, a re-cap of what we'd endured at Woodstock with a few of the band managers. Bill had created the best venues for live music in both San Francisco and New York City. The tickets were reasonable, the vibe was loose, there were shows every night with great bands and great sound. The Joshua Lightshow was totally psychedelic. I talked with my old friend, Jerry Pompili who was now running the theater, about Bill's attitude. Jerry said, "It's his stage. That's how he sees it. What can I say?"

This last comment "What can I say?", or some variation of it, about his scene, his head, his reality, his life, was obviously becoming a casual, well-used phrase, useful in any situation, showing an acceptance of individualism. In fact, it was the beginning of the new decade: the '70s, the "Me Generation", fed by the notion that if we, those of us who defined themselves as "the generation", couldn't change the world vis a vis Viet Nam, War, Peace, the race issue, feminism, sexism, every intense wave of emotion or action, maybe we could look inside and change ourselves. Take an emotional or spiritual path not a material or political one. It follows the old tale that God wanted to be present on earth but didn't know the best place to put himself (I won't say herself here because that's distracting at this point in the story). He thought and observed and finally decided that there was only one place to put himself: inside every human being. It would be the last place they'd ever look.

The beginning of the decade was discussed by CSNY, as we filmed them in a hotel room playing poker, hanging out, following Neil around Greenwich Village as he discussed D modal tuning with a Washington Square guitar player.

At this juncture, I have to admit to one of the worst things I ever did, or didn't do, as a crewmember. We were on McDougal Street and Myers was nervous which sometimes happened in crowds when he was filming. He was also tired from our late hours, traveling, hauling equipment, the rigors of the road. He took his camera and opened up the magazine cover. I was standing there and wasn't quick enough or willful enough to stop him. He exposed all the film we had just shot and then slumped over, realizing what he'd done. He looked at me like it was my fault, Larry looked at me, yelling why did I let him do that? It was fraught with so many levels of disappointment and consideration: the one girl on the crew didn't stand up to her boss; it was embarrassing to do this in front of Neil; they had lost faith in me as a camera assistant. I was crushed and there was nothing I could say except, I'm sorry. Joel Bernstein was with us taking pictures of Neil while we were filming, one of which became the cover of "After The Gold Rush", solarized to emphasize Neil's isolation. Joel gave me a hug and we picked up the equipment to carry it into a coffee shop to collect ourselves. We all agreed we were done for the afternoon and we should save our energy for what was ahead of us.

Back at the Fillmore, the crew was arriving, some of the cameramen who had been on the "Woodstock" shoot, Dick Pearce, Don Lenzer, Ed Lynch. Once again, gaffer, electrician extraordinaire, Marty Andrews, was with us, and we geared up to shoot multi-camera coverage of the band over a few nights. John

Binder also worked with us, helping Fred run the production, hiring crew, putting them to work in the loading pit or at camera stations.

The first night, CSNY was rocking with "Four Dead in Ohio", Neil's anthem, being sung by a thousand voices. Myers was on stage, getting in close and I watched from the wings as Bill Graham crept up to him and grabbed his belt and tried to pull him off the stage. No one gets on Bill's stage. John Binder went in and grabbed Bill, pulling him off of David. Both he and Johnson freaked out at Bill who was screaming back, ready to punch the closest filmmaker. Band manager Elliot Roberts weighed in with Bill, pulling him off-stage and that was that. Myers went in and got his shot.

CSNY was one of the heaviest groups in America, it had the best deal with their record company, Atlantic, negotiated by Elliot and David Geffen, and they could tell Bill Graham they owned the stage at that moment in time. Or, Bill would have a few empty houses. We filmed two more nights and got great footage. The nervousness that the guys, Neil, Stephen, David and Graham, had on the Woodstock stage was gone, the harmonies close and beautiful, and the energy electric. Bill was happy and so were we, amends having been made.

Myers bought me a wristwatch as he didn't like the dainty one I wore while working and I guess that was his way of acknowledging that my gaff was forgiven. Gee, you could've just said something at the time, Dave.

It had been great to be back on the mean streets of New York but we saw it differently having spent six months in California. The previous fall, Larry and I had also rented a place out of the city across from the Mt. Kisco reservoir where my Fire Island friends, Bernie and Penny had bought a deconsecrated church, rectory and barn that had been converted into a living space. We'd moved some things into the barn with hopes that it would be a weekend retreat. But, now we knew Los Angeles was the place for us and we made arrangements with our landlords before we left the city. New York had been good to me and for me, taking me in and teaching me some big life lessons, but a new chapter was opening and I was challenged again, a good thing.

We returned to L.A. from the tour with no place to live and lots of film footage to sync up and cut. Lookout Management, David Geffen and Elliot Roberts, had a small upstairs office on La Cienega, just south of Santa Monica Blvd. on the west side of the street. It was in a two-story, L-shaped building called "The Clear Thoughts Building." On the first floor, in a store front, was a great boutique owned by Pamela Courson, a pretty red-headed designer and model who clothed rock stars and their friends. She also was the significant other of Jim Morrison of The Doors who had an office on the long side of the "L" off the parking lot.

We had to move out of the Warner Bros. rental on Orlando Avenue within a week or so. We had to get the film into the lab. We had to get an office and editing equipment. The list ran long. The easy part was the cutting room as there was a small office just down from Lookout so we moved in with a rudimentary set up.

I was getting things in order when a California beauty came in the open door. "Want some coffee?" She was too nice. What does she want? You can tell by my suspicion that I'd been on the road, but I said, sure. She introduced herself as Charlotte, from the Liquid Butterfly just down the hall. She was also an actress, she told me. I learned later she'd worked with Elvis and had been married to Tim Considine who I loved in the "Spin and Marty" stories on the '50s "Mickey Mouse Club" TV show.

I followed her back to her studio/shop. She and a friend, Dani, had two rooms filled with beautiful tie-dyed clothes, peasant dresses, scarves, antique clothes, jewelry. A hippie delight. And that was the beginning of a beautiful friendship.

When she learned we needed a place to stay she offered us her apartment. Then Gary Burden did his magic. Jim Morrison and

Pamela were moving to Paris. They had a place in town and a Topanga house on Corvo Way. Both homes had people who wanted them. Gary told Jim, No, man, you should let Larry and Jeanne have the Topanga place. Jim was shy, hiding behind his beard and a few extra pounds. We told him we had just moved to LA, had worked on "Woodstock" and would take good care of his house and he agreed. We stayed at Char's for a few days then moved to Topanga. We hired a truck to bring out what was left of our New York apartments and we were in a new home. We bought a 1966 blue and white Volkswagan camper with tie-dyed curtains, a refrigerator and pull-out bed, a hippie dream mobile.

We were actually strangers in a strange land. Southern California was like no where else I had ever lived. I mean, look at the path: Wisconsin, New York, Colorado, New York. I never thought that I would live in Los Angeles. When a college friend chose to go to L.A. for a teaching job I though she was crazy. L.A. was a cultural abyss.

It was July when we moved to Topanga and it was hot. 116 degree heat out the back door. The house was built on the north side of a hill so at least we had that going for us. The lower floor had streamstone walls and a large wooden bar area. The next floor was all pine with a kitchen, living/dining room with a fireplace and lots of windows and a small bedroom. Out the back door were some stairs that led to a small tower room overlooking the property.

We adopted three cats, Rio, Willy and Gary, and couldn't believe how fast and sadly they disappeared as they became an easy lunch for the roaming coyotes who were ubiquitous in the Santa Monica Mountains. But we didn't know about this. I picked wild flowers up and down the road and mountain paths and came down with searing poison oak everywhere, and I mean everywhere. There were a lot of things I needed to learn about this move from the streets of New York to the rural back-alley neighborhood of Topanga.

Meanwhile, we commuted into Hollywood to the editing room putting together the footage. The drive through the San Fernando Valley on the 101 freeway was another culture shock. It was summer and the smog was so thick you could barely see the houses on the side of the mountains along the southern reaches of towns called Tarzana (because Edgar Rice Burroughs had lived and written his famous story there), Reseda, Encino, Sherman Oaks. The traffic crawled along and I couldn't imagine living in that air. Sometimes we'd take a dirt road off of Topanga Canyon Blvd. up through ranch land to Mulholland Drive along the top ridge of the Santa Monica Mountains into town just to get out of the traffic. Up there we would see deer, coyote, wildflowers and arrive at The Clear Thoughts Building with a better attitude.

Once we'd got the music footage in synch we continued to view the documentary material. It was iffy – some nice moments with Neil walking around the Village, some backstage conversations with the band. But the guys seemed stiff, not really ready to talk to the camera, except for David who discoursed on everything, playing the moments. The music was good and strong getting lots of applause and appreciation from the audience. We were pleased with the coverage and the quality of the sound, and it looked great. We worked long hours putting together a reel for them to view and gave it to Elliot.

Stephen Stills had recorded a solo album and suggested that we film him riding horseback out at a nearby ranch. Gary Burden and Henry Diltz were there to capture photos for the album cover and David Myers and Larry shot doc footage, which could possibly be used in the CSNY film too. I was there to assist them. We limoed out to Newhall to a stable that was owned by Glenn Randall, Hollywood's foremost horse trainer. The man had trained Trigger, teaching him all those tricks we'd grown up watching, and had supplied all the horses for "Ben Hur". He had several horses available to Stephen who was a bold rider dressed in a football jersey, racing a horse across the large riding ring. A photo Henry

Sharon with Josh and John Henry

got that day was on the back of the terrific album that came out a few months later.

Glenn had watched Stephen ride his horses hard so invited us up to a covered riding ring he had near the barns. He was dressed in good ranch pants and a jacket and he mounted a gorgeous horse which he then put through a dressage routine that was spectacular, man and horse in perfect communication. He rode up to us and said, "Anyone can ride fast."

One day our friend from New York, Sharon Binder, called us. She'd moved out here. She and John had split up and she was reinventing her life, not an easy thing when you have two small sons, Josh, four years old, John Henry, six months. Her sister Molly lived downtown with her husband George, who was a conceptual artist, and her young son, Aaron. Sharon had found an apartment near our office and wondered if we could help her move in, considering we had our VW bus. We could and did. We spent some good times with her and the kids, gathering up at Bob Maurice's classic Beverly Hills mansion around the pool. Michael and his wife Renee lived up there too, so it was as if some of our New York community had simply moved west.

Time went by. We didn't hear anything from CSNY or Elliot. Did they like the footage? What about our rough edit that we had poured our artistic selves into? Soon, they said. We decided to take a trip to Wisconsin in the bus. We camped out throughout the west and when the thing broke down, pushed it through the Badlands of South Dakota with a ninety-degree wind at our backs. When we got to Madison, we were welcomed warmly by Mom and Dad and my brother Charles who had decided to join my father in business. Not what I would have guessed he'd do, but there he was.

We were invited to a party at a neighbor's house and there were all the people I'd known for years. Everyone was affluent, drinking and enjoying the summer evening. My mom pulled me into a group that was talking about "Oh these kids today" kind of thing.

She turned to me and said, "Well, you don't take acid, do you dear?"
It was a decisive moment.
"Yes, Mom, I have taken LSD. It was a monumental trip."

What did she expect? She was aghast or whatever else describes the sudden panic a mother feels when her only daughter pulls out the stops and decides to revolutionize the neighborhood.

"I can get you some if you'd like to drop", I said pushing the envelope even further.

Boy, was she sorry she'd tried to make me an example of those who say no. It was probably safe to say that Mom never got over this, more for the neighbors' opinion of her outlaw daughter than anything. For sure, she never set herself or me up as a good example, asking questions she didn't know the answer to or probably didn't want to know what the answer would be.

On the way home to California, we hit horrible weather around Omaha, torrential rainstorms that kept us inside our camper for hours. Crossing Nebraska was so boring that I read Nathanial West's book "Day of the Locust" about the crushing influence of Hollywood on culture. Traveling west into the sun on our way to Denver, the experience gave me another excruciating corneal abrasion. We arrived at our friend's house and I was once again blind. Maybe Nathanial West was sending me a message and we should have turned around and headed back to Wisconsin when we still had a chance.

We were planning to stay with Bill McDonough in Denver and he rushed us to a hospital where I was given anesthetic drops and a patch and sent home. Recovered, two days later, we headed up to Aspen with McDonough via the road to Leadville then onto Hwy. 82, past Deer Park, up and over Independence Pass. Closed to car traffic in the winter as it crossed over the Continental Divide at about 12,000' and sometimes little more than one lane, it was a wild ride through the Rockies.

Bill had left the ad biz and moved to Denver where he set up several businesses that didn't fare as well as he had hoped. Now, he was going to Aspen to apply for a job in the ski business at Bert Bidwell's Mountain Shop. He got the job while we were there and that began a very successful career selling skiwear. Bill was very smart, funny and great company. At one point I thought he might be good boyfriend material, but he liked another woman and kept her around until she left him for "I am, I cried", Neil Diamond. I liked him enough to keep him as a friend.

Once again, the Chase family welcomed me with open arms and we stayed with them enjoying the picnic hikes up the Maroon Bells and sitting by the Roaring Fork River. They enjoyed Larry and he took to Curt who embodied the very best of the mountain man ethos. The kids were growing fast, Heidi already my size and smart as a whip. Jimmy was still so sweet and easy. Betsy and Curt had weathered the socializing that had entered their lives and were happy together again.

Back in L.A., Larry and I settled into our new city with new friends. Char and Dani moved their shop a few blocks west on Santa Monica Blvd. into a beautiful building. Gary Burden's wife, Annette, became a friend and good influence. She was an American sweetheart, a mother, baker, cook, dressmaker, gardener, the wholesome homemaker, included in Joni Mitchell's song, "Ladies of the Canyon". She started bringing things into the store that she'd found at swap meets and thrift shops, mostly hand-made things from earlier years. She also did lots of crocheted tops. Char and Dani hired me to work some hours and sell whatever I found on my trips with Annie. I bought a sewing machine and patterns and set up a work room in the basement bar of the house, no doubt a far cry from the activity Jim Morrison had brought into that space.

I'd taken sewing lessons at the Singer store when I was thirteen and had made a dropped waist cotton turquoise dress that actually fit. My grandmother Lylli was a very good seamstress, knitter, crocheter. She always had her needles with her when she'd come to visit and sit crocheting as she and Mom talked. She taught me how to knit and I always had a sweater going. This continued until I graduated from college. I made crew necks, a beautiful rust angora sweater for Mom, a turquoise one for me, even an Aran Island sweater with all the different patterns, and the obligatory red Wisconsin sweater.

Mom didn't do these crafts – she had grown up with home-made clothes. Now she lived in Shorewood Hills and could buy the best, and did. Dad always wanted her to look like the wife of a successful businessman and opened charge accounts at all the downtown stores. Mom had a nice sense of style and we loved to go shopping. When I was ten, I charged a dress at the department store, Manchester's, on the Capitol Square, a navy blue taffeta with a white lace collar. I brought it home and Mom and Dad were aghast that the store had let me do this. I had to take it back but this was the beginning of my clothes-horse life. I loved clothes and shoes. I threw a fit when I was five because I wanted to wear my flannel-lined jeans to school and Mom made me change. I knew at a very young age, that clothes are part of what defines you. They don't have to be expensive and if you're a good shopper you can always ferret out that great affordable shirt or jacket at a Goodwill or Bloomingdale's. I definitely had an eye for color, fabric and texture.

I knew I had to have a calling card item for the store. Char made colorful patchwork peasant dresses made sexy with elastic below the bosom and one on the waist. Dani did tie-dye velvet and crepe and intricate embroidery. She made beautiful shirts for Miles Davis, who she had met through her ex-husband/jazz musician Pat Senatore. Miles would come into the shop to pick them up, strolling in cool as could be, followed by a few of his jazzbo friends. We'd hang out in the back room, listening to Miles tell his stories in his raspy voice.

I settled on designing and making cowboy shirts with contrasting fabric for the yoke and cuffs. I did flat-felled seams so they had a very finished look, put in pearl stud snaps and I could turn one out in five hours. They all sold out and I began to get special orders. I was in business.

I stretched a bit and began to make women's clothes, simple pants with tunics, skirts, etc. The fabric was the thing and L.A. had great stores and factory outlets. I scoured antique and resale stores looking for Forty's prints, Twenty's dresses I could make over. The hard part was selling them rather than keeping them for myself.

Having eschewed the homemaker's tasks for a life in business, it was surprising that sewing was becoming a part of my life. I cooked meals at home and planted a garden with tomato plants and other veggies, having finally learned more about the

California growing seasons. It was the first time I hadn't worked at a career in a while and it was interesting to see what I found interesting. Cooking became an important part of my day.

Both Larry and I enjoyed our domestic life, the slower pace of Topanga country living. He'd play the Martin guitar he'd bought as a present to himself after "Woodstock", read a lot of newspapers, watch TV news, get sound gigs if they came his way. Van Schley and his girlfriend April bought a great thirteen acre spot nearby and some of their New York friends came with them. Gary and Annette bought Neil Young's house when he moved up north. Charles John Quarto, a poet friend of Graham's who'd been on the road with us, hung out wherever. Joel Bernstein rented a house next to Will Geer's Theatricum Botanicum and was joined by high school friend, Fred Weis. These two were all of eighteen years old, deciding to learn from life instead of college textbooks.

That fall we had the first taste of another California season: fire season. The Santa Anas, hot winds off the Mohave Desert, blew in raising the temperatures and drying out the chaparral that covered the coastal mountain ranges. Fires broke out along the freeways where cigarettes were thrown or along the back roads where arsonists did their crime. A fire started north of us, over the mountains in the San Fernando Valley, but with the winds coming from the northeast, it quickly became a threat. The fire engines' sirens screamed constantly as the crews kept changing their fire breaks. Larry and I packed up our most valuable possessions and put them in the bus, so no matter where we went there all of our stuff did too. We stayed home a lot in order to protect our house should the call arise. Finally, after a week, the fire was contained and we were safe. Smoke hung in the air, ashes covered everything, but the fire hadn't claimed us, our house or any near-by structures.

Gary Burden called and asked if he could come over. He didn't have good news. CSNY was breaking up. It was Neil and Steven who couldn't see eye to eye. What about the film? He didn't know anything yet, but would soon. Then it was silence.

In February, we experienced another of California's seasons, the Earthquake. It's epicenter was in Sylmar, about five miles as the crow flies from Topanga. We were rocked with a 6.7 Richter Scale roller. It happened early in the morning and we were still in bed. At first, I thought one of the neighbor dogs had gotten onto our roof, up the stairs that led to the little tower room. Then we realized what it was and tried to run out the back door. The house was bucking like mad, swaying from side to side. Then it stopped. They don't last long, really, it just seems like they do. One of those intense moments when time stands still. All was fine in the house, not a cup or plate broken, all pictures still hanging on the wall.

That night we went into town to the Beverly Cinema to see a Warhol movie, "Trash". Sitting in the theater, the aftershocks started to hit, shaking the whole place. Wondering how crazy were we to be sitting there, we exited. A few days later, Sharon called. She was taking Josh and John Henry and moving with her sister Molly and son Aaron to Ohio. They don't have earthquakes in Ohio. Two women on the move with their kids. Although they were afraid of earthquakes, I thought they were the bravest people I knew.

Maybe we were really crazy living in L.A. with the fires and earthquakes but we knew that we weren't up to going back to New York. If we wanted to be part of a large film community, we needed to be where we were. And we both were committed to this.

Larry's Oscar nomination was proof that we were on the right track. Here he was, twenty-four years old, and in line to win an Oscar! I've never been able to confirm this, but I bet he was and maybe still is the youngest person to be nominated for a technical Academy Award. The Academy recognized "Woodstock" in three categories: Best Documentary, Thelma for Best Editing, and Larry for Best Sound.

Larry, Jeanne, Dale and Margaret

So, now the big question was what were we going to wear? We went to Western Costume and Larry rented a beautifully-cut long jacket and ruffled shirt. I had found some beautiful lace curtains and made a skirt. Shades of Scarlett O'Hara. There was a store on Melrose owned by a Japanese woman who made dresses and I found a lace top that perfectly matched the skirt lace. I wanted really simple shoes, ala Greque, and ended up making them out of a leather sole and long ribbons that I criss-crossed up my legs. Basically, I went to the Oscars barefoot.

Larry's parents, Dale and Margaret joined us and Warner Bros. sent a limo to Topanga to pick us up and transport us to Hollywood Heaven. The first award of the night was for Best Sound so we didn't have a prolonged tense evening as "Patton", starring George C. Scott began it's sweep of nine awards. Thelma also lost, which was astonishing if you compare the complexity and the ingenuity of "Woodstock's" editing to "Patton's", a good but conventional film.

"Woodstock" did win Best Documentary and remains one of the most financially successful films ever made (gross vs. production cost). I thought, how easy! Work on a first film and it wins the Academy Award. We had a great time at the party. Gregory Peck and Eva Marie Saint came up to meet us, thrilled we'd won in the documentary field. Russ Meyer, famous for "Faster, Pussycat! Kill! Kill!" and his wife Edy, came over and pulled out a fat joint and asked if we'd like to share a smoke. Of course, we would so we got stoned at the Governor's Ball. We'd arrived.

Chapter Eight

Hallelujah

Ed Lynch called Larry. He was a very good documentary cameraman and had worked on "Woodstock" and CSNY with us. He had been contacted by two novice producers who had the rights to the story about a guy who was an evangelist, in fact, had been a child evangelist, and travelled around to churches and tents where they held revival meetings. The producers were Howard Smith and his girlfriend, Sarah Kernochan. Howard had a radio show in New York and Sarah did research for him. One night they had the preacher on for an interview and realized there was a movie in there someplace. The preacher's name was Marjoe Gortner. Ed told Howard and Sarah he'd put a crew together they could trust. Larry and John Binder would do sound, David Myers, Ken Van Sickle and Ed on camera, Fred Underhill was the production manager and I would do production and assistant camera.

There's a scene in the movie shot at a motel on Sunset Blvd. near the Seven Veils strip club Myers loved so much. We're all sitting around a small bedroom and Marjoe is telling us how to behave and dress, seeing as how we were going to be in religious settings with evangelists and their flocks of true believers. Larry and John had long hair. That had to go. I was going to be assisting either Myers or Ken and Marjoe said I had to wear a dress, nylons and flats. All this so we wouldn't offend the audience members or the preachers who would be in a tent somewhere in Orange County or a downtown hall in Any City, USA.

I wanted to be a good crew member so I pulled out a wrap-around skirt and top and wore my nylon stockings in a very hot

John, Marjoe, Sara, Ed, Howard, Agnes Benjamin, Fred

tent. My job was very active, bringing in film magazines, carrying cable, changing lenses. The cinematographers were covering everything from all angles. As I carried a magazine up the aisle to Myers, I felt a tug on my waist and with one swoop, my wrap-around skirt fell off. Juggling equipment and the cable, I picked up my skirt and found a chair to sit in so I could re-wind it around my body. So much for decorum. I'd have been better off in pants.

Marjoe had convinced several preachers that we were only doing a film about his life. In fact, the film was set up from the beginning to de-bunk the evangelist movement and it's penchant for taking a lot of money from gullible poor people, or people who should be spending their money on their families. A few of the preachers were quite wealthy and showed considerable glee when talking about their fortune and how they'd earned it. One of them boasted about the huge ranch he'd bought in Brazil, another one, we later found out, sold stolen cars in his tent to his flock for cut-rate prices. What would Jesus say? Two years later, "Marjoe" also won the Oscar for Best Documentary. Two in a row. Man, this was easy!

That summer, our friend Marty Andrews was getting married in London to Elizabeth Scott. They'd met when she sublet his New York apartment for a few months when he was on a film location and when he returned, they fell in love and she never left. Marty was a member of a distinguished eastern family, the most famous member being Buckminster Fuller, who was his uncle. Bucky created the geodesic dome, the dymaxion car, among many other inventions and was one of the most important thinkers in America at the time. He could take you on a philosophical journey that inspired. Marty had inherited a good sum of money and was intent on blowing the whole wad on his honeymoon trip and a movie about their travels. What could Liz say? She was so in love with this eccentric wizard, she said yes.

The second thing Marty did was invite all his filmmaker friends to join them on the honeymoon and to convey all of us on a trip through England, he bought a double-decker London bus. Larry and I went to London a few weeks early to help in the conversion from bus to camper. We stayed in an inexpensive bed and breakfast, chowing down on fried eggs, baked beans, scones and tea then took the tube out to Ealing where Liz's family lived and where the bus was parked. The seats upstairs were torn out and two large platforms running along the sides were built. These would serve as sleeping pads once the mattresses were put down. In the back, we built a "honeymoon suite" for the newlyweds. I went to work making curtains and dozens of pillows for the upstairs. Downstairs, we kept most of the seats but pulled some out to create a film equipment room and work space as there would be a lot of cameras capturing every exciting moment.

Marty wanted a professional look to this film, unlike a lot of the short films he had made which he ran on the walls of his apartment. He hired David Myers to come along to be the main cinematographer and so of course, I worked as Dave's assistant. Larry rented a Nagra in England and together they were a top quality cinema verite crew. Teddy Churchill, who had been at

Woodstock with us, Big Ed from New Jersey, were ever-alert cameramen.

We made time to have fun and Liz gave us great tours of London. She had a real grasp of history so we came to love the city as she did. All this and plan a wedding too.

Marty read in one of London's many newspapers that the Bus Transportation Department was going to give an award to one of its drivers for "Most Outstanding" performance. We all went to the ceremony and watched as a young man got his citation. Crowding around him afterwards were many of his colleagues, congratulating him. Marty pressed forward and asked if he could have a word with the Most Outstanding driver. The driver looked askance at our group, wondering what was going on. As Marty described his honeymoon plans the driver couldn't help but sputter and laugh. And then Marty offered him the job of driver and it turned out that he had some vacation time coming and as he wasn't married and hadn't planned anything, a paid vacation driving a bunch of American lunatics around the country appealed to his sense of humor. He accepted on the spot and we all knew we'd be in good hands with Mr. Outstanding.

More friends arrived and the big day was at hand. We all gathered at a lovely old church in Liz's neighborhood, cameras whirring, every moment documented by at least four cameras and Larry getting sync sound, teamed with Myers. During the reception, we all gathered around Buckminster Fuller who said he had many people for us to meet at Cambridge and Oxford, people who appreciated our double-decker living experiment, which Bucky called a true embodiment of "Spaceship Earth", a term he helped popularize with his book "Operating Manual for Spaceship Earth". Bucky had planned to travel with us for a few days but a bad cold sidelined him. The next morning, we waved good-bye to Liz's patient and tolerant parents and Bucky and his wife Ann.

Marty Andrews with the Bus and Auxiliary Van

Our driver pulled the bus away from the curb and signaled to our auxiliary vehicle, a van painted to match the bus, and we were off. There were fifteen of us intrepid travelers and our first stop would be Woodstock, England. How could we not? Rather than recite the entire itinerary of this wonderful journey through England, suffice to say that in three weeks, we saw cities and countryside, the Cambridge campus where we greeted the dons wearing animal masks, the lake country, artists, sheep farmers, castles and campsites.

We were an oddity to say the least. Our appearances at the camping grounds around the country drew a lot of attention and that was good as we were making a movie. The curiosity seekers usually wound up on film, joining in on our song fests and campfires where endless stories were told.

Jeanne at Cambridge University

Larry and I left the group before the end of the trip and headed back to London where we stayed with a friend of Van Schley's on Sloan Square, a posh city neighborhood. We had received word that the CSNY film might have a life after all and Larry was anxious to get back and see if there was anything real to the rumors.

And there was. Neil had offered to buy the footage from David, Graham and Stephen and he wanted to do some more filming. There was no script, just a rough outline of a story about a graduate and what a young man faces when he sets out in the world. It would be done in an allegorical style with more music from Neil. All of this would be intercut with the documentary and music material we'd already done.

In September, Larry went on the road with Neil, David Myers, Fred Underhill and Carrie Snodgress, Neil's new girlfriend who was a prominent actress. Myers now had a full-time assistant, George Stevenson, and Fred did the production so I busied myself with sewing clothes and working at The Liquid Butterfly. The custom cowboy shirts made of colorful fabric continued to sell well.

I loved living in Topanga. Char had moved out there too, into a house with a great view of the huge canyon park, with one of April's friends from New York, Doreen Small. Joel and Fred had found a trail and hung ropes to make the climb easier. We would take these challenging hikes up into parkland that had signs of primitive life. There were large sandstone bowls that had holes carved into the bottoms and sides, probably used by First Native women for grinding walnut meats or corn into meal. The ocean was a few miles away and Topanga Beach was famous for it's surf and loose beach culture. I was finally "getting" California. Initially, Los Angeles had palled by comparison to Manhattan. I'd thought it was so ugly as a city, so sprawling, no center, no great restaurants, no culture. But in Topanga, I was close to the earth, in the country on the land, living the hippie dream just as Joni Mitchell's song "Woodstock" had said and it made me happy.

I was working in town at The Liquid Butterfly one day when a ten year old boy came in with some beautiful velvet costumes. He also had his little dog with him. He and his mom were moving to Argentina, he said, and would we buy the costumes they wore to the Renaissance Faire? I looked them over and they were in very good condition. What about your dog, I asked. Oh, that's Fantasia, we have to give her up too. I took everything, the clothes and the black Skye Terrier/Poolie mix dog. And I didn't change her name. That night I picked up Larry at the airport. He'd been at Neil's ranch and as I pulled up in front of the PSA terminal, he opened the door and up popped this dog that had huge ears that stuck out of her head like a telephone handset. He laughed at the sight, climbed in and Tas (for Fantasia), as we would call her, settled into his lap. I would have this great dog for the next eighteen years.

WE WANT INTO YOUR PANTS
THE LIQUID BUTTERFLY·8709 SANTA MONICA BLVD.·657-5266

Two Customers, Dani, Charlotte, Jeanne

Larry reported that Neil was completely enthralled with the filmmaking process. He was hard at work on a new album which would become "Harvest", but he was devoting a lot of time to getting southern footage (for "Southern Man") and Nashville footage (a great scene with a barge being launched into the Cumberland River). Larry took him to his mother, Margaret's, hometown, Americus, Georgia where Larry reunited with the old black couple who had taken care of him as a baby. After that trip, we spent time on the ranch filming Neil and the musicians (Kenny Buttrey, drums, Tim Drummond, bass, Jack Nietzsche, piano, Ben Keith, slide guitar) that producer Elliot Mazer had introduced Neil to in Nashville.

Ben Keith, Tim Drummond, Neil, Tim Mulligan (bg)

Setting up in an old barn on the ranch, they put in a stage and left the hay bales. You had to sit on something. The hillside facing the barn had a herd of buffalo which would run toward the barn every afternoon around 5pm. Maybe they wanted to harmonize or were just enjoying the music. I felt very privileged to be there, listening to those wonderful songs that have become Neil classics, "Are you Ready for the Country", "Alabama", and "Words - Between the Lines of Age" (which we always sang as "Between the ears of Tas", honoring our little dog). It was a great part of my production assistant job.

Fantasia (Tas) and Jeanne on the ranch

Bad news hit. Jim Morrison was dead in Paris. A mysterious death it was too, happening in the bathtub. We mourned as did many of our friends who knew him well. Soon after, his lawyer called. Pamela, Jim's widow, was selling the house and were we interested. I thought a moment and then asked what the asking price was. He said $19,000. Hmmm. Pretty good price, I thought. But, we were moving to Neil's ranch. Did we want to be landlords? Would this be the place we'd want to return to? I told him we were hippies who didn't believe in owning property and that we would not buy the house. In retrospect, boy, was I stupid. But this was just another example of how I have never been motivated by the dollar, or, gee, maybe I am really stupid. All of my really important decisions in life have not had the consideration of money at their core. Other elements have taken precedent, what my heart, gut, head dictated. Not necessarily in that order. I'm sure this is a result of my protected childhood, my supportive parents, my own good luck and the times that were some of the most affluent in history.

That Christmas, we went to Orlando, Florida where Larry's parents, Dale and Margaret Johnson, lived. Dale had left the army as a colonel but was still part of the military industrial complex

Eisenhower had warned the country about, working for Martin-Marietta Corp. I didn't know what he did there and maybe he never told Larry, either. This was not unusual as Dale had worked for Military Intelligence – I know, it's an oxymoron – and over the years would at times disappear in the middle of the night, telling Margaret he'd be back from the current hotspot when he could. That might be a week, a month, or longer that he would be incomunicado.

Orlando was still pre-Disney World so we did the old touristy things like going to Sarasota and the Barnum and Bailey Winter headquarters; to Tampa and Ibor City which had been the center of the Have-a-Tampa cigar business and had good Cuban food; to Daytona Beach and Cape Canaveral. Dale had a VW bug and had offered it to us prior to our leaving L.A. Our plan was to drive across country in the bug then move to Neil's ranch in January. With thanks for a nice Christmas holiday, we set out.

A trip across country in a bug is a thing unto itself. The car never could travel faster than fifty-five which is fine except for when you're in Texas. We did the southern route and I was stunned when we got to the Biloxi/Gulfport area where my family and I had spent spring vacations starting in 1955, ten days of getting too much sun, too fast, swimming in the Gulf waters. I had told Larry about Pine Lodge, a nice motel across the street from the Gulf which had southern colonial-style cabins where we'd always stayed.

I couldn't find it. Then, we remembered Hurricane Camille, the 1969 storm that had hit the gulf coast and changed the town. I could find the Jefferson Davis home which had been the Confederate White House for a time and the Broadwater Beach Hotel where I'd been arrested for trespassing and sending a pompano through the waterfall/swimming pool complex one night a decade earlier.

It happened when I was in college and could be tossed off as a simple prank if not for the reverberations. Wisconsin High School friend, Bob Reznichek, and his family had been coming to Gulfport as many years as we had and another college friend, George Haberichter, was there with his parents. We'd been swimming in the Gulf in the late afternoon and had caught bare-handed a large pompano, the flat flounder-like fish common to the area. We put it in a bucket of saltwater then late that night took it to the fancy hotel with the three-tiered swimming pool with rapids and waterfalls in between. We thought the fish would enjoy it. When it got stuck, George took off his clothes and jumped in to free it only to be caught by a security guard. This man was not going to be deterred from his official duties and no amount of pleading and cajoling would persuade him to let us go. He called the cops and arrested us for trespassing. We had enough money to bail out George who had to go back to Pine Lodge, wake up our parents and bring them back to bail us out. My mother was horrified when she learned I'd been stuck in a cell with a murderess named Ponytail. The Police Chief said that they were not going to drop charges and the Judge was going to make an example of us, Northern college kids coming to the South in 1963, thinking they could get away with rude behavior. I had a court date before we would leave for home.

It turned out that my Uncle George Field knew some powerful Gulf Coast people through his oil business and he said there was one dowager I had to go meet, with my mother in tow. She lived next to the Dixie Whitehouse in a graceful colonial home with an expansive lawn and garden. We were invited to tea and arrived in dresses and heels. She was quite lovely and could understand that pranks happen but I really should watch myself in the future and definitely don't come back with any of those freedom riders. She called the Judge, her dear friend, who promised he'd only penalize us with a small fine.

Being a southern boy, Larry had complicated feelings about this part of the country. He still had a bit of redneck in him but knew that the south had to accept equality. We saw some slight changes as we kept going west, shared bathrooms, water bubblers and integrated restaurants, at least the ones we ate in. My prejudice, maybe, but the south still felt segregated to me.

We drove onward to New Orleans then south to Abbeville near LaFayette where some L.A. friends were living. Kate and Dave, our kind of people, had been disc jockeys at the KPCC FM station in Pasadena when they were fired and retaliated by locking themselves in that station to broadcast to the aficionados of alternative radio. A few years later, this story became a movie called "FM" and was shot by our pal David Myers. Kate and Dave were from Abbeville and had given up on Hollywood after their firing to come back and settle in with people they could trust. They took us out to their land on the bayou, to the diner in town where they served the best oysters and shrimp, etc. I think I have ever had.

Then, on to Texas. Man, it's a long way across that state and the day dragged on. I'm sure the locals laughed their butts off as they zoomed past the little beige VW with Florida plates plugging along with stuff on the luggage rack. We got to Dealey Plaza in Dallas where a crime of the generation had happened. It was just a circular road, a few buildings and the infamous grassy knoll, not much of a memorial to the murder of a man we had hoped would bring real changes in our lifetime.

Our next planned stop was Santa Fe, NM where our friends Michael Mason and Jemima James were spending the holidays with her parents at their adobe retreat. Michael's sister Judy was married to Fred Underhill. Michael and Jemima were/are wonderful musicians and free spirits. Michael and Judy's dad, an art book publisher, had edited a famous book, "The Family of Man", which had great photographs of people around the world that had originally had been collected by Edward Steichen in a monumental photography exhibition at the Museum of Modern Art. The James' house was a rambling adobe and we had our own room overlooking a desert arroyo, decorated with the colorful ristras (chili wreaths) and warmed by an adobe fireplace, It was an amazing resting spot after that trip across Texas.

On the Ranch - El Corte de Madeira Creek

Chapter Nine

Back to the Land

Larry was anxious to get back to L.A., are you seeing a trend here? By this time, he was called "L.A." for Larry Alderman Johnson, not for Los Angeles, he insisted. He went by that moniker on all his credited work from this time forward. We had to pack up the house, put most things in storage and move to Neil's Broken Arrow ranch. We were now a two-VW family with the bus/camper and the bug. We loaded up Tas, our orange cat, Hawker-Boy, and followed one another up Hwy. 101.

Neil's ranch was on the San Francisco peninsula in the mountain range that divides it north to south. The property had been a huge ranch that was subdivided into three parcels. He was offered the lower parcel of 1200 acres while the other two men, Djerassi and Zafferoni, Stanford University chemists who had patented the formula for the birth control pill, took the two upper parcels.

We exited the 101 Freeway near Palo Alto then climbed into the mountains to Skyline Blvd. The redwood trees towered above us and as we drove along the road and accepted that we were basically in the middle of nowhere. There was a small grocery store and restaurant at Skylonda Corners, called this because if you went straight you ended up in La Honda, home to Ken Kesey and his band of Merry Pranksters. We continued north on Skyline to a one lane ex-logging road through the thick forest with no guard rails and an almost ninety-degree slope plunging downward a few feet from the road. We traveled slowly around each bend, passing the other property owners' gates. Then the road broke through to an incredible view of bare mountain tops covered with tall green grass, the fog rolling in from the sea, and Neil's land in sight.

Neil and Carrie lived in a nice, redwood, four room house which overlooked a pond and had decks all around. It was cozy and beautiful. Up the hill from this was a redwood studio he'd built. Continuing on across the ranch about a mile, we came to several outbuildings. Next to them was a small white house, called "The Little White House" and up further was "The Red House". Beyond that and down a hill was "The Big White House" where the Hash family lived. The Little White House would be our home for the next year.

Since we arrived with only clothes and some personal artifacts, the house and our life in it was pretty simple. I put up the 1880's Crazy Quilt I'd bought at the Rose Bowl swap meet and made up the bed with nice linens, stored away some kitchen equipment and that was about it. You entered the house from a small porch into the kitchen which was lit by a bare light bulb. The floor was covered with horrible linoleum which we soon painted a cream color. To the right off the kitchen was a very small "living room" and believe me, I use that term loosely. To the left was a small bathroom and then our bedroom. That was it. The Little White House. But it had windows all around and we figured we'd be spending most of our time at the studio, which indeed we did.

Next door, in The Red House, lived Sandy Castle nee James Mazzeo and those names were completely interchangeable. Co-habiting with him was Kathy, a natural beauty, and her two kids. Sandy was a ranch hand/artist who made beautifully sculptured woodstoves, furniture, paintings and he could wax eloquently on just about every subject, especially if we'd just smoked one with our morning tea.

The Hash family seemed an anachronism on this rock and roll ranch. Bob was an old school ranch foreman and a pro. His

Carrie and Neil

wife, Geri, was also of ranch stock and they were horse people who had been hired from the neighboring Portola Valley. They had youngish kids, Clay, Craig, and Joe.

Over near Neil's place, there was another small house, a barn and a large seriously-built, fenced-in pen. Louis and Clara lived here and it was this Old Man who came with the ranch, who worked with Bob and did his daily rounds in his jeep with his cow dog at his side. "Old Man look at my life I'm a lot like you were. I need someone to love the whole day through." They had a kitchen garden and kept to themselves but were an important anchor for the place. Neil fully intended that his ranch was going to be the real deal. He had his herd of buffalo and also ran black angus cattle. That pen I mentioned held a huge stud bull, the reason for the extra-sturdy fence.

In the short span of two years, I had come from New York

106

Neil plays Horseshoes

City to Hollywood to Topanga and now to ranchland that was an hour from the closest real grocery store. We had all heard Joni's hippie plea that we get ourselves back to the garden but I never ever thought I'd be living this kind of life. If I had wanted to live in the country, I could have stayed in Wisconsin. Larry and I were news junkies and now there was no newspaper nor television. Being isolated on the ranch also deprived us of our daily fix. We were like a lot of '60s people who marched in the streets, advocated change, then suffered burn out and actually welcomed a retreat from day to day anger at the man and his bureaucratic system.

"Are you ready for the country? Because it's time to go." Neil's lyric has a lot of meanings. Is it just about going out of the city into the country? Or, are you ready for your country and ready to do something about what's happening to it? In both cases, we were ready. Nixon was president and my feeling was, "What can I say?" You want a man who even had to make the plea, "I am not a crook" to be the leader of the free world? I'll sit by, discuss politics with friends and let hoist himself on his own petard, which of course, is what eventually happened.

Meanwhile, the upside of it all was the work. Each day, Larry and I would drive over to the redwood studio where we had an editing room. The studio's front porch opened into a main room with a small kitchen, desk and telephone. To the right was the editing room; to the left the music room with a large stone fireplace and balcony overlooking the forest; and straight ahead was the mixing room, surrounded by a redwood deck, with beautiful wood furniture, designed and made by Morris Sheppard, encasing all the state-of-the-art technical recording equipment and a twenty-four track mixing panel. Neil had rented a KEM three-picturehead editing machine such as we had used on "Woodstock". A dutch door opened up on to the redwood forest surrounding us. Only a rich rock star could do all this but what was really impressive was the attention to details and the vision that had inspired then. Rock 'n roll ranch was heaven indeed.

Neil had entitled the film we were about to fashion "Journey Through The Past". A huge amount of footage had to be synched up and logged in. We had our original rough cut of the CSNY performance material plus all of the new stuff telling the story of a recent Graduate's plight as he made his way into the world. There was more of Neil and Carrie, and Neil doing weird-ass interviews and a lot of cinema verite shooting. It was going to be a challenge to put this into a film that could make sense. And, believe me, there are people who will swear to their grave that we did this and many others who deny it will ever make sense.

Night life on The Hill, as everyone called it, was centered around several places. The favorite was Alex's, a fun bar and restaurant run by Alex who was a great guy and welcomed you as if you were entering his living room, which in a way, his place was.

The restaurant at Skylonda Corners was more upscale and the Buena Vista, the BV, was even more so and it had the view of San Francisco Bay and the towns that surrounded it. Then, there was Boots and Saddles in La Honda and a few biker bars that we long-haired hippies didn't want to test. If we were really adventurous, there was Woodside and Palo Alto/Menlo Park/Atherton.

Money was not an issue. Larry and I didn't pay rent and Neil paid well for our services and so we could afford whatever we wanted. But if we worked all day, sometimes it was just nice to go home, cook dinner, relax and crash. This was 1972 and there was no satellite, no cable out there in the woods and our small TV didn't receive much over the air.

As we were still shooting scenes, Fred Underhill was also on the clock. He set himself up in the living room of our house and for a few months the three of us lived together. Judy and their daughters, Justine and Molly, were in San Francisco living in an apartment on Lombard St. and Fred would venture home on the weekends. Sometimes, we would go along too just to get some city energy.

Part of my job was to keep the studio refrigerator and pantry filled with food for us and the men who worked with Neil recording his music, which was on-going. The small kitchen didn't have much counter space for real cooking, which was fine because I was not yet a real cook. We made eggs and toast, sandwiches, some soup from cans. The primary occupant of the refrigerator was beer. I was getting into that head that if we want to eat good food, which we're used to, then I'd better come up with something.

We were thirty minutes from the Skylonda convenience store and one hour from a good grocery store, Roberts of Woodside. I drove down to Roberts on a weekly basis in our VW bus to load up on supplies. I used Neil's charge account so there was no limit as to what I could buy. I was trusted because everyone knew I was naturally frugal. It became a local joke between me and the checkers about what the bill was going to be. At first, they had a hard time connecting this hippie chick in a VW bus with hundreds of dollars worth of food, but then got the picture. Ohhhh, Neil Young, the famous musician/recluse, which was pretty much who he was at this stage of his life.

I took the time on these trips to learn how to shop. And that led to cooking, which we did at The Little White House. There were other workers on the ranch as well who lived on their own off the ranch. So, when dinner rolled around, there were always a few who might stop in. It was casual and unhurried and we were probably just going to go back to the studio to work into the night anyway. There was no clock, no 9-5, just the natural rhythm of the country.

I had a "Joy of Cooking" which I began to read. Fred was a good cook, a gourmet even, and he taught me details like cooking something, then letting it rest, covered, to settle before eating. His vichyssoise was amazing, silky smooth, penetrated with leeks and that earthy potato taste and smell. Just as I was learning the craft of the film editing room which took care and time, and timing, I was doing the same in the kitchen.

Larry was relentlessly quick-witted and kept us all laughing. For example, one day Neil came in to the studio and mentioned that he'd been approached by Hallmark Cards which wanted to use some of his lyrics. Without a pause Larry rejoined: "Old Man Lying by the Side of the Road. Happy Birthday!" Neil was stunned, then he laughed too. That deal was never made.

In February, Geri Hash knocked on my door. My mother was trying to reach me and because of our work schedule, had somehow missed me at the studio and at home and found herself talking to Geri. I immediately called her and she didn't have good news. My dad had hit a train. He'd been at a construction site in a small town south of Madison and was coming home on a snowy country road, traveling west, dirty windshield, sun blazing through. The railroad crossing didn't have wig-wags or any sort of warning light and with the windows up he didn't hear a thing. He smashed into the side of the engine and his new station wagon was pulled along down the track until it hit the mailbag pole that still stood beside the track. The pole pulled his car off of the train and probably saved his life. He was in the hospital and had a team of doctors attending to him. I asked mom what the prognosis was and she said he was fine. That sounded impossible. Should I come back, I asked. No, it's not necessary. Obviously, Mom was still in shock. I left the next day and went to the hospital from the airport.

Dad was in the ICU and the prognosis was not good. He'd broken so many bones, facial, ribs, right thigh bone shattered into bits, but the real danger was edema of the brain, which if he survived might still leave him with significant damage. There was a team of ten doctors on call for him and not one thought that he had a fighting chance. But they didn't know my dad.

Charles Frederick Field, known as Chuck, was the youngest son of Rose Hirsig Field and her husband George. They lived in Monroe, Wisconsin, Cheese Capital of the state, which is about sixty miles south of Madison where Grandpa George was a county assessor and had been a carriage painter. He was very low key and died when I was five so I barely knew him. Grandma Rose was another thing entirely. She had airs about her and was extremely prejudiced. If you weren't a Swiss Reformed Lutheran, you were no good. Like many people of that time, she came from a large family. Her brothers had done very well in business, they were Swiss after all, and knew how to rub two nickels together.

Rose's brother, Louis, had started a hardware business in Madison with two partners, Wolff and Kubly and that was the name of the business: Wolff, Kubly & Hirsig. They started with one store with three floors on the Capitol Square and eventually had four stores, a builders hardware department, a heating and air-conditioning business, and a fine china and silver store. My two Field uncles, George and Bill, had been sent to college but by the

Dad, Bill, George, Grandma Rose, Grandpa George

time my dad was of age, the depression had wiped out the money that had been set aside for his tuition and living expenses. Uncle Louis offered him a job and a place to live. Dad could sleep in the storeroom, get up at 4am to start the furnace and at 7:30 open the doors. He did that, learned the hardware business and soon was learning the builders hardware business, reading blueprints and writing bids for large buildings and homes in Madison. At home, Dad was a very positive person, willing to pitch in and get things done, drive me to skating lessons, away-games in high school, helpful, as I grew up and matured, with advice, a check, and love.

Uncle George had become a geologist and did very well in the oil patch, living in Mississippi, Texas and Oklahoma his whole life with his wife Gwen, the daughter of a University of Wisconsin Dean, and their five daughters, Judith, Nancy, twins Susie and Sally, and Debby. He was incredibly bright and the old saw was don't ask George a question. He'll take you back to Genesis with the answer. He was the first person I ever heard who said that the big money was not going to come from oil but from water some day. It appears history will bear him out.

Middle brother Bill was known around the state of Wisconsin as "Mr. Conservation", as he worked for the Department of Fish and Game and even took President Eisenhower fishing on the Fox River. "Toot toot, beanbag" was his sense of humor when addressing any of us kids but there was also a dark side to him when it came to ethnic people or other religions, if you get my drift. He, more than George or my dad, was carrying on that Hirsig sense of entitlement and dislike of people who were not just like him. His wife Bernice Adelman Field was also from Monroe and Grandma Rose thought she was perfect and so were her children, Barbara and Billy. She really knew how to cook all the game her husband bagged, and was blond, attractive and Swiss. They lived in Beaver Dam which is about fifty minutes north of Madison and Bill continued in his father's footsteps when he later took a job with the Department of Natural Resources acquiring land for the state and over-seeing wildlife refuges.

Into this mix came my mother, Viola Hjordis Landvick, a first generation Norwegian from Stoughton, Wisconsin about twenty miles southeast of Madison. Her father Earling owned a restaurant and bar and a ski jump. He died in a car accident when Mom was fifteen leaving her mother, Lylli, and sons Earling, Jr. and Robert behind. This was in the depression so life had been tough for Mom. A man in town offered to send her to college but she didn't want to be beholding to anyone and struck out on her own, moving to Madison and getting a secretarial job at the Court House. My dad fell in love with her right away after they'd met through friends at a bar in the Bush, a rowdy Italian neighborhood in Madison. When I asked her how had Dad proposed, she said, "He didn't. He pulled out the blueprints for the house he was going to build in Shorewood Hills and said, 'Here's our house'." Mom's brother Robert was killed in a bar fight during WWII, Earling Jr., in a car crash in 1955, and Grandma Lylli, died of a sudden heart attack soon after that, leaving my mom as the sole survivor of her immediate family.

Mom - Vi Field

Now here she was, seeing her husband lying in the ICU and it was a very hard for her, dealing with all the doctors, getting sympathy from neighbors, family and friends, all very difficult. Mom was a woman who liked to be alone. She wasn't a joiner or a "do-er" like her husband or for that matter, like me. Not that she wasn't social, because she was. She loved beautiful clothes and had them, looked good in them and always took care of herself. She played golf at the nearby Blackhawk Country Club but didn't seek out the committee chairmanships or stay around the club for hours lunching, playing bridge, staying away from home. She loved being at home, being a good mom.

My brother, Charles, at this time was twenty-six and had gone into business with my dad. Charles, who was known to everyone else on earth except Mom and me as Charlie, is funny and thoughtful and he was his mother's son as I was my father's daughter. We had always gotten along but as I was three-and-a-half years older, we weren't in each other's spheres in school. Now, he and I knew that a big part of each day would be making sure Mom got through it. He filled me in on what was going on in our dad's life that might have put him in this precarious situation.

Dad was the Vice-President of the company. Duke Kubly was President and Fritz Wolff was Executive Vice-President. The Board of Directors was made up of Louis Hirsig's sons-in-law and a few local businessmen. Ace Hardware had come to town and, typical of a national chain, had made a lucrative offer for the company. My dad was the only one who didn't want to accept it as the store and his work were his life. At fifty-seven, he wanted to keep things going in the very successful way they had for years. The post-war period of the fifties and sixties had seen a building boom as the University and the State government in Madison had expanded and Dad was a favorite of the architects and contractors, his bids were fair and he delivered on time and on budget. Frank Lloyd Wright's school, Taliesan, was in near-by Spring Green and

Charles at the Shack in the country

he and his architecture students had come to rely on Wolff Kubly & Hirsig for all their building needs. I had met Mr. Wright one day as he parked his huge old car curbside in front of what we always called "Dad's store" and swept in with his broad-brimmed hat and cape. He'd come to make sure he could still get credit even though he'd defaulted on other past invoices. Of course my Swiss dad said "No, C.O.D. only". A world famous architect wearing a cape and gigantic hat might impress some people, but my dad thought every man should pay his bills. That conviction defined Chuck Field.

The Board voted to accept the Ace offer for all the real estate and inventory. No executive personnel would be retained. Mom, Charles and I conjectured this was what was occupying Dad's thoughts as he sped home to Madison on that winter afternoon. His

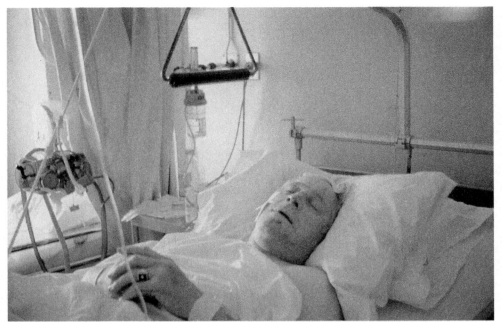

Dad

mind was a million miles away as he tried to understand why his partners would sell the company. It was a blow to our family too. I had worked at the Capitol Square main store many summers and during the Christmas rush. Eventually, I got the prime job for a teen-ager in the record department where I was relied on to listen to the new 45's and be the "hit-picker" when the label reps would come to town. And now, this chapter would be over. The sale was going to close, my dad and brother would have to move on.

In the hospital after the accident, Dad was conscious but drifting in and out. I came in, opened the window curtains and took pictures of him. I was clueless as to how serious it all was and probably thought this would buoy his spirits. Dad always loved to take pictures with his "Tampax" camera as he called the Pentax SLR camera he always had with him. The ICU was under strict supervision from the nurses and only one family member was allowed to be bedside at a time and then only for ten minutes each hour. Dad was being attended to by these pros so that once I had seen him, we left to get me settled at home.

I was back in my old bedroom, with my custom-made bed with a bookshelf behind the pillows, my collection of Storybook dolls on a wallshelf, the walls painted a light turquoise, my favorite color my whole life. One window overlooked the front hills sloping down to the street, the other was a dormer-style window that had a copper-lined nook in the roof line where I would tuck myself between reflective sheets and try to get a tan in early March.

Coming in from Broken Arrow Ranch, it was a shock to the system that here I was, back home again, but with a very real crisis on my hands. I would sit in the ICU waiting room, surrounded by people who had a family member in that grey area between life and death and waited my turn to go in to see Dad. Each day, one of these families would be gone, either because death had claimed the patient or they had improved enough to go into a hospital ward. I almost didn't want to get to know anyone well as it was too painful to see how they each dealt with their own medical emergency. Some people would weep continuously, inconsolably, slumped in the uncomfortable chairs, barely dragging themselves into the ICU for their ten minutes at bedside.

How each of us manage a crisis of this magnitude is personal and telling. I didn't really know how I'd handle it. I was frightened but also bold. Perhaps one fed the other. The one thing that came through to me was that this experience was not about me, it was about my father and it was my "job" or duty to wipe away the emotional component and take care of business. In effect, I was saving myself from myself. I also wanted to be brave for Mom who had more experience with death than all of us but this was a very debilitating time for her and she was hanging on by a thin thread. It did take it's toll on me one day while I was finding my way to the lavatory. I felt very dizzy and once inside the private room, fainted dead away. I revived quickly, I think, drank some water and went back to the waiting room.

We would leave the hospital each day to return home where we would usually find a casserole dish sitting on the frozen front step. There were many friends and neighbors who were concerned about us and that translated into the "food for the weary" program. We would eat something, anything, watch some television then go to bed early so that we could be at the hospital early enough to catch some of the doctors.

Dad was improving at an amazing rate. His vital signs were very strong and his will to live even stronger. I went into see him about a week into the ordeal and he called me over as if he had some secret to tell me. He said I should go home and get the butcher knife and cut him out of there. The nurses had wrist restraints on him as he wasn't always the best patient due to the swelling of his brain and had tried to rip out his IVs. I said I'd think about it. Then he instructed me to make a phone call. He had it in his mind that there was a company Board of Directors meeting and he wanted to let Duke Kubly know that he couldn't attend. I asked one of the nurses if I could use the ICU phone and she said yes. I dialed the store, got Duke on the phone and gave him Dad's message. Then I held the phone up for Dad and that was when I almost lost it. He was being so brave and trying to conduct business as usual under these impossibly extreme conditions, another example of the things that defined my Dad and it just about broke my heart.

His condition stabilized after three weeks in the hospital. His neurologist still warned us that the swelling of the brain might have caused permanent damage but it wouldn't impede his recovery nor his quality of life once he got out.   By now, the medical team acknowledged that he was going to make it.

I made my plans to return to California and went in to see him before going to the airport. Mom, Charles and I were at bedside and I leaned over to give him a kiss and say good-bye.

He said, "Good-bye? You just got here."

"No, Dad, I've been here three weeks."
He said, "I didn't know that. How long have I been here?"

Three weeks, we answered. We then realized he had been in a fog of the trauma and the drugs. I promised I'd return when he was released to help him and Mom make the transition at home.

Back at the ranch (isn't that a phrase you have always wanted to use), work was progressing slowly but then, what was the hurry? We were living in a redwood paradise, surrounded by interesting people, making money, getting high. Two new ranch hands were hired, Larry Christiani and his friend, Sandy Kroopf. They had both grown up in the Palo Alto area and fit the profile of Neil's workers: young, strong, independent, artistic. Tim Mulligan, who was also a musician, rounded out the crew, having been brought in by Carrie who had known him from Chicago. Christiani had spent nine months in jail as a war protestor and all-around Stanford hot-head and once he was back on the streets had high-tailed it to the woods on land owned by Jimmy Wickett which was called Star Hill and was west of Neil's ranch.

Jimmy was in his twenty's and invited all sorts of hippies to come and live on the land. Christiani had staked out a place far from everyone and built a geodesic dome that he hung on three redwood trees high above the roaring creek fifty feet below. His girlfriend, Johanna Putnoi, a dancer and teacher, lived with him in this rustic situation. They had to drive down an old logging road which had two-foot-deep ruts caused by the tremendous rain storms the coastal area got, park the mud-packed four-by-four they drove, then walk several hundred yards to their home. They had a generator near the car park, located there because then you wouldn't hear it when you were in the dome. They could run it for a few hours to provide the only electricity. The kitchen was run on propane and a wood-burning stove gave them heat. You entered the dome into the kitchen and bathroom level then climbed several steps up into the living room area. Above this was a sleeping loft.

Sandy Castle (James Mazzeo), Tim Mulligan, Larry Christiani

It was a wonderful space, with rugs and pillows on the floor and colorful fabrics covering the dome wall.

If they wanted to be part of the Star Hill community, they would walk or drive up to the open acres that looked out on the ocean where about twenty other people had built their homes, all of them small but most of them, artistic wonders. Sandy Castle had lived up there too before he moved to the ranch. He built a beautiful tree house that someone else now called home. It was way up high, an almost scary trip up a redwood, and had several levels. A perfect icon for life at Star Hill.

The redwood forest can capture you, the huge trees surrounded by lush ferns and dogwood, the wonderful smell of the needles and cones. Behind our house there was a wide fairy ring of smaller trees, ones that grew from the parent tree that had been cut down. I'd escape to the woods, think about my Dad, or try not to, focus my camera lens on the beauty surrounding me, huge and miniscule. I'd always loved being in a woods, sometimes pretending it was a primordial experience, and here at Broken Arrow, the path led me into sanctuaries that could either speak to me or listen quietly.

Doreen Small, who was still sharing a house with Charlotte in Topanga, called one day. She had signed on to a film production that was being done at the American Film Institute by one of the fellows there. AFI matched grants for the filmmakers but they had to raise the money before AFI would put up their side. She was hoping that she could get an interview with Neil in hopes that he would help a starving artist. Larry invited her to the ranch to show the film student's previous efforts and have an audience with Neil. We all met at the studio in front of the KEM editing machine and watched David Lynch's short, then heard about the feature film he wanted to make which was called "Eraserhead". It was about a young guy who could barely utter a word, probably because of the cretinous industrial society that had stolen his soul. His girlfriend, Mary X was pregnant and when the baby arrived, it was a creature. He had pangs about the woman across the hall and visualized a midget in the radiator. Wow, what a blockbuster. Neil passed but I actually decided I wanted to work on it. They would start shooting in the summer and I could stay with Doreen and Char.

My social life beyond my work at the studio was checkered. Neil's girlfriend, Carrie, now the Queen Bee, was as mercurial as a hurricane. One day, she was your best friend, incredibly into you, the next, you were stung practically to death. There was no indicator as to which Carrie you'd get. Her best friend was Gigi who had come out from Chicago with Tim Mulligan, and they lived in a two room house near our turn-off on Skyline. Sometimes, I'd stop there on my way back from the grocery store, and Gigi would be out of it. I didn't know what drugs she did but she was a tiny, pale-faced urban girl with long black hair, goth before goth was even a hint in anyone's mind. Another friend hung around as well. Betsy Heimann was also from Chicago but unlike her friend Gigi, had a lot of energy and opinions. She liked to take photos and struck up a friendship with Joel Bernstein.

They were Carrie's pals and it was hard to break into their circle. Carrie seemed to need these friends around, as if to validate her decision to leave Hollywood just as her career was taking off. Monique James, the head of casting at Universal, had discovered Carrie and put her in several small roles before casting her in "Diary of a Mad Housewife". In this seminal role of a woman not clear on the marriage concept, knowing she was being pulled in two directions, one the loving wife, the other, the bright New York woman who had the world nearly at her fingertips, Carrie had given a mind-blowing performance, one that won her an Oscar nomination. Neil had seen the movie and it won her his love. As he says in his song, "Man Needs A Maid": "I fell in love with the actress. She was playing a part that I could understand."

When Neil wanted to meet Carrie, he was in the hospital nursing an incredibly painful back. She had no idea who he was but Gigi told her and Elliot facilitated the meeting. Neil ended up having a spinal fusion and Carrie was there to help him when he was released. She told me that she fell in love with his pain. At the time, maybe because of my Dad's situation, I didn't have a lot of patience for game players. Jack Nietzsche and his wife Gracia, who lived in a house nearby, had more patience with Carrie's mood changes than I. Gigi and Betsy did too.

A few weeks had passed since I'd returned to the ranch. Dad was gaining strength and ready to come home, so I went back to Madison. We set up a hospital bed in the living room as he couldn't yet climb up stairs to the second floor bedroom. Mom's anxiety had calmed but I could tell that having full responsibility for him was difficult. There were no nurses or aides to pitch in when she or he got tired. It was all on us. Dad was a battered mess. His facial bones had been shattered as had his teeth. His right leg was now held together by a long steel rod which ultimately was never removed. But he was so glad to be home that this emotion replaced all others. We were glad he was home too and whatever came next, we would handle. Friends and relatives stopped by, giving him additional strength and he in turn never showed an emotion less than chipper.

Mom was exhausted, as usually happens with the "survivor". She'd had the emotional upheaval, the countless trips to the hospital not only to see Dad but to confer with doctors, conversations with insurance auditors, and her unspoken desire to sue the shit out of the railroad. The crossing where Dad had hit the train was in the country and had no warning signals of an approaching train. Wasn't the company responsible? But this was not a litigious time and I recall that our neighbor and lawyer, Vernon Molbreak advised against it. Dad was also a proud man and the thought of admitting any kind of mistake or fault in the accident, much less living it all over again, was not in the cards.

Meanwhile, the sale of the company was proceeding and Dad had many other things on his mind, especially the formation of his own company, carrying on with long-time clients with my brother at his side. His brother George encouraged him to create his own hardware store and offered to invest in the large overhead that would require. But Dad declined the offer and said he would make bids on buildings as he did before and if he was chosen, then he would get advance money for the needed supplies.

Another big consideration was the "shack" that Dad and Charles had started building a year before the accident. This was a cottage on forty acres of land out in the country near the small town of Barneveld about thirty miles west of Madison. It was heavily forested with red oak trees and brush, had large rock outcroppings and was part of a parcel that a friend of Dad's had bought. They had split the costs of building a road, bringing in electricity, gas and water. The house had a garage and tool room on the lower floor, a kitchen, bathroom, two bedrooms, living room and screened-in porch on the main floor, then a sleeping loft/attic above. We all had gathered large streamstones for the fireplace. It was a simple place but perfect in Dad's eyes and he was dying to get back there. That was the first outing we made so that Dad could survey the place and assess how he could move forward on the work despite his infirmities.

Knowing that I had done as much as I could for the moment, I returned to Broken Arrow Ranch where spring was in it's glory. That winter had seen particularly heavy rain fall and it was great now to not have wet animals, dirty boots and ponchos in our little white house. The Hashes were very open about us using their horses and the rides through the countryside, down the dirt roads toward the ocean were incredibly beautiful. Carrie was pregnant and she and Neil were thrilled with this. All seemed right in rock 'n roll heaven. We were a community with Neil at the center.

I needed another outlet for my city energy and an idea kept gnawing at me. Having been a Political Science major in college, I saw the Viet Nam war in terms other than many in the anti-war movement. I saw a bigger picture beyond a body count, one that the Nixon administration was not acknowledging. I had an idea for a play. Called "The Brothers", it would delve into the underpinnings of the war, the fall of the French at Dien Bien Phu because of the American failure to provide air cover during significant battles. The growing American presence that John Foster Dulles, as Secretary of State under Eisenhower, and his brother Allan Dulles, as Director of the CIA, initiated with the Catholic Diem brothers, Ngo Dinh Diem and Ngo Dihn Nhu, drew me in. Stanford University was an hour away and had a huge cache of information about the politics of South Viet Nam. The Diems were assassinated during Kennedy's term, no doubt engineered by the Dulles brothers, and all the promises and the lies passed as diplomacy, done between these two sets of brothers. But the drama of this was beyond my writing skill. I read as much as I could put my hands on and attempted to talk with friends at the ranch, but I was on my own on this one.

Work on the movie was going slowly. With so much to choose from, Neil being a novice film editor, and Larry too, for that matter as he had spent most of his time at Paradigm doing location sound recording and/or post-production duties which involved sound, they tried several versions of the story without mapping out what it should or could be. My duties in the editing room were as an assistant, cleaning up, making sure that outtakes were re-wound and put in boxes that were carefully labeled and organized.

Doreen called from L.A. to say that David Lynch had raised enough money to begin work on his film. I confirmed my interest in being part of the crew and she said of course I could stay in Topanga with her and Char, who was also going to work on the film. It was going to be a rigorous shoot as the sound man, Alan Splet, had a real job and couldn't show up until 5pm which meant that we would work nights. Doreen was the production manager and David's "go to" girl. She was also sleeping with him as he seemed to be breaking up with his wife.

David had built his sets in the carriage house of the Greystone mansion that housed AFI in Beverly Hills. It was the old Doheny mansion which we always referred to as "Ned's House" after Ned Doheny, a musician we knew peripherally through Lookout Mountain Management. And had his family history been a bit different, it really would have been his house. I soon learned that AFI considered David the fair-haired boy. It was the first, and last, full-length feature film that would be authorized there.

The main character in the movie, Henry Spencer, was played by Jack Nance who was married to Catherine Coulson. They both would become regulars in David's later movies and television series. Each afternoon, Catherine brought food for the crew then did Jack's hair which meant lots of back-combing and hair spray. This gave Henry his extra special surprised look. Jack was a very nice guy, funny, laid-back and a committed actor originally from Texas. His existential performance in the movie was also part of his personality as Jack could just "be" like very few others.

Charlotte boldly threw herself into her role as his angry pregnant girlfriend, Mary X, who lived with her parents. Pretty as she was, Char had never been afraid to look horrible in a film role, "Anything for the movies" being a mantra she could murmur at length.

Each day David would come to the set wearing two ties, an affectation he thankfully dropped later on when he was more famous. There was no script that any of us could read, but one must have existed in David's mind because he knew exactly what we were doing each day. We'd all sit around eating dinner and he would go through the scene. Then we'd light it and shoot it.

I worked with the lighting cameraman, Herb Cardwell, setting lights, running cable, loading magazines. When some of the special effects were to be used in a scene, I would also participate in these. We were very low tech as David had built all the equipment we operated. David had started out as a painter then was drawn to film which was why he was at the AFI. He was a very handy guy, driving a VW bug on which he had rigged a rooftop carrier for lumber, equipment, whatever the shoot required. In one of the early scenes, Henry had come for dinner at Mary X's house. Her father was ranting and raving and attempted to carve some little chickens his wife has prepared. Unfortunately, every time he put the carving knife in a chicken, it jumped and wiggled. I was under the table using a tube and plunger gizmo that David had made and it was this that made the chickens move. (What, leave show business?) Another special effect was the mutant baby Mary X has. We are all sworn to secrecy about what was in the bag that formed the baby's body so you won't learn that here. But, the baby had about forty separate moves and once again, yours truly was behind the scenes plunging to beat the band, making the baby do things that drove Henry crazy. Crazy enough to be seduced by the beautiful woman down the hall who took him to her bed where they almost drowned in a sea of milk. Really, I'm not making this up. Crazy enough that he saw a midget dancing in the radiator. Crazy enough to think that his brain would be better off used as pencil erasers. Ah, ha, we have finally gotten to the big plot point. And so it goes.

After each night of shooting, Char, Doreen and I would get in our separate cars and drive home to Topanga. Some nights or dawns, as the case might be, I didn't even remember the drive home. I'd fall into bed and as I was sleeping in the living room, try to get at least a few hours before the daylight drove the sandman from my head. I'd go to the beach, see friends, then go back to the movie set by 5pm.

This went on for several weeks and during that time we only had one day where we shot outside. It was the scene where Henry wandered through a field of oil derricks which was actually in Beverly Hills near the high school. We had reached the end of the script so far and David decided he needed to put together what he had before he filmed more material. He also had to raise more money. He would spend the next four years working on the film but it set him up to be hired by Mel Brooks to direct "The Elephant Man".

Returning to ranch life after my time in L.A., I realized that Larry and I were drifting apart. I thought that some of this problem was Fred Underhill who still would spend time in our little house, leaving his family in their apartment in San Francisco. But, it also turned out to be Carrie who would gossip with Fred about everyone, including me. Carrie the actress had brought her melodrama to the country and I feared that Larry was somehow caught up in it too.

Neil was essentially a loner and we knew he liked to keep ranch drama at a low roar. At the end of the day, after spending hours editing, he usually ambled home for a quiet evening. So it was surprising that one night he came to our little house and plopped himself down at the kitchen table. He stayed for dinner and we talked but I could tell something was up. I didn't really want to pry but mentioned that he seemed a little uncomfortable.

"Yeah," he said, "it's America."

"You mean, politics, the war. "

"No, I mean America, the fucking group that sang "Horse With No Name"."

I had to laugh. "Yeah, everyone thought you wrote that song." I did laugh at Neil on occasion and Larry would get so mad at me, as he thought I was disrespecting the star.

"That's the problem," Neil said, "I hate that song. Those guys are at Elliot's house and he wanted me to meet them." Ah, the truth. Neil was hiding out and figured the last place Elliot would look for him was in the little white house, too far to drive along that dark windy road with a group of musicians who'd come to make nice.

We were now in post-production with the picture locked, so Fred and Larry were spending a lot of time in Los Angeles dealing with the lab. I stayed on the ranch and hung out with Johanna who cleaned the studio. I worked in the editing room getting things ready for the mix which we were going to do ourselves using an Ampex system Neil had bought and the great mixing board he used for recording.

Johanna and I had a good connection as we were the worker bees on the ranch. She'd studied in France, New York, was a dancer and practiced tai chi which she taught me out on the studio deck. We both felt we were just on the perimeter of the ranch social scene, meaning Carrie's group. She was a good horseback rider and the Hashes trusted her so we could take the horses off the ranch out onto Star Hill where we could ride for miles.

Johanna and Larry Christiani decided to get married. It wouldn't really be official, more like a hippie wedding but it was the thought that counted. They made their plans to gather at Star Hill

Johanna, Jeanne & Larry

in a beautiful meadow overlooking the sea. Johanna's parents arrived and it was obvious that she, too, was her father's daughter. Dr. Putnoi had spent a career in the army, some of it in New York City on Governor's Island or at other more exotic posts. Mrs. Putnoi had been a nurse and had that crisp demeanor one learns in an institution, hospital or army. Johanna's sister, Sue, was so unlike her as to wonder which one was adopted. She was an upper eastside NYC housewife who had bought into a conventional life early on. All three of them were gracious in the face of the very unconventional, hippie life the youngest daughter had chosen.

Johanna had asked me to be her maid of honor and I did my duty by getting her righteously stoned on a bomber in my VW bug as we ventured up to the wedding site. Walking with her and Larry C. with Larry J. at my side, we had a view of the tribal event of the year. They had invited some friends from the Hill, and of course, those had invited others. Dogs ran through the crowd and the biggest and boldest was Larry C's dog, Smack, who proceeded to take on all comers during the short ceremony. It was a portentous beginning. Following that, the guests swarmed on and over the beautiful buffet table and everything was gone in about fifteen minutes. None of us got a lick. But it was a grand gesture from a mother and father who were relieved their youngest had found marital bliss with a rag tag coupling that was becoming more common.

At Broken Arrow Ranch, across the road from our little house was a small pig pen with four large pigs. Although they were well taken care of by Bob Hash, I did my bit by bringing out vegetable leavings whenever we had them. I liked the pigs and it was one of the signs we lived on a real ranch. One day it was decided that like all good ranches there would be a summer bar-b-que. There had been the castration of the calves born that spring and the resultant rocky mountain oyster buffet and there also would be a roast pig. What? Not one of "my" pigs. Oh, yes. Bob Hash whipped out his .45 and put it behind the ears of one of them and the deed was done. But that was only the first step. Next, they had to cart the carcass over to the barn near by and clean it up. I didn't leave the house. Fred and Larry joined in the shaving of the pig using extra sharp knives to get every last bristle, drinking tequila by the quart as they did so, following Bob's instructions. Next, they had to dig the pit. They chose a spot outside of the studio and dug down about five feet, layed in firewood, aromatic branches, charcoal to start, got it going, then added the pig. They covered it with more branches and firewood. The thing cooked all night.

It was a major festivity. Neighbors from all over came, all of the ranch workers, Jack Nitzsche showed up with Charlie Watts, the Rolling Stones drummer. Dr. Joe, the rock and roll MD and his wife Diantha flew up and Fred brought his family down from the city. Dave Myers was there with Barbara and of course Elliot with his family. Everyone was loaded on something when they uncovered

Ranch Group Photo

the pig, the piece de resistance. Much as I had mourned it's passing, I had to admit it was delicious, but is there any wonder? I'd fed it really good food.

In September, Zeke Young was born. Dr. Joe was scheduled to come up and be with Neil and Carrie for the home birth they wanted to have. Carrie's contractions began early in the morning and they called Joe who ran to the airport. But Carrie's pain was too intense and as they knew that Zeke was a breach baby, they chose to get in a car and race to Stanford Hospital where Zeke was born. Joe was disappointed that they didn't wait as he felt he could have delivered Neil's first son. We all gathered at the hospital to congratulate the new mom and dad.

After the slow and steady editing work, Neil was now very busy, caught up in his own world, finishing the film and planning a new tour that would go out after the New Year. He'd walk from his house to the studio, following the muse and would sit down at the desk or in the music room working on new material for the tour and record. Working quietly so not to bother him, Larry and I were in the editing room putting up film tracks for the mix, which we mixed down with the help of Tim Mulligan who ran the board. We were working fifteen hours a day trying to finish up before band rehearsal began.

Neil had done his albums "Everybody Knows this is Nowhere" and "After the Gold Rush" with the first incarnation of the Crazy Horse band. Danny Whitten was part of it and had a voice that could partner up with Neil's for an arresting affect. Neil hadn't played with Danny in a few years and wanted him to be part of the new tour with the Stray Gators, who had backed Neil on "Harvest". Word had it that Danny was living in the Inland Empire working in a diner owned by his girlfriend's family. Crazy Horse had not been doing much since Neil had joined CSNY and the time had not been kind to Danny. Neil's song, "Needle and the Damage Done" chronicled that split. Neil went to L.A. to see Danny and invited him to come to the ranch for rehearsals. Leo Makota, who had been on the CSNY tour as a roadie and bodyguard, brought in an Airstream trailer which he set up right outside the studio. It was approximately ten steps to the front door. They didn't want to take a chance Danny wouldn't make it. Johanna came over in the morning, fixed breakfast for Danny, enough to sustain him for the long rehearsals held each day. All for naught as Danny couldn't remember or learn a four chord song. Leo kept an eye on him to make sure he didn't shoot up or sniff or whatever he was used to doing to get the drugs into his system, but Danny was too far gone to let an ex-Hell's Angel biker like Leo trump his play. His stay on the ranch only lasted a few weeks and then with heavy heart, Neil told Danny to go home. Leo drove him to the airport, gave him some money and wished him well. Very early the next morning, Leo was at our door. He came in for coffee and gave us the sad news. Danny had landed in L.A., gone to Topanga, scored some smack and had OD'd. He was dead.

We could barely move around the studio. Everyone cried and the loss completely enervated all of us. Neil became a demon pushing everyone to keep on, focus on the business at hand. Carrie begged him to stop, to take the time to grieve, but it wasn't to be. She became furious with Neil, trying to get all of us on her side, which didn't help matters at all.

In December, our job was done. Neil was focused on the tour with his crew which included most of the guys who had worked on the ranch. Larry Christiani became a roadie, but his old buddy Sandy Kroopf did not, choosing to pursue his photography and eventually his screenwriting. Mulligan would mix the house monitors in the venues. Johanna didn't want to be left behind and went to Carrie to offer help with Zeke and was invited along. Larry C. was not that thrilled with this, especially when the other roadies kidded him about his old lady being on the road, often seen as a curse. Sandy Castle went out on tour and with his exit, Kathy and the kids left the ranch. 1972 was ending with a whisper and a tear.

134

Lamp Light

Chapter Ten

Crash Landing

Larry and I returned to Los Angeles and rented a wonderful compound at the foot of Topanga Canyon. It was owned by Dr. Joe and his wife Diantha who were moving up to Montecito and it was a good deal for all. The house was in a place called the Rodeo Grounds, owned by the Los Angeles Athletic Club which had plans to develop the land and the beach into a huge marina with homes and apartments. People could own a house but not the land. You turned off of Topanga Canyon Blvd. then traveled down a dirt road, crossed Topanga Creek, then passed three other homes to arrive at a very high fence. Behind this was a large yard surrounded by foliage. To the left was an office which was separated by a deck from the main house. To the right of the house was a patio then a glass house, a small structure on a raised platform built completely of old windows someone had scavenged, heated by a lovely old pot-bellied stove. The house was rudimentary with an eat-in kitchen, living room, bedroom, extra room and a great bathroom that opened up through French doors to a back garden that had the mountain as it's far edge.

Topanga Creek could be a roaring river or a very small creek depending on the season. As we were arriving in January, we could expect the worst. When the water was too high, we would have to leave the cars in a parking area then cross over on a swaying foot bridge that hung by cables from poles on either side of the water.

Larry and I got our things out of storage and into the house, then went to Wisconsin for Christmas. We both were too edgy for the holiday season. The last event at the ranch had made us withdrawn and morose. We stayed in Madison for a few days and then the "Time Fades Away" tour with Neil and the Stray Gators came to play the Coliseum there. Neil was staying at the Edgewater Hotel on Lake Mendota which was frozen solid. Larry and I took ice skates when we went to visit him and the three of us skated out on the lake. I also had a small blanket we could take turns attaching to our ankles and hold up like a sail. We took turns scooting over the bumpy surface, carried by the northern wind. Being Canadian, Neil loved it; being Southern, Larry was miserable and so we gave in and hit the hotel bar.

When we were invited to go to Milwaukee where Neil and the band were performing then follow them to New York and their stop at Madison Square Garden, my parents were a bit put out as they'd hoped we would spend more time with them. Dad was doing alright and the dentist and doctors had helped him mend. He had new teeth and walked with barely a limp. The sale of the company had brought a good windfall to them and Charles and Dad were doing well in business. He had his humor back because when we went out to eat, he ordered a steak and when the waitress asked how he wanted it, he said, "Just hold it under your armpit as you walk to the table."

Now, I was pulled in two directions and chose to go with Larry hoping to keep our partnership alive. We couldn't seem to let go of our friends from the ranch and yet everyone had moved on in an emotional way. The tour was a difficult one and, as close as Neil was to his crew, it soon became apparent that the partnership in the country all of us had did not lead naturally into life on the road, especially with the schedule as tight as it was. Carrie was bringing Zeke to the huge venues and we all wondered about that, with the crowds and the very loud music. Johanna seemed to have brought the shadows of the forest with her and Larry C. was not handling it well. The music was raw and compared to the opening act of Linda Ronstadt with her back-up band made up of players who would form the Eagles, very ragged. Neil's emotions were shut down and he was remote to us, almost as if we had done our time and now it was onto the next. But, that's Neil. He can be so focused that if you're not in the currant purview, he doesn't necessarily take the time. He'd say hello but he had a lot on his mind with the shows and as this tour said, time fades away.

Both Larry and I were betwixt and between when we returned to Los Angeles. The movie, "Journey Through The Past", was not a Hollywood blockbuster and critical acclaim was withheld. No one knew what to make of it. Neil had created a company for the film, Shakey Pictures, and the credited director was Bernard Shakey. Was Neil hiding behind the film, not ready to admit that as a novice filmmaker he hadn't quite accomplished what he set out to do?

Honestly, I've always loved the movie but then I was drawn to film not by plot, action, and Hollywood stars, but by the mood, the moment in time captured in an artistic way. It takes a special eye to see a person or an event and think they can use it, put it in a movie and let it stand by itself or make a comment. It's a genre unto itself and so what if only a handful of people get it. If you're driven by critical acclaim or box office grosses, originality can go out the window. Neil proved he was still an original with his cinema verite style.

Several years later, I was introduced to the Russian filmmaker Andrei Tarkovsky whose meditative films draw you in by repetition, startling imagery, poetic scenes that are one long shot. In "Journey", there was a scene of Neil and Carrie driving one of Neil's old cars on the ranch road. They came to a narrow wooden bridge that spanned the creek that ran through the ranch, stopped the car and got out. It's a peaceful, beautiful moment that Myers shot, rolling for minutes. Neil and Carrie shared some juice, silently enjoying themselves. Then they got in the car and rolled on. That's it, and it was the essence of love and life in the country.

Elliot, busy with the tour, was remote and seemed to be embarrassed by the film. I'm sure he was only mirroring the responses he got from his Hollywood buddies, agents he had come up with at William Morris. Neil was weird, the movie was weird. Carrie's career was over. Next??!!

Compared to this, what turned out to be next was even harder. Larry had continued to be distant and it wasn't just the move or the movie. We had bought a 1966 Lincoln Continental convertible with the suicide doors. The hardtop came up and glided down into the trunk. It was a classic. The VW bus was history from the rigors of the mountain roads, so we had the VW bug, the Lincoln and an army jeep that Bob Hash had put together with spare parts from a kit he'd bought. Larry would usually drive the Lincoln and I'd use the jeep or the bug. One day, I needed to go to a fabric shop and drove down Neilson Way in Santa Monica. Along that road, there were two high-rise apartment buildings where Doreen Small's mother lived. I looked over and couldn't believe that the Lincoln was in the parking lot. All of a sudden, it was like I was hit by lightning. The reason for the brush-offs, the reason for the cool, was that Larry and Doreen were having an affair.

There had been hints of this along the way, but I am naturally a trusting person and had not taken to heart what should have been obvious. That, and the fact that none of our mutual friends had said anything once we had returned to Southern California. There had been the time that Larry had come to L.A. for lab work on "Journey" when I was shooting "Eraserhead". I suggested to Doreen that we just drop in one morning after shooting and it was an uncomfortable moment. She'd attempted to beg off but I had insisted. There was the moment when I'd asked Larry if we had a problem and was told that we didn't. I wanted to believe that and so I did.

When I confronted him, all he could say was that his stomach was killing him, his way of begging off, asking forgiveness. He didn't want to break up, at least not then. I was in turmoil.

Meanwhile, Larry was on the phone with Carrie a lot. One of the band member's wives had a meltdown on the tour, actually closer to an OD. Larry told me the wife would come stay with us for a few days while she cooled out. We went to LAX and I was stunned by what we met there. The bandmember's wife was on the nod, in a wheelchair, and in need of real help which I didn't think we were capable of giving. But here she was and there was nothing I could say. About it or anything, as it turned out. She sat in the sun in our yard and threw a tennis ball for Tas for hours and eventually was healthy enough to go back on the tour which she joined at the Forum when Neil and the band came to town.

Larry got a quick job in New York and decided he would also go to see his parents, alone. He flew to Florida and was gone for weeks. He met Doreen down there and they went to the Caribbean island of Dominque. I called Dale looking for Larry and he intimated that there was a rough road ahead, saying that I had taken a lot of money from Larry, that I spent a lot of money, things I was aghast to hear, as it was just not the case. Any money spent had been to get our new digs in shape, Topanga-style.

I called Charlotte. Doreen was her roommate, surely she knew all of this. Yes, unfortunately, she did. And didn't I deserve a word? Well, she didn't think it was up to her, wasn't it up to Larry? Yes, it was but... he wasn't up to it.

My mom came out for a visit and I couldn't tell her about Larry. I had to make it seem like he was still on the East Coast job and that all was well. It was a nightmare. I was barely holding it together. The relationship I thought was my "picket fence family" was gone, the romance that included riding out the hard times, there for the good times, kids, pets, growing up and old together. For four years we had accepted each other for who we were, not like other couples we'd seen who had fallen in love and then made one or the other change their attitude, their style, and their habits. We'd rolled along until we didn't.

After a few weeks, Larry called to say that he would be back in a few days and we'd talk about it. I was so nervous I didn't know how to handle it. I dropped acid. I sat in the living room staring at a Navaho rug we'd bought, a Two Grey Hills pattern, and the power of the symbol, the weaver, the culture it came from, pulsated off the wall. Every minute was an hour and I was immobilized. I thought of the past and questioned what had I done to destroy this partnership. I remembered Gary Burden saying that the thing about Larry and me was that I was always around. Gary was a traditional man and his wife Annie was at home, caring for the two kids, baking, cooking, sewing, hanging out with her female friends. And, he was right. In our relationship, I was usually there, with Larry and the men he, we, worked with. Had we just burned out? Do relationships have a tipping point and we had just reached it quickly? Larry was a Gemini, I, a Libra. We thought we'd been made for each other.

I wept, paced, watered the garden. Time still crawled. And then the phone rang. I answered it. Charlotte was calling and she later said my voice sounded like it was coming from the back of a cave. I spoke as much as I could at the moment, basically just getting out I'd dropped acid. She said she and her boyfriend Peter Butterfield would come over. A while later, they walked through the big wooden gate, across the lawn and brought me a beautiful blouse with cut-work embroidery on the front. I slipped it on, it fit perfectly and I felt delivered. Peter asked if I wanted to play ping pong and we had several great games, due to my being so loose and focused on that little ball flying around the covered patio.

Then some other friends showed up. J.P. Jones and his girlfriend, Karen Stern, arrived unannounced from their home close by on Topanga Beach. John Binder had lived with Karen for a while in New York then stayed with her and J.P. after he came down from a year in Sonoma. I'd met her through John and agreed with him that she was one of a kind. Unfortunately, a San Francisco friend, Lee, who carried bad vibes, came with them and now, in my super-inflated state, he seemed like the Devil to me. But soon, I reached the point in the trip where everything is funny and nothing was going to bring me down. So with a little help from my friends I got through what could have been a bad solo acid trip, something I never attempted again.

The next morning, early, Larry showed up. I almost didn't recognize him. I thought he was the Gas Company meter reader with a short haircut and dressed in grey shirt and pants. Neither of us had much to say to the other, so we relied on the practical to get us through the visit. He'd be moving up north to Santa Barbara with Doreen, I could keep the house which was too expensive for me on my own. But, at the moment, I didn't have an alternate plan.

It all happened fast. When Larry was motivated, he moved quickly and efficiently, working to get in and out as fast as possible. A Master of the Fast Exit. He took the black leather antique chairs, the office furniture, his personal effects and the Lincoln. I kept the rest of the furniture, kitchen equipment, the VW bug and the spare parts army jeep. I felt like I was a collection of spare parts too. So much of my life had depended on Larry. He was my other half, maybe my two-thirds. So much of what I had done work-wise had come through him. He was the one they called, but I would work the long hours too. Now, Doreen filled that bill. In fact, a few years later, I was interviewing for a job and the person said there was someone else with the same credits. He showed me the resume and it was Doreen's and she had actually listed all the films I'd done as ones she'd worked on. What a girl!

Friends visited to cheer me up. I spent long hours at Topanga Beach which was a short walk down the creek. John Binder lived a few miles up Pacific Coast Highway and would stop in to wash his car and have a beer. His girlfriend, Gloria, would come by. Karen and JP always welcomed me and we would crank up the Champion juicer and make wonderful combinations, especially, my favorite, carrot/beet juice. Karen did a lot of sewing and inspired me to do some things again. I interviewed for some film jobs which I didn't get. And the depression set in. I was sad beyond words. I ate very little during the day. I was so enervated that food, drink, etc. didn't interest me. I dropped to ninety lbs. and realized that I had always wanted to look this skinny, especially since Topanga Beach was the bonanza of undress and I could wear the skimpiest bikini with no shame.

I spent the summer on the beach and have always loved that I had that time, watching the lines of surf, the timelessness of the waves. But the sadness continued and I couldn't shake it. I bottomed out. Flashes of my dad post-collision came to mind as I felt as banged up emotionally as he was, everything in a sling, bandaged face, broken teeth, mumbling words. Philosophically, I knew this was temporary but I was wallowing in the pain and loneliness, feeling unwanted, invisible, so numbed I couldn't fathom a future.

Kit Carson, who I had known at Paradigm from "David Holzman's Diary", his girlfriend, Pup, and good friend, Papaw, were in Los Angeles and came to visit one day. Kit saw that I had a nice place, was in need of friends; he was in need of digs, and they all moved in. Rent wasn't an issue because they had no money. What they did have though was good energy and conversation.

Papaw took one look at the army jeep and came to me with a thought. Back in Texas, he'd been experimenting with a methane-driven engine and proposed that he try it on the jeep. All we'd need would be his adaptor and a good supply of animal waste. We just happened to have that near by at Louis Marvin's Moonfire Temple in La Tuna Canyon, the next canyon over. Heir to the S&H Green Stamp fortune (there used to be books you'd get at the grocery store and every time you bought something you got stamps, which you'd put in the books and once it was filled you could redeem it for money or goods), Louis was a vegetarian warrior who went everywhere with his llama, sometimes a goat and one of his dogs in his large convertible with the backseat removed. The animals also lived in the temple with him.

We went up to visit him and explained the project and he was all for it – free llama and goat shit anytime we wanted it. What a pal! Papaw mounted a fifty-five-gallon drum on the back of the jeep, filled it with the soon-to-be fuel and some water and the damn thing actually worked. We'd tool all around with the jeep, as ugly a vehicle as you can imagine and it had an exhaust smell all it's own. Within time, however, Kit and crew were a little much for full-time residency and I had to ask them to move on to another encampment. But, it was good while it lasted and Kit remained a friend for a long time.

Bob Greenfield, Rolling Stone writer and Charlotte's ex-boyfriend, came by to visit. He'd done the amazing magazine interview with Keith Richard in the south of France two years previously and was in town on business. He was making his way up into Topanga to see some old friends he'd met in Italy. I offered him some mushrooms but he passed so I ate them and Bob and I wandered around the beach area. My VW had broken down and he helped me take it to the gas station which normally would not be a big deal, but I was just coming on to the psilocybin high, and it became hilarious, to me at least. Not so much to Bob who had to translate my "vision" of what was wrong with the bug to the impatient mechanic who was only trying to be helpful. I'm sure this guy had seen a lot of Topanga freaks in his life and I was no different than any of them as they kept our clunkers on the road far longer than the typical life expectancy.

Leaving my car to the expert, we set out for The Smoothie Bar in Topanga Canyon Center. This hole-in-the-wall place was in the middle of Topanga and one of the few commercial spots in the canyon. It was funky before they had a word for it. A long Quonset hut surrounded by parking lots on the edge of the Topanga River, it had a few restaurants and stores. To the left of it, was the grocery store owned and operated by Joe Creek who owned the place, although he lived in Brentwood. To the right was the Post Office. It really was the center of the community as so many residents came there on a daily basis to collect their mail, gas up across the street, and buy the few food items they forgot to get in the Valley or Santa Monica. Krikor The Tailor and the Vintage Shop also pulled people in to browse. Krikor made the off-white muslin drawstring pants and tops that started the uni-sex look. Some of these would then be dyed or tie-dyed into the hippie garb we all would get sick of none too soon.

The Smoothie Bar was between these two shops and there we found Carl and John, Bob's friends. He'd met them in Rome where they were living and working as the American dubbing group for the Italian film industry. They were part of a theater ensemble that had been founded in Rome by Tom and Kathy Hunter. It was a group of about a dozen people who did street theater and staged plays but who made their real money doing the voiceovers for all the movies made in Rome at Cinecitta Studios. Italian movies are done MOS, mit out sound, a term that was coined by Stroheim or someone German when the camera rolled and there was no location sound being recorded. They usually did a scratch track so they had something to go by, but the production sound was done in post by ADR, automatic dialogue replacement, and in the many languages that coincided with the distribution of the movie. For example, a Fellini film probably was seen all over the world, so "La Dolce Vita" or "8½", would be dubbed into many languages by foreign speakers. Carl and John, etc. had done a lot of movies which would be shown in the US.

Tom and Kathy had broken up and that spelled the end of the time in Rome. Kathy and their daughter, Kaki, had come to Los Angeles and so had Carl Miranda, John Thompson, Mickey Fox, Joe Williams, his girlfriend, Roxanne and their baby, Baba. Now they were all working at The Smoothie Bar because Kathy had caught the eye of the owner, Terry, who had wanted to make movies and here he was running a smoothie bar, albeit a successful one. They all lived together at the end of Happy Trail, a one-lane road off of Topanga Canyon road which crossed over a stream then dead-ended at their house. There are a lot of these in Topanga.

Bob Greenfield & Carl Miranda at the Smoothie Bar

I watched as Bob greeted two very good-looking men. Carl had lots of dark curly hair surrounding a handsome Spanish face made surreal by bright blue eyes, a trim body barely clothed in tank top, shorts and sandals. John had long brown hair and a sophisticated manner that belied a wonderful sense of humor. They were just getting off work and wanted to hit the beach, so off we went. We laughed a lot because I was still tripping and that sort of high is infectious. Then, the day was done and I headed back to my lonely house.

A few days later, I was sitting in the living room reading "Daniel", the E.L. Doctorow book about the Rosenbergs (Was I a glutton for punishment??), the controversy about treason, their trial and their death, when the large front gate opened up. In walked Carl, bare-chested, dressed in shorts and sandals, carrying a large leather bag with fringe and beads. A stranger contradiction you could not find between my book and a friend. He'd just been surfing at the beach and did I want to hang out, get dinner, whatever. We all know what the "whatever" consisted of. Carl became my savior, the sponge that sucked up all that hurt, all that anger, all the leftovers from a love affair gone bad. He would hold me for hours on end, meeting my eyes, absorbing my pain, until it left me. He also was my entrée into my next incarnation: waitress.

Terry had sold the restaurant and the new owner of The Smoothie Bar had big plans. He and Krikor made a deal and the wall between the two places came down so that the clothing shop and the bar was one. New tables, chairs, equipment made the place into a hippie fantasy with avocado/sprout sandwiches, home-baked pies by Kaki, and any kind of fruit smoothie a stoned-out hippie could imagine. Plus, you could buy a Krikor outfit, made to transform the most up-tight banker into a hippie-for-a-day.

With this enlargement, they needed more workers and I was ready. Number one, I wanted to be around these vibrant people and two, I needed the money. Not only did I take this job but I took in a roommate. Ella was a friend of Kiel Martin and Jan Michael Vincent who had homes just up the creek from mine. They were actors who were doing pretty well. Jan was a pretty boy who got lots of TV and film work and Kiel, having just divorced his wife who was the daughter of Dean Martin, was staying as invisible as possible because Dino wanted to kill him. Ella was Brazilian whose heart was as big – not quite - as her tits. She worked at The Troubadour as a waitress and was famous for her forward-moving appendages which were encased in the latest hip T-shirt. She was really a wonderful person and the fact that we were such different people made for a close friendship. She took the smaller bedroom in the back of the house and was a godsend when I needed it. She also loved the house and gardens and appreciated that I had opened my house to her. Jan and his wife Bonnie, Kiel and whomever would drop by for a coffee or beer. Michael Green, an actor and activist, was also in the neighborhood and it was good to be part of the community there.

Carl and John were also good musicians. They always had their guitars at the restaurant and would pull them out to play their own songs or the latest sing-along hit. Kaki's boyfriend, Gary, was a piano player and brought in a piano at the restaurant so the music would get going and the energy would flow. The Oingo-Boingo band would show up in the parking lot, gather a crowd, which eventually would spill over into the restaurant.

I was beginning to feel whole again. I was casually pursuing my film career but it seemed to be closed to me. The few jobs I interviewed for never called back. I did a few shorts and a documentary covering a Spiritual Convention but they were freebies. At the Convention, my eyes were opened up to the many religious/spiritual belief systems that offered solace to the challenged and the bereaved. With more time on my hands than I wanted, I was able to read and talk about the paths to peace and freedom. Los Angeles and the surrounding southern California areas were home to many of the greatest spiritual thinkers and writers of our century. Yogananda had been encouraged by Vivekananda to come here from India to spread the magic of Hinduism and he'd started the Self-Realization Fellowship. Krishnamurti was in Ojai three months out of the year, speaking and holding informal sessions during March, April and May. Many others came through the city to give lectures, lead meditation sessions so finding God in your own way was very possible and real.

Karen introduced me to a spiritualist, Javen, who gave readings and did astrology charts. I decided I should really find out who I was and asked her to do mine. I knew my sun sign was Libra but didn't know the positions of any of the other planets. It turned out that I had lots of Libra in my chart: Sun, Moon, Venus, Mars, Mercury, Uranus, Neptune all were in my first house of Libra which made my rising sign Virgo. I was all cardinal Air so thank the lucky stars that I had that Virgo sitting on my horizon which would keep my feet on the ground and eventually, my hands in the dirt, gardening, as it's a mutable Earth sign. I found these astrological readings fascinating, buying into the idea that someone can look at a chart, see all the symbols of the planets arranged around a circle, know my past, my present, my future. I honestly can't remember whether Javen could see the dissolution of my relationship, the current unknowing of the present, or what the future held, but it was a good introduction to information that I could use or ignore, depending on my need.

I found that I liked personality systems and accepted that they can show us new sides to ourselves, some we weren't even aware of. There were so many tests out there, based on the work Carl Jung did, the Myers-Briggs typology test, Numerology, much later, the Enneagram, based on Gurdjieff and Sufi spiritualism. So, I chose the solitary route of reading about myself as opposed to finding a therapist who would see me on a weekly basis where we could delve into the dark reaches of my pain and suffering and disillusionment.

I was now thirty years old and I knew that this was the real beginning of my own life. The past years belonged to the "me" who had been reared by my parents and the educational system. Even in our twenties, we are still choosing and following the patterns they set for us. I was on the cusp of my own adventure, finding out who I was, determined solely by me and who and what I chose to bring into my life. From my Topanga point of view, Hollywood seemed very far away. My year on Broken Arrow Ranch had taken me out of the slipstream of the business and I wasn't finding a way back in. The path of least resistance seemed to be up canyon, to the Center, to the new improved Smoothie Bar. I asked if I could work there and was hired immediately. Me, the Waitress, avocado sandwich slinger and new improved woman.

When I'd lived in Topanga before, I hadn't really plugged into the Canyon community. Larry and I had our friends who we would see, but didn't hang out at the bars or restaurants there. Now, I became a real denizen, at the Center several days a week and a regular at the Topanga Corral which was a real scene, gathering the disparate groups of Topangans: old-time locals, hippies, musicians, drinkers, pool players, druggies, bikers, Canyon-wanna-be's from the Valley. Canned Heat, which had made a real showing at Woodstock, was a local band. Spanky and Our Gang would show up. And Neil, trying out some songs with Crazy Horse, even played a night. Anytime we fell into the place at night, there would be good music, a few friends, and a game of pool, if you put a quarter on the table and waited your turn to play.

The restaurant was minting money. It was a very successful summer. Kathy and friends turned the place into "dining as theater". Every day was a new scene with the same main cast but with new supporting "actors" sitting at their tables ordering food. If someone sent something back to the kitchen, it became guerilla theater. Once, a customer said his eggs were overcooked. He got another plate – still overdone. Then he got a plate with two raw eggs puddled in the middle. He got up and walked out and we all wished him well.

About half-a-mile up canyon was a place called Elysium Fields. It was a nine-acre site up above Topanga Cyn. Blvd. and had several meeting houses, a tennis court, swimming pool and was "clothing optional". The man who founded the place was Ed Lange and he was well-known in the naturalist communities around the country. One day, he came into the restaurant and said he was hosting some large gatherings and could use a catering company. On a daily basis, his kitchen could provide food for the members but on these special occasions, he needed outside help and were we interested. We discussed it and said we could cater these events, providing lunch and dinner. We drew up a budget and he accepted it. So, in addition to the food we were preparing at the restaurant, on certain weekends, we would go up to Elysium Fields. As many of the participants weren't wearing clothes, we decided that it would be prudent, not to mention good business, if we would do the same so we bought cute aprons that covered certain parts but when we walked away, well, you get the picture.

I came home one day to find a large, damaged cardboard box on the front step addressed to The Eagles. Then it occurred to me that Dr. Joe had been the go-to doc for the rock 'n roll crowd and whoever had been asked to deliver something to the band might have thought this was the right house or at least it would get to them. I opened the box which had a vegetable smell and looked like it had come quite a distance. Inside were several thousand peyote buttons and I'm not kidding. They were still green, looking a little puckered but good and ripe. When Carl came over, he couldn't believe it either. We called John Thompson and a few more friends and set about cleaning the buttons, carefully carving out the white wooly hairs which we thought gave the cactus strychnine. This turned out to be an urban legend but someone must have figured that anything that makes you that sick had to have some poison in it somewhere. We all gathered in the glass house and started eating peyote. It's bitter taste makes it really hard to get down. And, once in your stomach, it is so nausea-inducing, you have to fight to keep it there. Eventually I threw up and fell asleep. I awakened to one of the best highs ever, energized, visually stunning, and we all had a great time. As the night retreated and dawn promised a beautiful sunrise, we walked to the beach and plunged into the ocean. A week or so later, Carl and I drove the box minus all the peyote we had eaten or made tea from, up to Eagle guitarist Bernie Leadon's house. He'd bought Neil's old house from Gary Burden when Gary decided to join Joe and Diantha, Larry and Doreen, up in Montecito. We left the peyote on Bernie's door step.

John Binder's girlfriend, Gloria, came to Topanga Beach one day with John's kids, Josh and John Henry. The little boys were eight and five and couldn't believe that all these adults were walking around naked. I wore a bikini but there were a number of people who were militant in their clothing-optional stance. That day, the Pacific was just that, smooth and quiet, which was unusual as Topanga was known for it's good waves. Carl asked John Henry if he'd like to ride on the surfboard. We walked out into the water and John Henry got on in front of Carl who paddled out, slipping easily through the soft surf. They didn't go out very far but then

Carl saw that a wave was coming in. It was not small and they were right in its path. We all watched from shore, Gloria freaking out, because what could she ever say to John if she'd lost his youngest in the ocean. We saw John Henry lie down and grip the board, Carl stood up and they caught that big wave and rode it into the beach. When he waded up to us, John Henry's eyes were as big as saucers and a grin covered his face. He'd done something his big brother hadn't and it felt great.

As summer turned to autumn it became obvious that our boss, the construction company guy who'd overbuilt the restaurant, was in big financial trouble, leveraged to the hilt. Without any warning, we were all out of jobs. Joe Creek, who owned the Center and ran the grocery store, said he'd still like a restaurant in the space, so along with Kathy, I spent the last of the money I'd saved over the year, to take the lease. We had to completely start over at the restaurant as all of the fittings, equipment, tables and chairs had been re-possessed by the previous owner's creditors. The wall was put up between us and Krikor and we set about rebuilding from scratch. It was now our place, Everybody's Mother, with it's motto, "Eat Here Now".

Carl also worked at The Great American Food and Beverage Restaurant in Santa Monica, known for it's musical waiters. and huge wooden trays laden with food. Its owner, Poppy, liked us and guided us through the process with the licensing, getting equipment and even gave us a Squirrel Cage which in restaurant vernacular is the stove ventilator that sits on the roof and exhausts all the cooking heat, grease and smell. We put out the word that we were a Canyon charity. Tables, chairs, even a wood-burning stove was donated. I had boxes of hand-sewn quilt-tops that Margaret Johnson had bought at a Florida retirement home and we draped them on to the ceiling of the quonsut hut. I moved in a nice wood-framed sofa and a coffee table from my house. And best of all, there was a large round community table which could seat a dozen customers. Kaki also used it as her baking table and they loved watching her make the delicious pies we sold.

When we were ready to fire up the equipment, our gas line kept giving us trouble. I called the Gas Company and they couldn't figure out what the problem was. There was another eatery a few doors down from us, The Center Restaurant, which was a smoke-filled dive, greasy spoon, with a pool table in the middle. The regulars were what we called "De-horns", shaggy, funky guys who lived on who knows what and never came to The Smoothie Bar. We had a paranoid hunch that Ed, the greasy spoon owner, might just be the cause of our problem. One morning, I took my camera and sat in the back of the rear parking lot. Sure enough, out came Ed holding a huge wrench. He walked to the junction of all the gas lines that fed the Center shops and turned the knob of our line to "Off". I caught it on camera and yelled, "Hey, Ed, I gotcha." His goose was cooked and we were in business.

We designed an open kitchen plan, something quite new back then, inspired by the fact that we didn't want to get stuck in the kitchen. We wanted to be part of the scene. We collectively created a menu that appealed to us and the vegetarian residents of the Canyon, letting it change constantly, relying on the seasons. We didn't know about Alice Waters, who always gets credit for doing this, but we were on the same wave length. Kathy and I would run the kitchen, Kaki was the baker. Carl, John and Gary, worked in many capacities, greeters, waiters, busboys, musicians. Priscilla, whose day job was at the Jung Institute, came in at night to wait on tables.

The work in the restaurant meant long hours, little pay and communal living. I gave up my Rodeo Grounds house. One, it was expensive and two, that fall a fire had come through. Driven by the annual Santa Ana winds, possibly arson-set, the fire had started way up canyon in an area that was a State Park. Burning the dry chapparal, it moved at a frightening pace as it created it's own momentum. The fire storm sent sparks flying everywhere in advance of the actual fire and within a day, it had reached the bottom of the canyon where I lived. A slight ocean breeze encouraged the firefighters to set backfires behind each house and I

Outside the Rodeo Grounds House, Topanga Fire, 1973

was evacuated to the beach. I put sheets over all the furniture to save them from the ash that was falling all over the neighborhood, put the dogs in the VW bug, and parked it down on the PCH - the Pacific Coast Highway.

Then I went back to the house with my camera. The backfires were moving slowly up canyon fueled by the natural vegetation that covered the mountains, catching some of the large trees on fire that exploded from the heat. The place was an inferno but the houses were saved. Bereft of it's covering, the mountainsides were just dirt

and burned wood and that didn't bode well for the rainy season that would soon be upon us. Indeed, after I left, the storms ravaged the area turning it in to a huge muddy field, destroying the road, the creek bed and the place never looked the same again. The Rodeo

Grounds as a living area ceased to exist a few decades later when the Marina company that owned all the land sold it to the state for park land.

My new residence was the converted garage aka "The Bunkhouse" at Kathy and Kaki's house at the end of Happy Trail. Carl and I shared a fifteen by twelve room which was quite a come-down from my Rodeo Grounds compound. I'd traded, sold, or given away furniture, clothing, other household items. My kitchen was now in the restaurant. John had been living in the Bunkhouse and, as that was just too crowded for me, he moved up to Kathy's room on the second floor of the house. Kaki and Gary had a bedroom on the main floor across from the kitchen. The bathroom was outside the kitchen door, unheated, cement-floored, and primitive, with just a toilet and shower. It was now November and temperatures could get to down to the high thirties so the run at 6am from the Bunkhouse to the bathroom to get a quick warm-up shower and then dress was a warrior woman routine.

Our restaurant opening was a canyon event and Bernie Leadon came in with some of The Eagles to rock the night away. We bit off more than we could chew when we set the hours at 7am to 10pm, seven days a week, but we thought that this was the optimum for the folks who lived in the Canyon. There were commuters who stopped in for breakfast, especially for the espresso coffee, a novelty at that time, Kaki's muffins, egg platters or tofu with scallions, mushrooms, and tumeric. Others were lunch regulars still craving the smoothies and sandwiches. And then there were our delicious dinners, cooked by vegetarians Mitch (Mexican Mondays) or Rita (Indian Thursdays), Dorothy's fried chicken and Jewish specialties on Sundays, Kathy's pasta, and my current specialties, chicken and meat dishes or grilled fish. The selections changed with our whims and the market and the only

Kaki, Jeanne, Kathy, Kedrick, a good customer

menu was a chalkboard on the wall. Mickey, a three-hundred-pound vivacious red-headed character who was loved by Fellini when she was an actress in Rome, manned the cash register at the front door. We still had the music from Gary on piano, accompanied by John and Carl on guitars. Our walls sported photographs and paintings by local artists. Sheila Schoonhoven waited tables for us and her husband, Terry, brought in a huge new painting that covered one wall. Charlotte was a very popular waitress whenever she wasn't working as an actress in Hollywood.

I was immersed in recipes, cooking techniques for a large crowd, cooking to order. Kathy and I went to the market at 4am in a green van purchased for just that. The Central Market was in downtown L.A., as were other suppliers, and we bargained with all

Lane roasts his Topanga Thanksgiving goat

of them for good prices. We would hit the Mexican outlets, meat and poultry purveyors, stop for a quick breakfast then headed back to Topanga. We had a refrigerated walk-in outside the back door that held all the supplies.

We decided to take a break at Thanksgiving and were invited to an annual Topanga feast by one of our neighbors, Lane. He ran the bar-b-que pit and said there'd be lots of food, especially if we brought some side dishes. We took the time to create the usual go-alongs for the Thanksgiving table, yams, mashed potatoes, green beans. We were stunned to arrive and see that this particular celebration had it's own roasted creature, a very skinny goat. We hung out for a bit then went to the restaurant to scavenge something out of the cooler.

As the months went by, we fell into a good pattern at work. We had a good flow of customers who appreciated the home cooking attitude we brought to the business, our weekend brunches were filled to capacity with L.A. friends coming up to enjoy a Topanga day. John Lennon even stopped in.

One night, Priscilla was feeling very stressed with her day job, her night job and the four kids she single-parented and she cut her hand making an avocado sandwich. She took a break and went out to the Center bathrooms across the parking lot from Everybody's Mother but didn't come back. Someone ran in and said that two Sheriffs had apprehended her. I went out to discuss the matter. Two burly cops had Priscilla handcuffed and were about to put her in the car.

I asked what the charge was and they said "Drug dealing, she was trying to sell some speed."

This was such a lie, it was ludicrous. She was my only waitress that night and I needed her back at work and by the way, did they know they were on private property? They cursed me out and that drew a crowd.

"Who the fuck are you," they said.
"I own this place and you're not taking her."

They threw her in the backseat of the cop car and she cried out that her hand was bleeding. They jumped in and were going to leave. I reached in and grabbed the keys out of the ignition. What was I thinking? But, it was all going so fast. I threw the keys into the parking lot and the driver jumped out, grabbed me so hard I flew out of my shoes and he bent me over the hood of the car saying did I know what he'd do to me if there was no one around. I spit in his face. That was it. He handcuffed me, put me in the backseat with Priscilla.

As we drove down the canyon to the Malibu Sheriff Station, the cop in the passenger seat began to talk, somehow trying to make the situation better. He knew it had gotten way out of hand. I told them I was going to make a big stink and knew I had the witnesses to back me up. The cops discussed taking us back but the driver was still very angry. We were booked, fingerprinted and put in a cell.

I was an outlaw, my second time in jail. I smoked pot, did other drugs, and had been through two illegal abortions. Otherwise, I was a clean citizen. Legality in 1974 was up for discussion. Was the Viet Nam War legal? It hadn't been officially declared and millions of people died. Richard Nixon was in deep doodoo over the Watergate break-in and the erasure of tapes that probably implicated him in that crime and others. Draftcard burners went to jail, Daniel Ellsberg had been indicted over the Pentagon Papers. The rules and regulations were made to be broken if morality trumped the criminality of the event. Spit in a cop's face? I'm cool with that.

About 5am, Carl bailed us out. I was exhausted but intent on getting into the injustice of the arrest. Kathy and I went to Joe Creek and let him have it. How could the Sheriffs come onto his property, make false allegations and violently treat two women who worked there? He called the Malibu Sheriff Station and the County Supervisor's Office and we got into it. They sent a Public Relations Liaison for meetings. I suggested that if the sheriffs had taken the time to know who any of us were, stopped in for a cup of coffee and a piece of pie, none of this would have happened. We belonged there. The PR man explained that these cops usually worked South Central Los Angeles for three weeks, then cycled out to Malibu for three weeks. Unfortunately, they brought their inner-city tough guy approach with them. Nevertheless, they were still going to press charges. I talked with a lawyer friend from the Rodeo Grounds who did a lot of work with the beach crowd and surfers and he took us on pro bono. Ultimately, he got the charges against Priscilla dropped and I got a plea deal and paid a $25 fine for disturbing the peace, record to be expunged. I made the lawyer a nice cowboy shirt for payment.

Years later, this altercation had another connection. I was walking in Westwood with my then-husband Steve who pointed out a soda shop he and his friend Mike Mdivani used to come to. I couldn't believe my ears as this was the Sheriff who had beat me up. Steve had known him from school, the tony John Thomas Dye private elementary school in Bel Air. I learned that he was the son of oil fortune heiress Virginia Sinclair and David Mdivani who was one of the "Marrying Mdivanis", three noble expats from the country of Georgia who all married very wealthy American women. Mike's uncle, Alexis, had married Barbara Hutton, one of the world's richest women. Why was this guy a cop? Turned out, little Mike was all mixed up when he was a teenager and had set fire to something and in return for not charging him, he had to spend time with a Sheriff's department outreach program. That put him on the road to police work. When his mother died, he inherited millions and Malibu property. But, it didn't make him a happy man and he committed suicide in 1990.

The Topanga winter rains were heavy in 1974. They washed down the burned-up mountainsides that rose steeply from Topanga Canyon Blvd. as it winds down from the Santa Monica Mountains that divide the San Fernando Valley from the Pacific Ocean. The road was and is a major route for commuters, beachgoers and surfers, and because of it's grand natural beauty, weekend drivers. We depended on this road for our supplies and customers. In February, the native plants covering the hillsides could no longer hold the heavy mud, shale and gravel and it all came down, closing the road for several months. It devastated our canyon, our business, and eventually, our spirits.

The twice-weekly drive to downtown L.A. now meant going through the San Fernando Valley, down the 101, adding a lot of time to the trip. Carl was getting on my nerves and there seemed to be a schism in the crew. Kathy and Kaki only worked with each other; John was tired of cleaning the griddle every night; Carl spent more time working at The Great American in Santa Monica, sometimes staying out all night. Our regular customers' work life was badly effected by the weather and road closure and so were their paychecks. Week-end brunches didn't attract people to Topanga because they couldn't get there.

Everybody's Mother had become an albatross around my neck. Restaurant work was the hardest work in the world. Of course, the long, much too long hours we were open, didn't help. And, the fact that no one had had a vacation and barely a day off for a year added to the weariness. Our dishwashers had their own subtle schedule known only to them, but try replacing them. Would Zero, one of the homeless Creek freaks, roll up his sleeves for a few bucks and a meal? Wouldn't think of it, even though we frequently fed him and his pals leftovers out the back door. I finally had the revelation that if I was going to work this hard, I should go back to the film business. I talked with Carl and he said to do what I needed to do. I said I'd be leaving but I'd be near by and that was

Carl Miranda

fine with him, he said shrugging. Carl did not believe in stress, or agro, as the surfers called it.

I sat down and talked with Kathy. She was such an accepting person and said she understood, all would be okay. It was hard to leave but I knew I had done what I set out to do with the restaurant. We'd created a place where only fresh food was served and done with a smile or at least with gratitude to the paying customer. We'd satisfied the varied tastes of the long-time middle-class Topanga residents, the hippies, the working men and women, the tourists, the surfers. Kathy bought me out and Charlotte offered me a bedroom in the house she shared with Peter on Observation Drive. I sat down to think about things, to observe and notice the significance of what was being scrutinized. Was this when that rinky-dink phrase came out? "Today is the first day of the rest of your life." In any case, I took it seriously.

The house on Observation was two stories, built on the side of the mountain with a large deck looking south. My bedroom had it's own bath, windows on two sides and was off the living room. Next to that was a dining room then the kitchen. Downstairs, Char and Peter had their bedroom and a music room for him. It was a domestic paradise compared to the end of Happy Trail and I was very comfortable for the first time in a long time.

I was physically exhausted from the restaurant work, standing at the sink, the prep table or the stove, lifting heavy stock pots full of soups or stews, waiting on tables, going back and forth on the cement floor between the kitchen and the dining area. I needed to stretch, relax, give my body a break. The deck was a great place to do yoga, write my city girl, country girl thoughts, and just not think too much, or "nothink" as i call it now.

Up in Ojai, J. Krisnamurti was giving weekend talks and Tuesday and Thursday discussion sessions. It was a beautiful drive up the coast to Rt. 33 into the valley where Hollywood shot a Shangri-La movie years before. I passed a family farm that grew apples and sold cider, past little houses owned or rented by working folk, mostly Latino, to Meiner's Oaks where the Krishnamurti school was being developed. I parked the bug, then walked through the open land to an area marked off for the lecture, an idyllic spot under the huge arms of ancient oak trees. A small stage was set up in front with a solitary spindly wooden chair on it. As people gathered, they rolled out a mat or spread a small blanket, talking quietly or not at all. It was a serious, respectful crowd of all ages and colors.

At the appointed time, it grew quiet, and from a hidden place to the right of the stage, Krishnamurti would appear, step on the stage, afix his small microphone and say, "Let Us Begin Together." This was a key phrase because the basis of his teaching was the Observer separating from the Observed. Once this happens, things change. No surprise then that physicists were drawn to him, as wasn't this part of the Heisenberg principle. K, as he was known casually, was a very passionate speaker, raising his voice when need be, when he felt like people were losing attention, or was he attuned to us far more intimately than an ordinary lecturer? In his last year, he published a book in which he admitted to having extra-sensory perception about people and the cosmos, but it wasn't what drove him in his teachings.

I went up to Ojai as much as possible, joined by Carl or other friends who also were interested in a spiritual path. I read the books and meditated on them, searching, hoping that the Way would become obvious. Of course, this wasn't how it happens. It came to me slowly, day by day, step by step, over many years. But, it opened me up to acknowledge my intuition, to trust it, to even question it at times. This was the "Me Generation". We didn't know what else to believe in anymore so we learned to believe in ourselves. If we couldn't change the world we could change ourselves.

The world, though, had changed. President Nixon was caught in the web of the Watergate break-in and brought down by two young Washington Post reporters. The Viet Nam War was almost over as the U.S. was withdrawing its support of the South Vietnamese army. Racial equality was being achieved on a personal level in Los Angeles through the arts if not on a grand scale in schools, housing and employment opportunities. Social and political policy have their own clock, frustrating at times, but also surprising when all of a sudden, an issue has the collective mass to become a real change.

164

Flower in the Crannied Wall - Taliesin, Spring Green, WI

Chapter Eleven

Little Old Madison

I was now feeling I was on solid ground and maybe it was a good time to go back to Madison to visit my dear Mom and Dad. Of course, they were happy to see me. Dad was getting around okay, steel rod still in his leg, taking lots of aspirin to quell the constant aggravation. Mom had pulled out of the shock of his accident and was looking vibrant again. Charles was healthy, living on his own, working with Dad, handsome at twenty-eight. Visits back to Madison revolved around seeing old friends and neighbors, playing rounds of golf, swimming in Lake Mendota or at the Village pool. It was great to be back home and I was more comfortable being there, probably because I was in such a reflective frame of mind, perhaps at the end of one chapter and approaching the beginning of another.

In my early thirties, unmarried with no prospects, I knew my parents were concerned. Okay, it was good to want to be productive and have employment, have your own business, but what about family, kids, settling down. None of this was said, but I felt the watchful eye. I'd always been a good kid, wanting to please my parents, glad to get the approval when it came. All my life, they had been very accepting of both Charles and me and neither one of us was very neurotic. In fact, I had always believed we both had a very strong core that could withstand the tough times that can come along. Dad's accident had shown all of us that when it came to the real moments, we were a good unit, working in agreement.

Out on the golf course, I swung at the ball easily. It felt good to be back at Blackhawk Country Club, a place I'd loved since the age of 10. The Village owned the land the Club was on so there was reciprocity for residents which allowed them to play a few rounds each year and also offered free lessons to kids every Monday morning. My dad put together a few clubs and a small bag and each Monday, I'd sling it over a shoulder and bike up to the Club for my group lesson. The Pro's son, Butch, was in my class and he was already really good. He gave the rest of us something to shoot for. His dad, Kelly, was an iconic golfer, tall and loose, relaxed in his swing and his teaching method. He took the mystery out of it as he helped us develop our natural swings with a wood, our technique with the irons approaching a green and the patience and eye to scope out the lay of a green. As my interest in golf continued, it inspired Dad to join the club. It was a good business move and he got Mom to take up golf as well and volunteer for the Women's committees. Mom enjoyed it in a limited way which was probably just as well as some of the women played their golf matches, then had lunch, played cards, drank cocktails into the late afternoons. Mom put herself above these boozy dames and knew there would be hell to pay if Dad's dinner wasn't ready when he walked through the door.

As I grew older, I became active in the Junior Golf program which met every Tuesday morning and I eventually won the Girls' Eighteen Hole Tournament when I was a teenager. In college, I'd play all summer long, going up to the course by myself, hoping I'd be able to go out solo and hit the ball, concentrating on the shot, not the score. On occasion, I'd play twenty-seven holes straight just so I could get past the frustration of bad shots, learning the meaning of consistency. Golf demanded that. Now on the course after a few years off, this lesson came back to me and I promised myself, I'd apply it in a new way, on a new path if it ever appeared.

Our house was a short block from the Elementary School yard where there were tennis courts, a baseball diamond, a large field for track, football, Capture the Flag. Growing up, I loved tennis and baseball and would usually go over there after dinner in the summer and find a game. When I was eleven, I was a baseball fanatic. There was a club for boys called the Knothole Club and it took a busload of kids to Milwaukee for a Braves game. Somehow, I got it in my head that I had to do this too and was able to convince the adult leaders to let me in. I broke the gender barrier of the Knothole Club. This gave me lots of cred, especially when a Braves pitcher, Joe Black, threw a hardball to me at one of the games.

There was a Little League team in our Village that played the other Madison teams. In the middle of the summer schedule, one of the kids got sick. He had cancer which was almost unheard of back then. Polio was even more common than cancer. Lawrence had been the pitcher and he was through. The team was short a player and there I was, a Knothole regular and a good all-round player. They asked me to join the team and I got my shot. Or course, they put me play right field. I picked up a uniform, got my glove in real good shape and was so excited. The day before the game, something horrible happened. There was blood in my undies. I showed Mom, expecting the worst. She confirmed I'd begun my period. Ohh, my life was over. The little handbook she'd given me had said that girls shouldn't swim or exercise when they were having their monthly. I told her there was no way I was missing the game the next day and she knew there was nothing she could say. She showed me how to clip the Kotex pad to the skinny elastic belt. The thing was so bulky I waddled like a duck. Then I put my uniform on, the cream colored pants and blue shirt. I just knew everyone could tell I had that bulging cotton pad between my legs. I reached in my pants and tried to squeeze the thing smaller but then realized that could have undesired results if the blood started flowing.

Game day, I was there early to work out and loosen up. We all threw the ball around, the other team arrived. Our team took the field and as I headed out to right field, I was still so conscious of the wad in my baseball pants. As we played the game, I forgot about the strange convergence of these two events: I was the first girl playing in a boys' Little League hardball game and I had just got my period for the first time. I got a hit and made an out. No one thought I looked or ran funny. I played the next few games to end the season with the team. But, it was made clear that this did not make me eligible to play next year. It was a boys' team only. I thought of Lawrence, dying from his cancer, and knew I was one very lucky girl.

Next summer found me on the tennis courts and that's where I stayed, not intent on pushing myself into situations where I wasn't welcome, nor did I want to test the very real friendships I had with the boys in my class. These friendships started out with sports in grade school and continued in the extracurricular programs the Village offered. Besides the skiing we did on our ski jump and little local hills, we had a great skating rink. Every winter the Volunteer Fire Department flooded a large section of the school yard which was across the street from the Village Hall/Fire and Police Station. They took very good care of the ice rink which also had a cute little log cabin with a stove for a warm-up house. This was later replaced by the Heiden Haus, named after neighborhood boy, Eric Heiden, who won an unprecedented five individual Olympic Speedskating Medals and set four Olympic records in 1980. Eric's success typified the emphasis Village parents put on sports as an important part of a kid's education.

All through the winter, we had nightly figure skating lessons, learning the compulsory exercises of the figures, the three and eight, which give the sport it's name: figure skating. Professor Sorum who taught chemistry at the U.W. was the head of the program and had recruited other skaters to work with him. Once we learned how to find the inside and outside edges, how to glide and stop, make turns, we learned jumps and spins, and the dances, the Dutch Waltz, the Swing Dance and the Fiesta Tango. And if you were going to dance, you needed a partner and that's where the boys came in. The boys usually came to the skating rink to play tag, hang out in the warming hut, throw snowballs at the girls and as we got older, it was a place to be with a girl they liked. If they were part of the skating class and learned the dances, they could partner up with her, holding her close. Music was piped in from the Village Hall and it good wholesome fun. I would skate after school, go home for

Gossiping on the Rink

dinner, and be back for night skating, either lessons or practicing my jumps and spins.

In January, when it was guaranteed to be really cold, there was a Winter Carnival, a weekend event with races on Saturday and an Ice Show on Sunday. I loved the races and was a fast skater, winning lots of blue ribbons but also some red and white ones too, as we tore around the outside lanes of the rink. That night, the firemen would spray the ice, making sure to get a really smooth surface. The Annual Ice Show featured each level of skaters, in costume, performing a number to music, nervous parents hoping their kid wouldn't fall and start to cry. Mom was a willing volunteer, making costumes, helping with the practice sessions, keeping us warm with hot chocolate. In my early teenage years, I was good enough to be chosen to perform a short solo piece, choreographed with the help of one of our teachers to music. My grandmother, Lyllie, made me beautiful skating costumes, a turquoise one with white lining and angora embroidery, a purple one with a knitted ear warmer to match. I felt like Tinkerbell out there on the ice, skating fast into a jump, doing the spins, even the camel, which you had to do slow and was technically challenging.

The Dancing followed and led by Prof. Sorum who was old yet splendid in his love for skating. I'd pair up with one of my classmates and glide through the pattern, held tight by my partner, enjoying the spectacle, being applauded by all our neighbors. It was community in the best sense of the word.

The Phy Ed teacher and Recreation Director at our school was Dick Miyagawa, an amazing man, a gymnast, teacher, and ukelele player. He was a Japanese-Hawaiian who was short and muscular, full of energy with a quick smile. It was a tribute to the liberal feelings of Madison that Dick had this job so soon after the end of WWII. He introduced tumbling to all grades and I loved that, taking his Saturday class, learning to do flips, handstands, the splits. We had track and field as part of gym class, racing Fifty and Seventy-five yard dashes, broad jumps, high jumps, which led to Field Day, with families gathering in the spring to watch their kids compete for ribbons and end with a picnic. In Seventh grade, I set the school record for the Fifty-yard dash and the boys in my class weren't happy about that. Mom and Dad were very proud and so was I.

Summer mornings I rode my bike to Shorewood Beach on Lake Mendota where I eventually earned my Jr. Lifeguard badge. There were piers jutting far out into the lake with a high dive on one side and a diving board on the other. In the afternoons at the Summer Playschool, we learned archery and tennis, drawing and painting, arts and crafts. Dick brought in a woman from Hawaii to teach the hula and we made our own hula grass skirts. Some kids learned to play the ukelele and we had a traveling troupe that went to old folks' homes, hospitals and Camp Wawbeek across the lake that was especially for handicapped kids. When this broke up in the afternoons, I'd be off to the beach again, to work on my tan, swim, gossip with friends, watch Phil, Tim, Peter, LaVerne, Ted, go off the diving board and hope that one of them might like me and walk me to my bike.

Shorewood School also had a football team and that meant that there had to be cheerleaders. Dick organized a small squad from the tumbling group and I was on it. He taught us some cheers with moves and integrated some handsprings and round-offs to make it interesting. I loved it right from the beginning and cheerleading became a big part of my identity.

When I went to Wisconsin High School for eighth grade, I tried out for cheerleading and got on the squad because of my gymnastic chops. My winner was doing a cheer, then running into a handspring, landing in the splits. No one else did this at Badger Prep and it won me the most votes among the girls trying out. I was thirteen and on the High School squad. I was noticed at an early age and that certainly helped the dreaded transition of entering a new school. I was a cheerleader all four years and even tried out at the U.W. and was on that squad too, traveling to other Big Ten schools to root for the Badgers.

Women's sports in the '50s and '60s didn't have a Title IX to give and demand support so there were no teams we could join. We played half-court basketball and field hockey and that was it for girls in high school. Cheerleading gave me another outlet to be athletic, have a relationship with the Coach at our high school, and be a real supporter of the teams that represented our school and our spirit. I loved being on the football field, on the sideline next to the team, yelling for a first down, a touchdown, an extra point. Willing the team to Defend, Tackle, and Intercept to Beat Them. Cheering in the basketball arena, close to the crowd, we'd run out on the floor during a time out, exhorting the kids and our parents to make some noise, show the team we knew they could win. And when they lost, literally crying for the boys that came up short. We'd paint banners to hang in the stadium or fieldhouse, make up cheers like "Extirpate East", "Go Team" which was done with just one movement in a lunge, a cheerleading zen moment. In my senior year in high school, I went to a cheerleading convention and saw the sad handwriting on the wall. Phy ed teachers began choreographing routines that required huge pep squads, long hours of rehearsal. It took the action out of the excitement of the moment when the team does well and turned it into a showgirl-type movement regardless of what's happening on the field. Nevertheless, I knew cheerleading was in my blood and it became a positive energy I could apply to a lot of situations at work or at play.

Athletics and sports were a large part of my life during school and was how I thought of myself. I was a golfer and I loved to ski on water or snow. I was an ice skater. I wasn't a musician or a good artist, I was an okay student and I had a lot of friends. In these formative years, we grope for descriptions, self-knowledge, identity. Who Am I? Maybe Popeye said it best, "I yam what I yam."

Religion also had an answer. I was a Lutheran. My parents weren't active churchgoers but did attend a Christmas Eve service, tithed to the church so it could do it's good works for the poor. I went to Sunday school, sang in the choir. Dad would drop Charles and me off, preferring to spend his Sundays outdoors, working in the garden or on the house. I went to my friends' churches too, sampling the Baptists, Congregationalists, Episcopalians, curious to know if they were similar or really different. Kids want to know what category of religion they belong to. If for no other reason, it's important for parents to address this and tell them and if they happen to be agnostic, say that, then take them to the Unitarian Church, or a community meeting, so it puts the question to rest. I went to Confirmation class which was a big deal at our church, spending every Saturday morning the first year reading the Bible cover to cover and being tested on it, then learning the Lutheran creed the second year incorporating biblical studies. I even went to a Bible camp one year, sent by my church.

At different times, I met people who were still searching, joining cults, seeing shrinks, trying to figure out where in the universe they belonged. I knew where I belonged. Being a Lutheran worked through high school; in college, I learned I didn't like organized religion when I saw holier-than-thou people who came to church on Sunday to show off their new clothes then did shitty things on Monday. In the end, I still think it all came down to the Golden Rule and non-judgment.

The last day of my visit, we all went out to our forty-acre country place, The Shack. Dad and Charles had designed and built it on a hill surrounded by beautiful tall oak trees. It had just been finished as Dad's accident had interrupted the work. The house inside was furnished simply in a Scandinavian style. Outside, they'd stained the wood a dark green and added small orange shutters which also gave the windows protection from the hunters and farmers' kids who might trespass on occasion.

Dad always had projects to do in addition to the prodigious workload he carried at his company but this one had been the most complicated ever. After they'd finished building the house, there were still some little jobs to do – cut and stack firewood, plant some of the 3,500 trees he got from the DNR (Department of Natural Resources). They had carved hiking trails through the woods which ended up on a hill next to a farmer's corn field and these were also cross country ski trails in the winter. There was an old mill down the road on a beautiful country stream that provided a pastoral place to watch the water go by as it turned the wheel. The Wisconsin River was a few miles away for canoeing or fishing and Taliesin, Frank Lloyd Wright's school, was there too. We sat on the deck and ate lunch, talking some, enjoying the quiet, took a walk, then packed up and headed back home. I loved my family. At home before leaving for the airport, Mom said she hoped I'd find my next job or whatever it was I was looking for. Dad handed me a check to help out and gave me a hug. Not a lot but the care and consideration it represented meant the world to me.

Lake Mendota - Madison

Chapter Twelve

Roll Camera!

Back in LA, I made some calls, talked to some Topanga film people and in a short while, I'd scored a job at a Hollywood commercial company. On my first ad, I was asked to find a donkey that could sit down. I spent a week canvassing equestrian stables around the county, no luck. Then, I found a very smart mule who could be taught the trick in a short amount of time and I was elated with my success. I went to the director only to learn they'd scrapped that storyboard, hadn't I been told?

We shot the commercial up in Ojai. I was the production assistant and had to be on set early to make coffee, set out the craft service table, be on hand to do any other detail. On my way to the location, I drove past the school bus that was going to be in the shoot. I stopped to help the driver and was chewed out by the production manager. So far as I could tell, none of the crew was pissed their coffee wasn't quite ready when they arrived. This was a food commercial and there was a stylist on hand. She prepared a ton of fried chicken all of which was tossed at the end of the day because she'd sprayed it with a glossy greasy substance to make it camera-perfect but inedible. Everything about this experience just reeked because, well, it was commercial. Compared to my film experience up until then, this was bullshit.

Charlotte, too, was feeling some angst about her life. Peter had secretly had an affair which surprised both of us, but was an indication that all was not well with their relationship. Char was going on lots of auditions which meant driving into Hollywood, meeting the casting director, maybe even the director, reading the sides, then driving back home, a round trip of about thirty to forty miles. Sometimes, she'd get home from a morning interview, get another call or a callback, have to jump in her car and return. And, she had to look pretty and perfect for the role. It was too much. She took things in hand and left. She rented a studio apartment in West Hollywood and that was it for Topanga. I didn't want to take the lease and neither did Peter. I was on the road again.

It usually took a few months to find just the right place to live in Los Angeles. It's a huge place with so many really great areas and people but you also have to be geographically desirable for work, play and romance. Charlotte eventually landed in the Hollywood Hills with a great view of the Capitol Records building and the thousands of city blocks that stretched southwest to the Ocean. The old Woodstock office had been in this east Hollywood neighborhood, so I took some time to drive around investigating the possibilities. I put out the word I needed an apartment and got a good lead. My old Aspen friend, Diana Stamberger Burden was living in L.A., married to a doctor, David Sachs. His ex-wife's boyfriend knew a guy who knew a guy who owned a house in Beachwood Canyon. So L.A. The owner, Gene, lived on the first floor with his wife and baby and they were renting out the lower floor which was a long four room, two bath apartment, with a huge deck out front for the astronomical price of $275. I'd be hard pressed to make this rent but figured this would be an incentive to get good jobs. I moved in and was glad to be on my own.

Within a few months, I had a job working at Paramount. Ronee Blakley had set up a meeting for me with Fred Roos who was producing a film with Coppola. They were months away from production on a Viet Nam movie but he knew a director who was looking for an assistant. The film was "The Big Bus", directed by Jim Frawley, written and co-produced by the very funny Fred Freeman and Larry Cohen, produced by Julia and Michael Phillips who had shot to fame with "The Sting". It had a huge cast starring Stockard Channing and Joe Bologna who are caught on a runaway nuclear

Hollyridge in Beachwood

bus, slowly falling in love. A Disaster Comedy. Working on a film with a big budget compared to my previous jobs was an education, especially because Jim wanted me at his side during the meetings with the head of the studio and their appointed production overseer, Howard Koch. I was privy to all the concerns, the artistic decisions based on the budget, the day to day running of a complicated production with experienced department heads.

On Set in Tujunga

I was paid well enough and continued into post production assisting Fred and Larry as well as Jim. I celebrated my birthday on set and was serenaded by the cast which also included Sally Kellerman, Ned Beaty, Rene Auberjunois, John Beck, Ruth Gordon, Richard Schull, Jose Ferrer, Harold Gould, Larry Hagman, Richard Mulligan, Lynn Redgrave, Howard Hesseman, and even Mickey Fox, who I was able to get hired as a passenger on the bus.

Jim was so generous, teaching me about script, inviting me to parties with his friends who were some of the top producers in town. We went to good restaurants and I hadn't had food like that in a long time. Great salads, seafood, pasta opened up my palate to the meals money can buy. A friend took me to Little Tokyo and

Jeanne & Jim

introduced me to sushi and sashimi. A Thai restaurant had opened up around the corner from the Los Feliz Theater on Vermont and I had pad thai, green papaya salad and their wonderful bar-b-cued chicken and shrimp for the first time. Hollywood had always been a melting pot and these post-Viet Nam years had brought countless people from Southeast Asia to California.

There were small restaurants that were great. The Black Rabbit Inn on Melrose was a country dining room with fireplace, area rugs, and home-made food. But, these were the mid-70s and Chasen's, Musso & Frank, Scandia and Perinos were still the places that were famous with their red-leather banquettes, dark lighting masking Hollywood stars out for an evening, hiding illicit affairs, serving steaks, fried food, creamed vegetables and chili. I'd taken a break from cooking. I don't remember one dinner I cooked in these times. My working hours were long so lunch was the primary meal. Good food was easy to get, Charlotte and other friends lived near-by, so I was out of the kitchen and back in the film world.

I never did get a job on "Apocalypse Now", the film I had met on with Fred Roos. Another job I missed was "Days of Heaven" with Terry Malick who I met at Jim's house and he offered me a job but I was still working with Jim and felt loyal to him. Jim got a call one day from George Carlin's manager, Jack Lewis, saying that George was interested in doing a film about his stand-up comedy act. They wanted to book George into the Roxy on Sunset and cover it concert-style with several cameras. I said, I know how to do this and Jim trusted me.

I'd met a great cameraman who'd mostly done commercials but had a big personality and the confidence to match. Michael Watkins had dated all of us, Charlotte, Ronee, but was still married. We'd all partied a lot together, digging the Hollywood scene with cocaine, marijuana, beer, tequila shots and Courvoisier to smooth it all out. We hung out at someone's pad, listened to music, played backgammon, did drugs and slept around. All in a day's and night's work.

Michael brought in his crew, we hired three more cameramen, soundmen and we were down with it. We shot doc footage backstage in the miniscule dressing room with George warming up, greeting friends, then filmed all three nights of the show. It was an overflow crowd and George would always be one of the best things I ever saw on stage.

He did his Seven Words, *"Shit, piss, fuck, cunt, cocksucker, motherfucker,* and *tits.* Those are the heavy seven. Those are the ones that'll infect your soul, curve your spine and keep the country from winning the war." He did his growing up schtick, he was brilliant and hilarious. I was ecstatic to be back in a film milieu I could really understand.

Jim wanted to take a break. He'd put in almost a year on "The Big Bus" and definitely deserved a vacation. But, what about editing our Carlin footage? I asked. He told me to get it together. Enter Larry Johnson, cued up and waiting in the wings. Well, not quite. In fact, he was a mess.

I'd actually re-connected with Larry the year before when he blew back into L.A., engaged to be married to a woman who'd been on the periphery for the last few years. Leslie Morris had worked for music producer Nick Vinet when we were doing the "Woodstock" pre-mixes at the Record Plant. She'd worked for Elliot Roberts at Lookout and then connected with Larry after he'd run through his relationship with Doreen, much to my delight. After a whirlwind courtship, they were getting hitched at Joni Mitchell's house and needed a caterer. I offered to handle it and although she was not sure what to make of all of this, Leslie accepted. I called Kathy at the restaurant and they planned the feast. Larry's parents flew out. It was great to see Dale and Margaret again and I felt like I'd gotten part of my family back.

Then, a great job cropped up and Larry went on the road with Bob Dylan's Rolling Thunder Review which featured The Band, Ronee and Joni, Joan Baez, with Sam Shepard along to write the book. David Myers on camera, Larry on sound, they were the B crew to whom Sam dedicated his tome, "The Rolling Thunder Logbook". Mid-way though the tour, Leslie joined up in New York, at Niagara Falls. There, after four months and seventeen days of marriage, Leslie said it was over. It rocked Larry's world and as much as I thought he'd finally gotten what he deserved, I felt sorry for the bastard. I saw him when the tour had ended and Ronee

182

threw a party for cast and crew at her Hollywood apartment. Larry was out of it, stoned on red wine and reds, singing loudly, out of tune, embarrassing himself in front of these amazing musicians. Someone had to take him in hand. I called him up and said I had a job for him. Let's get Wadleigh's KEM and do the Carlin documentary. It was the spark he needed, or at least it was a flicker.

Michael was living and working in West Hollywood with his girlfriend Dulcie who he'd met the spring before we did "Woodstock". Jim McBride also lived at the house while he was writing a script and helped Michael who was flying back and forth to London on a sci-fi project. Our rental of the office with the KEM would help with the overhead.

Jim Frawley met with us at the editing room, took a perfunctory look at some of the footage and went on vacation. He'd be back in six weeks. We got to work on the thousands of feet of film, synching it up, using all three picture heads to get a feeling for what kind of film we had. We knew George would be coming by to check it out so we wanted to make the experience, sometimes excruciating for the talent, easy and fun. We had to get leader to fill in the spaces on the film when a camera was not running so that all the footage from the cameras would run in synch. Instead of black leader, we got some old porno footage and slugged it in upside down and backwards. Larry had done some crew work on a film based on the book "The Secret Life of Plants". He had liberated a galvanometer from that job which they had used to read and analyze a plant's response to stimuli. We brought in a huge spider plant from the patio, put it on a table next to the KEM with the meter attached to it, then ran the footage. The galvanometer would groan and whine, screech at times, depending on the sounds and maybe even the sight of George.

As a cutting device, we used George's dressing room warm ups which he did with a tape recorder. He'd always listen to his routine before he went on. We started the film with George listening to himself and his reactions, quipping to a friend, then cut on stage to the show. We could go back and forth and it gave great insight to his process.

George came to see the rough edit by himself. We sat him in the chair, turned on the galvanometer hooked up to the spider plant, then the KEM and let the film roll. George loved it and the plant loved it more, noisily reacting to every joke. We told him that the plant's reaction was determining the cut of the film. He couldn't believe that we'd put the crazy porno footage in there and almost wanted to use it in the final version. We were elated and having the time of our lives.

Jim returned to the city and hated it. Or at least, that's what he said, probably because it wasn't his idea and he'd had no input in the edit. Even though he heard from Jack Lewis that they were thrilled, he was very angry with me. I'd gone too far. Then, Jack called again with bad news. The project was off. Something about George's health, or the film was too close a look at him, didn't have the mystery that a star like him needed to hide behind. We were done. Not so funny.

I wrapped the editing room, had all the work print delivered to Jack's office, made my amends with Jim. But, most importantly, Larry and I were friends again, maybe co-workers even, should something come through.

Larry introduced me to Waterbarrel Productions run by a nice man, Frank Kratochvil, who was an editor. He got lots of jobs he couldn't do himself and was glad to have some help. I cut a Hyatt Hotel infomercial, even sending Neil Young out to shoot some footage of the Hyatt in San Francisco. I could safely say I was the only person to hire Neil as a cameraman and I paid him. Other little jobs came through and I was making my nut.

The VW bug irrevocably broke down and I needed a vehicle. I wasn't upset about this as the little beige car was not really how I saw myself. I was working in Hollywood and needed a good set of wheels. Especially, because one of my mantras was, "A girl's best friend are her wheels." "Is her wheels?" I could never figure that out but I meant it. What if I was with a date who was disgusting? I had my car. At a party where it was looking creepy and dangerous? I'm parked outside. Wanna drive up the coast? I could count on my car.

My first car had been a TR-3, a baby blue 1960 Triumph that Dad bought. I was in college and I loved that car. What other sorority girl drove a sports car like that? Couldn't think of one. High school friends Dave Gernon (yes, he moved to Aspen) and Steve Plater had Triumphs too and we'd go out in the country and drive the two lane county roads, up and down the hills, around the tight corners hoping a farmer on a tractor wasn't pulling out of his field.

Now, in need of a great car, I didn't want to settle for a boring old Ford or even a new Ford. But, I would buy a Mustang. And, I found it. A 1968, 287 engine, bronze body, white leather seats and a white convertible top, you heard me right. It was so hot and it was only $700. Mom wired me the money so I could jump ahead of the other buyers and it was mine. It never gave me a lick of trouble until a Salvadoreno immigrant hit me from behind when I was stopped on La Brea Ave. at a stop light. But that was not for a few years.

Marty Scorsese was in town working on his film, "New York, New York" with Bob De Niro and Liza Minnelli. I was dating a writer, Chris Hodenfield, who worked for Rolling Stone Magazine and he was assigned an article on De Niro. He was going to the set and asked if I'd like to come along. I hadn't seen Marty in a few years and it would be fun to watch him make this big feature film. We were both welcomed warmly by him and ushered on to the set. Marty and I got a chance to catch up as Chris talked with Bob.

I told him about the Carlin film and that Larry and I were looking for other films to do. The A.D. came up and told Marty the

D.P. was ready to do a take. Marty walked in to call action. Then, the A.D turned to me.

"Mr. De Niro has asked that you leave the set."
I looked at him, not quite getting it.
"There's the door."

I was being thrown out. I turned and left wondering whether I should be really hurt or maybe pleased that Mr. De Niro thought I was such a big distraction. I never asked and it wasn't really important because in a few weeks, Marty called and asked Larry and me to come to his office at MGM. He was doing another film and wanted our help.

Noah Purifoy Collage - Joshua Tree Outdoor Museum

Chapter Thirteen

Action!

Robbie Robertson had befriended Marty and called him about The Band's last concert at Winterland in San Francisco on Thanksgiving Day, which was three weeks away. The list of musicians coming in for the performance was mind-blowing. The house was sold out and Bill Graham was producing. Jonathan Taplin, who had done "Mean Streets" with Marty was producing a movie. This was huge and Marty gave us the gig. We immediately went into first gear and worked with them to pull together the crew. Michael Chapman was the D.P. and had his gaffer, electricians and grips. Boris Leven, who was the Production Designer on "New York, New York", went to the San Francisco Opera House set shop and chose a painted backdrop and rented chandeliers not only for the stage but for the audience section. Laszlo Kovacs, who had shot "Easy Rider" and was shooting Marty's "New York, New York", would be on stage left; Bobbie Byrne, stage right. Larry and I pulled in David Myers to be roving on stage along with Hiro Narita who we knew from "Journey Through The Past". Marty wanted Fred Schuler, I suggested Fred Elms and Michael Watkins. Fred was in but who was this Watkins guy? Didn't he just do commercials? Yes, he did but high end ones and he was right for the job. I called Michael and he was ecstatic to be part of it. Vilmos Zsigmond, a legend and friend of Laszlo's, dropped by Winterland on Wednesday and asked to be on the crew. We built a shooting platform for him in the back of the hall.

Marty wanted to shoot 35mm, all Panavision cameras. No one had done this before for a live performance film and for good reasons. First, the film magazines hold only four minutes of film and the change over and cleaning takes more time than just snapping on a 16mm magazine. Could Panavision even get us eight camera bodies, magazines, and all the lens components we'd need? Michael Chapman made the call and they could for him. We needed an assistant for each camera, loaders, runners and then Marty dropped the big one. He was scripting the entire shoot with Mardik Martin who'd written "Mean Streets" and "New York, New York". Therefore, he would also need readers at each camera station, reading to the cameraman, telling him which musician he should be shooting, how wide or close, when to make a zoom, a move, all choreographed. And, how would any of these people talk and hear over the very loud music? They'd wear headphones, everyone would be on a set. Marty had really gone Hollywood. We had always relied on the cameramen to know what to get, to feel the music and go with it. But, Marty had a point. There could be eight or ten musicians on stage at the same time and he didn't want all cameras focused on Robbie or Van Morrison or even Bob Dylan. With Mr. Dylan, that became moot as the directive came down that only two Dylan songs could be filmed. And who rolled through the other songs Dylan did? Michael Watkins. He covered up the little red light on the front of the camera, focused in on Dylan and sat back, getting every moment.

The first glitch in the production came on Tuesday at the Panavision equipment house. The IATSE union was striking and there was a circle of members picketing. Michael Chapman's Assistant Cameraman, Tibor Sands, was there to oversee the load-out and worked with the union guys and called friends to help get the gear out the door, past the strikers and onto the truck. The second glitch was that once the lights were hung, the chandeliers set, and everything turned on, it was really hot on the stage. The light level had to be high for the 35mm film. Time was now running out but we had to get silent air conditioning units up from L.A to cool the place down or the musicians would be drenched with sweat. The third glitch was my own damn fault and due to my being too sentimental about Thanksgiving. One of the truck drivers had brought his family with him so they could celebrate the holiday together and he asked me to give his two teenage daughters wristband all-access passes. I did this, with the plea that they not put them on and come to the ballroom before the concert. Good luck with that. They were teenagers and they wanted to see the musicians. Bill Graham saw them walking around and stormed into our office, screaming at the top of his lungs at me, accusing me of breaking his tight security. I denied it to the hilt and with the help of Larry and Jerry Pompili, who was still with Bill and didn't want to see me get thrown out, got him cooled out believing the girls had stolen into the office and taken them. Bill went off to the next horrendous problem that only he could see. But, I had to hand it to him, he was a detail guy, and that was impressive. Maybe that's what it took to run rock and roll palaces as well as he did.

Roc Brynner arrived and it was great to see him. We'd met a few years earlier when he lived at Topanga Beach and was friends with Karen, JP and John Binder. He was Yul's son and had lived a star-studded life and knew everyone in the film business. The chandeliers and the reason for them was that Roc had hired and coached a group of dancers who would actually do "The Last Waltz" in the Winterland Ballroom to start the concert.

Thanksgiving had never been like this. Bill Graham fed the crew, musicians and five thousand concertgoers. Roc's dancers glided around the ballroom floor under the glowing chandeliers, the cameramen, assistants, readers, loaders, soundmen took their places and at 9pm, The Band came on stage and swung into "Up On Cripple Creek". Marty and I were on stage left, both on headsets with scripts in front of us. As he talked to his cameramen and they responded, I made script notes. The readers, also on headsets, were directing their cameraman. It was so loud it soon became obvious this was not a workable system and everyone was on their own. Larry patrolled the camera positions, the loading area and checked with the recording truck, making sure we were all in sync and operating.

After The Band did their top hits, Ronnie Hawkins and Dr. John came on, followed by Paul Butterfield, Muddy Waters and Eric

Clapton. Neil and Joni did his song "Helpless". Joni, the only woman on the stage, sang "Coyote", then came Neil Diamond, a little too pop, but a friend of Robbie's. Van Morrison got the crowd rocking with "Caravan" and that brought out Dylan. Then it was a free for all jam until 2am. We burned through film faster than anyone expected and decisions had to be made as to what not to shoot, what songs could be covered by one or two cameras just for the record. Our readers attempted to hear Marty's Off or On directions and more or less it was effective. Gov. Jerry Brown had joined us on the side of the stage and greeted the musicians as they came off. Neil introduced him to Bob Dylan and they all faded into the night.

An after-party was the destination at the Miyako Hotel across the street. Unfortunately, I was overseeing the wrap, sitting at a desk with two accountants paying the crew in cash, as we added up their chits, their day rates and mileage. It was grueling work, especially coming at the end of a very long day. I got over to the party at 5am just as most people were leaving but was able to give Neil a hug.

Back in L.A., MGM was not sure whether to be angry that Marty, who was under an exclusive contract for "New York, New York", had stolen away to do the film or to get all the publicity they could for it. They, at least, insisted that all the film be developed in their lab so they could make money off the processing and negative cutting. They put a lot of pressure on Marty to get back to work so Larry and I took up the slack setting up post production. Yeu-Bun Yee, an editor who we had worked with on "Woodstock", was available and knew Marty from back then so he was brought in along with his friend Jan Roblee. I had to go to David Braun's office, Dylan's attorney, and play the scratch track for him, editing out all the Dylan tunes. He put it in his vault. More shooting was done but Larry and I weren't involved because of the union rules. That was fine by me as I was onto another job. We had been part of a crew that pulled off an amazing feat, and on viewing the work print as it started to come together we knew it was a film for the ages.

What I didn't do during all these preparations was get a written agreement, a contract, that said I was the production manager and that Larry was the line producer. As Larry would say, "You fucked up, you trusted them." Larry got his credit but because MGM took over after the shoot, the production became a DGA guild shoot and I was not a union member. Some MGM guy got my credit and I was listed as the Assistant Production Coordinator.

Question: "Why did God make men?"
Answer: "So they could screw women."

The guy who got my credit wasn't even at the concert and I was. It was a great experience, worth all the sleepless nights, and the worry, the money, as at least we were well-paid. So screw the MGM guy.

●<●>●<●>●<●>●<●>●<●>●

TVTV - Top Value Television - was a rad group of six people who did gonzo video. When the Sony Portapak came out, which was to video what the Éclair and Beaulieu were to film: hand-held systems that allowed the user to shoot in a cinema verite style, Wendy Apple, Paul Goldsmith, Alan Rucker, Hudson Marquez, Megan Williams and Michael Shamburg, were in the forefront of a new wave of television. Larry had worked with them on "Superbowl", a crazy look at the NFL with Bill Murray and Christopher Guest interviewing the players, coaches and owners. Now, they had been given one of Loren Michael's slots at NBC. The Saturday Night Live producer had four of them to use for other programming and thought that TVTV would bring a fresh look to late-night television. "The TVTV Show" would be scripted by a team of comedy writers, directed by a good comedy director, Alan Myerson, starring Howard Hesseman, Bill Murray, Dan Ackroyd and Rene Auberjonois. It was a satire of TV news and was hilarious. The budget was tight, the crew was small and it was very hard work. I was the production manager and it was like herding cats as none of the TVTV people had ever done a fictional show like this. But, we had tons of fun and I dated Bill Murray.

It all started when Shamburg asked if I could go to dinner one night. He was married, so I wondered what was up. In fact, he was asking me for Billy Murray who was too shy to ask me himself. It was Bill's birthday and he wanted to celebrate. I thought it would be a group of us so agreed to go. Billy showed up at the office at the end of our day, dressed in baggy shorts over long underwear, a sweatshirt and reeked of cologne. Michael said he'd drive and off we went to a French restaurant on Sunset Blvd. It was just going to be the three of us. We slid into the red banquette and ordered food, making small talk and it was basically a disaster.

A week later, I got a call at home and it was Billy. What was I doing on Wednesday? I wasn't about to have a repeat of his birthday dinner so I said I had some plans. Too bad, he said, someone at NBC had laid two tickets to the Bruce Springsteen concert at the Santa Monica Civic Auditorium, and he thought I'd like it. Ohh, would I. Springsteen was the new kid on the block who was amazing. He had everything, or so we'd heard. He could write songs that captured his life in New Jersey blue collar towns, and deliver them with extreme soul. I paused. Maybe I could change my schedule around. Bill said, great, I'll pick you up. He arrived on a 1000cc motorcycle that he'd borrowed from the TVTV office, cleaned up in jeans and a leather jacket with a small bottle of tequila in the inside pocket. We were Born to Run. He fired the thing up and we sped across town to the concert. We sat way down front and were spell-bound by the music and performance and tramps like us yelled and danced all night long. Bruce really gave you a lot for your money and became known for his four-hour shows.

Billy and I started hanging out, riding around in the pink Nash Metropolitan he called his comedy car. Once he stopped being shy, he was funny, smart and ambitious. And, that was when he got the big call. Lorne Michaels hired him to join Saturday Night

Live. TVTV had to re-write his part in the show so he could zip back and forth, becoming a bi-coastal entertainer. Romance was not in the cards and I couldn't blame him. Look where it took him. He made overtures one night when we were doing a difficult shoot and I wasn't in the mood nor had the time to really talk. He and Dan Ackroyd were playing undercover cops breaking into a house, a location I'd rented from my old friend Peter who now lived in the Valley. The actors had overacted to the point that they'd broken the front windows off their hinges, trashing the house inside. Just another headache every production manager has to make right. Besides, I had started seeing the gaffer, John Lindley, a New Yorker who I liked a lot, and was a lot less complicated than Mr. Bill Murray. I'd see Bill over the years and it was always friendly, sometimes hilarious, and he certainly got what he wanted out of life, if not out of me, and he deserved every bit of it.

Life and work were good. I picked up little jobs here and there, commercials, short films and began taking headshots of actor friends for their portfolios. I inherited photo lab equipment, an enlarger, trays and chemicals and installed it in one of the bathrooms and developed my own negatives. I loved living in Beachwood Canyon and had a fun group of friends who lived near by. Some of us would meet at the small restaurant there on Saturdays, sing the Breakfast Club song, drink coffee, share stories and suggestions for how to get ahead. The neighborhood had been the home of Aldous Huxley and his wife Laura who admired Krishnamurti and had befriended the Vedanta community which also included Christopher Isherwood. There was a very spiritual vibe here, with it's narrow, winding streets that led to well-tended Spanish-style homes, quiet at night, except for the odd police helicopter shining it's spotlight on the sides of the mountain trying to pin down a perp. I continued reading the books, Krishnamurti, "Autobiography of a Yogi" about Vivekinanda and Yogananda, Madam Blavatsky, Ouspensky and Gurdjieff. I put in a small garden down the terraces of the lawn and planted vegetables. I listened to a lot of music. I felt centered, alone but not lonely, with my dog Tas and a few cats.

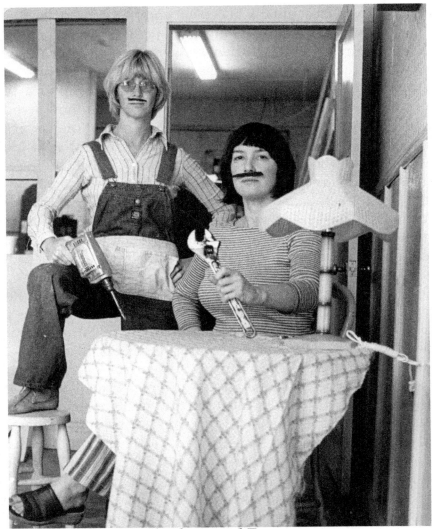

Charlotte and Eve

Char and I hung out at a great Hollywood restaurant, Ports, which was across from the Sam Goldwyn Studios. It was always fun and lively, had a good eclectic menu, run by a great couple, Jock and Micaela Livingstone. In true Hollywood fashion, you could always see a "star" or well-known producer, but who really cared about that when we had our good friends around. I knew I could always stop in for a drink and there would be someone to talk to. We even pitched in to help Micaela turn a room they acquired next door into an English tea shop, a decided left turn from the dark bar and restaurant she owned. Eve Babitz helped out too, taking a break from her writing. She was famous for her chess game with Marcel Duchamp in which she challenged the dadaist while naked and for her Buffalo Springfield record cover '60s montage.

Kathy Hunter called me to say that some FBI agents had been down to Happy Trail looking for me. She told them she had no idea where I was but did learn it had to do with David Sachs. Diana's doctor husband had gone rogue the year before, touting the positive medical attributes of cocaine. I had tasted some of the coke that they always had with them and it was fine. No wonder, as it was pure, uncut Merck crystals. Unhappily, I learned that they had used my name to get prescriptions of the drug at pharmacies all over Los Angeles County.

The hammer came down on David and Diana when he accepted a FedEx package of six pounds of coke sent to him by the Merck company in St. Louis and they were charged with a string of felonies. My name went on the list of unindicted co-conspirators. I helped Diana get a lawyer who saw me when I walked into the court room on the first day of the trial and told me to get the hell out. The FBI could subpoena me to testify. I took his advice and left town.

Once again, I headed to Aspen for some skiing and stayed with Bill McDonough and his wife, Joelle. Their house up Independence Pass looked over the Roaring Fork meadow north of town, with a view of the snow storms that came in and renewed the cash crop of the town. His sportswear store was doing a booming business and I worked there part-time, making enough to pay for the trip. One night, right after the store had closed, we had some royal visitors. King Carlos of Spain was ushered in and we showed him Bogners galore, the best ski clothes money could buy for him, the Queen and his prince and princesses. Curt and Betsy and the kids were thriving and we all skied together, trying to keep up with Heidi and Jimmy.

Aspen was changing a lot. It had become a magnet for Texans and very wealthy people from other parts of the country. Small homes from the mining days were going for almost a million dollars and became vacation homes, used a couple of weeks a year. The neighborhoods were going to the hogs and lost their friendly feeling. Cocaine was also really popular and this brought a different vibe into the nightclub scene that was always just beer, margaritas and pot.

In February, I made plans to meet John Lindley, who I'd met during the TVTV shoot, who would fly out to New Mexico. I drove the Mustang, running down the road for fifteen hours straight, and picked him up in Santa Fe, then headed to Taos to explore that amazing area. One of my favorite writers, D.H. Lawrence, had lived there in the '20s and his stories about the "Woman Who Rode Away" and "The Plumed Serpent" reverberated in the landscape. We ventured north to Canyon de Chelly, walking along the narrow path down the moutainside to look at the White House ruins in the cliffs above the river. It was February and we were there alone, warmed by the winter sun, aware of the connection between the present and the primordial past, sensing in these parts, on the Indian lands where time stops still, everything is the same as it's always been, sensing the oneness with the world, no need to look back or forward, to just be, meditative and peaceful and just right.

Work trickled in, commercials, one with Jonathan Winters, a documentary with cameraman Paul Goldsmith that I edited about Vermonters and their rural lives; another one with Paul at Santa Anita Race Track which required me, the Assistant Camera, to go into the jockeys' dressing room which totally freaked them out. They thought I'd brought bad luck with me but if that was so it didn't show up on the track as every jockey on every horse finished the race. I went to New York to see John and we drove out to Montauk where his mother had a beach house near the old

Bob & Janice

lighthouse. We swam, fished, took photos and ate simple dinners at home.

Janice Pober, one of Bob Greenfield's long-time friends from Brooklyn, moved to Los Angeles from Carmel Valley where they both had been living. She stayed with Char until she found a great spot and a good job, working at A&M Records. She rescued poor Tas one night who became frightened by a freak electrical summer storm, escaped from my deck and ran all the way across Beachwood Canyon to Char's apartment. Janice heard scratching at the door and there was the shivering wet dog. This forever endeared her to my heart and Janice became a great addition to our korass.

In August, I went to south Texas, to the Rio Grande Valley, for a feature film with Ronee Blakley, who had recommended me for a job on the film called "She Came To The Valley". Also in the period western cast were Dean Stockwell, Scott Glenn and Freddy Fender, playing Pancho Villa. Albert Band, an older European director, hired me to be the script supervisor. The actors weren't

Dean & Ronee and their on-screen kids

happy with him and wanted me to become the director, but I pointed out that Albert's company had raised the money from some of the local landowners and I had never directed before. The movie was an adaptation of the autobiography of a woman, Cleo Dawson, who grew up in the area. Her parents had come from the north in the early 20th century, some of the first snowbirds from the Midwest, to start the citrus business that grew and made them wealthy. The towns of McAllen and Mission became the bastions of white people surrounded by Mexican families who had long eked out poverty-level lives ranching and farming. The border was porous and in fact, at some of our locations, I simply walked from the U.S.A. to Mexico across a very shallow Rio Grande River.

As hot as it was down there, triple-digit, very humid temperatures, I loved it. We had a great crew, with D.P., Daniel Pearl and his wife, Dottie, Head Makeup Artist, Jim Bogard, his

The Crew on R 'n R

gaffer. The Pearls had worked with Tobe Hooper on "Texas Chainsaw Massacre" who Daniel had met at U.T. in Austin. The Texas connection was important as Daniel's friends would visit on the weekends for partying, peyote and local tips of where to go in Reynosa across the border for R&R. We had a lot of night shooting which was great considering the daytime temperatures and yet, it was still in the high 90s at midnight. I came out of an interior set that was probably 120 degrees and felt the cool 90 degree breeze. Ronee was drenched from the heat which made Dottie's job all the more difficult. We'd wrap at 6am and still wired from work, head across the border for dinner/breakfast washed down with tequila and beer.

Scott Glenn & Jeanne

Robbie Romero, a friend of Ronee's, actor, musician, worked with us for a few weeks. His mother was Rita Rodgers who had been a long-time lover of Sam Peckinpah's and was still a beauty. Mary Alice Artes, another friend of Ronee's, played a part. Her current boyfriend was Bob Dylan whom she claimed for Jesus. I always thought Bob wrote "Sweetheart Like You" about Mary Alice, "the most beautiful woman who ever crawled across cut glass to make a deal". Scott Glenn brought his family, wife, Carol, a ceramicist, and their young daughters, Dakota and Rio, with him and they were fun to have around.

Being on a film location is a fascinating experience. I was with a crew of thirty people for three months, working hard, long

Feeny Jield

days, hanging out on the days off, making money, getting per diem, fed on the set, so I was banking a lot of what I made. Then, everyone flew out, back through San Antonio to LAX, and you might never see some of those people again. Yet, during that time, we were close friends, getting each other through the day or night.

When I was working on "The Big Bus", the D.P. Harry Stradling, Jr. commented on that. His father had been one of the first feature film cinematographers who worked with Mary Pickford, shot "The Picture of Dorian Gray", "A Streetcar Named Desire", "My Fair Lady" and he had no other thought than to follow in his footsteps. He told me he'd run into a crew member on a studio lot, they'd look at each other, and say, "When was it? What movie did we do together?" They might or might not figure it out but there was that connection, the "Family of Man" feeling all crew people have with each other. I did see some of these new friends again, worked with Daniel and Dottie, had dinner with them.

Ronee is a friend to this day. I worked with Dean down the road and that will be another story.

One of the things I really loved was going into Mexico on our days off. We'd shop for serapes, boots, hats, peasant shirts, have a great meal then head back to the motel to swim, sleep and prep for the next day of shooting.

One of Daniel's good friends from college was from a very wealthy and powerful Texas family in Starr County, our location. His father was a state Senator, owned land on both sides of the border, holdings that were measured in miles not acres, and also owned a bridge that crossed the Rio Grande. There are twenty-seven bridges that cross over and only three of them are privately owned. That owner could control what comes in and what goes out. The two sons realized while they were at U.T. that they could do pretty well selling pot to coeds and frat boys. Their business grew to the point they were trucking the stuff in not just for Texas potheads but as far away as New York, New Jersey, Boston. One dark night in the midst of a deal, the two brothers were attacked. They fought, then tried to get away, but our friend's older brother was run down by a fast moving car and didn't survive. Daniel's friend still did a little dealing, not that he needed to, but he brought a big bag of peyote buttons to the set one Friday. Scott took a handful and lit out onto the desert and we didn't see him again until Monday. He said he had a great trip. I knew that this was not the time for me to take any and we could party without them.

I was having some difficult phone conversations with John and it was looking more and more that our long-distance affair was getting threadbare. He had a great loft on Crosby St. in lower Manhattan, an area that was just beginning to become popular with artists and although he traveled a lot for work, he wanted it to be his home base. I was not interested in going back to the city, surprising myself that I'd turned into a real California girl.

I'd also been seeing someone else in Los Angeles before I went on location. Craig was a budding film producer working with a successful producer/manager who had offices at Paramount. We liked each other and he was still reeling from a split with his wife who ran off with a friend of mine.

He was pushing to get serious and I was still wondering where the relationship with John was going. Now, I knew. Craig was calling a lot, wanting an answer. Did I want to get a place together? I'd been on my own for three years and while I loved my Hollyridge apartment, it was enticing to think that I could have a nice place with an interesting guy. We were almost finished with the production so I told him I was leaning toward saying yes but I wanted to wait until I got back to L.A., to look him in the eyes and see if this was the right move.

The shoot was going well. We'd gone over to Padre Island to do some "desert" scenes, when the Midwestern family is caught in a sandstorm on their way south to Texas. But, the weather was getting hot and heavy, a sure sign of the famous Gulf of Mexico hurricanes that could sweep onshore and destroy swaths of homes and the citrus orchards. We hurried back to Mission to shoot out some exteriors that still remained to be done on the set we'd built. Freddy Fender as Pancho Villa was going to swoop into town and Mary Alice had to drive a horse-driven wagon to get the kids to safety while Ronee, our heroine, would convince the Mexican Revolutionary Army to not destroy the farm they'd worked so hard to build. We did a few nights, getting most of the scenes, and then the hurricane winds started to blow. The storm was expected to hit us so all the businesses got their windows boarded up and our crew pitched in to help. If it did come, we'd lose the set and have to figure out how to make up the shots we still hadn't done.

The winds were now over a hundred miles per hour, a Stage Two hurricane, bending the tall palm trees in half, pounding rain onto the motel where we all gathered in the dining room. It was pitch black at noon and this wasn't the real storm. That never reached us. It turned south before it hit land and crushed a small Mexican fishing village below the border. We felt terrible about these poor people, but pleased we still had our film set. It took a few days for the dirt streets to dry out but we were able to get back to work and wrap up the film.

Once again, I'd loved being in Mexico but the obvious division between the white business people in South Texas and the Mexican laborers was glaring. Any dating or other sort of fraternizing was not accepted and any discussion about whose land it really was, not mentioned. Yes, it's American land now, but as I said, you could walk across thirty feet of shallow water and be in Mexico.

I was glad to be home in Beachwood, bank account bursting with all the money I'd earned and barely spent on location. Tas had been well-taken care of at Charlotte's, the bronze Mustang was ready at the curb, and where was I going next? I didn't have a clue. Craig was pressing me to make a decision. He was losing his apartment in West Hollywood and had found a great house on Woodrow Wilson Drive, modern, two stories with a pool, overlooking the Valley. I was tempted but it felt rushed. I didn't have a lingering feeling that my relationship with John was going to be re-kindled. I thought Craig had real possibilities and his best friend was an up-and-coming actor named Richard Gere who kept telling me to just do it. We went to see the house and it was really nice if unconventional. The entry way was on the top floor along with three bedrooms. A wide staircase went down to the lower level which was an open plan living/dining/kitchen area with glass doors all across the front leading out to a patio and swimming pool. Gee, could I actually afford to live here? It was almost too good to be true. Judy, the landlady, lived in a nice cabin below the house and wanted us to move in. She made it very possible.

I'd also just had a visit from Larry and Neil Young who'd just popped in at my apartment one day to say we were going to make another movie. It was still in the planning stages but it was going to happen. Dean Stockwell, who I'd just worked with in Texas, had come up with a story and it also involved Russ Tamblyn. They were working out all the details and Neil was stoked about this and about a new album he was recording in Hollywood. I'd hear from them soon. I figured I probably had more money coming in, so yeah, I'd take the big house with Craig. We'd see how the blooming romance would work out.

We moved in and it was a little iffy. Craig was a large personality from big Chicago money and he wanted things his way. His big waterbed went into the main bedroom, he chose his closets, set up his office in the next room with his TV, leaving me a smaller bedroom for my office and private space. We weren't a perfect fit but he went to work everyday and I had the place to myself.

Instead of some downtime, relaxing by the pool, I got a job working with Larry on a low budget film that an editor friend of ours, Jim Beshears, was going to direct. Larry was the Production Manager and I was the Assistant Director on "Junior High" now known as "Homework". It was a teenage romance with Joan Collins starring as one of the mothers. Carrie Snodgress and Betty Thomas did us favors and played small parts as did some other good Hollywood actors. The money came from Max Rosenberg, a ringmaster in the low budget movie world. He was about eighty years old and a real character, tough, but once we proved we knew what we were doing, he stayed out of our way. Considering we were so low budget, we had a great crew, Paul Goldsmith, D.P., Tom Stern, Gaffer, Peter Hlidall & Hudson Marquez, Sound, Ernst Van der Bovenkamp, Art Director and his sister Elsa Zamparelli, Sets, Betsy Heimann, Costumes, John Thompson from my restaurant days as the 2nd Assistant Director. We did good work and had a great time doing it. The downside was working through the holidays which saw me eating crackers in bed on Christmas day, Craig having gone to Vail to meet his parents for a few weeks of skiing.

One important lesson I learned on this film is that I wasn't an A.D., the person who runs the set, determines the schedule, gets everything ready for the director who has prepared with the actors. Larry and John Thompson were helpful and there to take command when I was feeling like I was not in control of the production, but it was still a blow to my self-esteem. It was probably a gender issue and none of us were willing to admit it. I'd always been friends with boys, now men, and had learned how to keep sexual attraction out of the equation over the years. I liked my masculine side which allowed me to function in business without tempting or capturing, weakening the energy in the room. Feminism was still a dreaded word with a lot of men who were caught in their parochial and patriarchal attitudes about us, while they held on for dear life to their number one position. They could be threatened, feeling timid and unsure of how to talk during meetings if a woman was there and they blamed this on us. This uncertainty and their feelings that they were being compromised overrode their own rationality that women should do and could do the jobs they were asking for. This brought up competition. Some men felt very uncomfortable if they thought a woman was competing with them. In the movie business, women had been working in the editing, continuity, costume and make-up departments. Or as a secretary to a producer but running a set was a whole different thing.

So the next job that came around, what did I do? A.D., on the new Neil Young film that was starting up in San Francisco. Glutton for punishment, I guess, or I just had to prove to myself that I could be the one out front. Larry didn't want the job because he needed to be everywhere at once, checking the sound, talking with Neil, so I agreed.

Chapter Fourteen

Rock 'n' Roll Will Never Die

Neil was playing a week at a small club in San Francisco, The Boarding House. It was just him, solo acoustic, with a few of his Wooden Indians standing on stage with him and he sang to the audience and to the Indians. He was working on a new album and trying out some of the new songs in small venues. That would be the anchor for the shoot, but there was a twist. This was the beginning of "Human Highway", with Dean Stockwell playing a music promoter/businessman/shyster and Russ Tamblyn was the bumbling friend who always gets Neil in trouble.

Surrounding this were girl groupies, one was a paranoid mess, played by Sally Kirkland, and only Neil could be her heart of gold. When she poured out her love and sorrow to Neil in a scene, his answer was, "I'm just a knob. I'm nothing to you," referencing radios that played his music and could be turned off or changed by a flick of the wrist. I have always loved that line even though it's not in the movie.

Dean's girlfriend was Toni Basil who was a choreographer and very trendy person and she'd seen a band in Berlin called Devo. Dean wanted them to be part of the film as adversaries to Neil's homespun ways. I called Gerry Casale, the guitar player and leader of this Akron, Ohio-based group and we made plans to fly them out to join the cast.

Neil had a new man working for him, David "R.D.", for Ranger Dave, Cline. He'd actually been a forest ranger earlier in his life and had been hired as a ranch manager. He had lots of people

Ranger Dave - David Cline

skills so was now also a road manager. He enlisted me to work with him running backstage during the shows in addition to my film production work, so I was on call day and night.

Craig was planning to come up to hang out with us but I had to call him and tell him to stay home. I didn't want to have to factor in downtime with Craig into an already maxed-out schedule. He was very upset and this was the beginning of the end, as he made clear on the phone. I wasn't up to saving this relationship at this point in time, but I was disheartened. Again, was this man-woman competition? It felt like it.

Neil was a huge draw in San Francisco which was as close to a hometown as he had at this point. The concerts had sold out, as this was a very prolific period in his life. "American Stars and Bars", and "Decade"had been released in the last year or so and he still had new songs to sing. We were shooting the shows with several cameras which David Myers oversaw and recording with the Wally Heider truck, so Neil figured we'd shoot scenes during the day that he, Dean and Russ had come up with using a few Hollywood actors. This was kind of sprung on me and we didn't really have a crew to do all this, so I didn't have a moment where I wasn't on the phone, A.D.-ing a scene, doing the schedule for the next day. It was too much and I needed an assistant.

I put out the word to the San Franciso-based crew and hired a great woman, Amanda Heming, who had worked in editorial but was smart enough to catch on quickly to the chaos that reigned at The Boarding House. And Larry really liked her. Within a few weeks, they were a couple.

We shot a scene at the Mabuhay Gardens on Columbus Avenue, in the thick of the strip clubs and raunchy bars. The owners of this Filipino restaurant/bar/nightclub had put out the word and the place was packed on a Saturday afternoon. Devo played on stage and Neil, carrying a very small instrument case, tried to push his way through the crowd which held him back as he shouted, "I can play, I can play." He finally made it to the stage and pulled out his ukelele.

Then it was off to a recording studio with Devo and Neil playing "Hey Hey My My, Rock and Roll will never die", with Mark Mothersbaugh sitting in a crib with his Boogie Boy mask on. R.D. and I found a woman in the neighborhood who was happy to sell her crib for a fistful of dollars. Recording all of this was David Briggs who had golden ears for Neil's sound. He was the person Neil would listen to after each take and he insisted on raw, authentic rock and roll and nothing else would do. He was also sexy as hell and even though he was in a long-term relationship, I couldn't help myself. He was also very amazed by me and that I was the one who called for "Quiet" before a take. I was one of the few women he accepted in his world besides the singers Neil worked with, Linda Ronstadt, Nicolette Larson, Emmy Lou Harris.

Neil was happy with all of this and plans were made to keep working on this unscripted, improvised fictional film. We decided to take a break with plans to pick up the production in a month. I headed back to L.A. to try and figure out what my domestic life looked like and discovered some other woman's clothes in my closet. Craig was sending a huge message which really was unnecessary as we were mutually in agreement that our trial attempt didn't lead to a long run. I moved into my little room down the hall and we began to live separate lives.

Larry and I worked out of David Geffen and Elliot Robert's office, Lookout Management, on Sunset Blvd., planning the next phase which included more shooting up north near the ranch then a road trip to Taos, New Mexico where Dennis Hopper was going to host the production. More actors were added to the cast who we would fly out to Taos, Myers pulled together a small crew, Neil and his new girlfriend Pegi Morton would travel in his tour bus, Pocahontas, along with Russ and Dean and we'd travel in a 1950's bus he also owned. We were on the road, Larry and Amanda, John Thompson, me and Tas, the dog.

The gist of the movie was that Neil had these psychic connections with the Native Americans and their land as represented by the wooden Indians who we'd brought with us on the trip. He was an artist seeking the muse that brings the brilliance but people kept getting in the way, women, businessmen, hobos, poets, other musicians, who needed help. But, then, the Wooden Indians are mysteriously gone, stolen from the back of his pick up truck. So he sets out to find them and more adventures happen.

As with "Journey Thru the Past", this was a visual expression, free-form, "let's put on a show then figure out later what we've got", production. And no one said we couldn't do it. Dennis offered introductions to his Taos friends and there wasn't anything we

Pegi Morton Young - Ready to ride.

couldn't have as a location. He would drop by unannounced at our film locations, accompanied by young women who would love to be movie extras if we needed them.

We took great advantage of the natural Taos landscape, rafting down the Rio Grande River, where Trish Soodik was a poet on a rock in the middle of the river and when no one listens she steps off of it to be swept away. Shades of Virginia Woolf. We shot on the Rio Gorge bridge, 1000' feet above the river, for a day. Neil's car has broken down and he's stranded. Up comes an old car and they offer help.   When Neil opens their car's trunk to get a jack, out

212

Danny Tucker and John Thompson

jumps a vagrant street band from San Francisco playing "Boulevard of Broken Dreams."

One night we filmed a dinner scene with all the cast and Dennis at the home of the late painter Leon Gaspard, a beautiful old home with dark red walls covered with his paintings. The caretaker had two llamas which he put in a fully-decorated Spanish style bedroom.

Jeanne, Dean & Neil with Tas

South of Taos, near Española, north of Santa Fe, was a famous ruins, the Puye Cliff Dwellings. They were on the Santa Clara Reservation and were generally off-limits to non-Natives. Neil was intent on shooting there and I was dispatched to make it happen. Carpio Bernal, the son of a Taos Pueblo elder, and a dancer, artist and cast member, gave me the name of a person to talk to and I made an appointment. Neil gave me some records and I bought some food gifts to give the family who was welcoming me.

I drove out of the mountains and reached the pueblo in an hour. I knocked on the door of a house close to the entrance and was taken to meet the Tafoya family. They were very friendly and we sat around their small living room talking quietly. I gave them the gifts and explained that we knew they were very protective of Puye and it's significance as their home since the 10th century. The original structures were no longer livable but there was a kiva that they still used for ceremonies which barred the attendance of non-natives. I noticed that there was a lot of Maria Tafoya's pottery in their home – the beautiful blackened vases, bowls and plates she was famous for and we discussed her method. We drank some coffee and then they said, yes, we could shoot there for a day. I asked if they would come up and they thought about it a moment, then said yes, they'd tell everyone to come, dressed for filming.

A few days later, the whole company left Taos for Puye. To get up to the mesa, we traveled along a dirt road up to the top of it, buses, trucks, cars, carrying our cast and crew. The weather was volatile, with storm clouds off to the west and bright hot sunshine to the east. Myers did a panning shot during the day which started on the darkening sky and as the lens got to the middle of the horizon where black meets blue, a huge lightning bolt cut it in two.

We continued to shoot with the actresses, Sally, Geraldine Baron, Trish Soodik, Karen Jumper, who connived to see who Neil would fall for; Neil, Dean and Russell prowled around looking for the missing Wooden Indians. As dusk approached, cars started to arrive, a hundred of them with the Pueblo Indians, all in native dress. Fires were built, Neil sang and played while Santa Clara young men carried the Wooden Indians to the fire and laid them on the pyre. The fires blazed, eating into the Cigar Store Indians, throwing flashing light on to Neil as we filmed him singing and playing, Indians drumming and the actors and Pueblo Indians dancing in a circle around them. Everyone stayed until the Wooden Indians were nothing but charred wood and ash. The scene captured the spiritual mystique that haunted Neil's music, his ethereal connection to the land and the tribes that had lived there for years, his recognition of their rights and the white man's diminution of these when they made the Wooden Indian statues and put them outside of tobacco stores.

We were done shooting so it was time to go back to California and see what we had. Larry, Amanda and I opted for a plane trip to L.A. so headed down to Santa Fe where we enjoyed the restaurants, galleries, the festive streets and squares. I also had to figure out where I was going to live and Craig was on my case to move my belongings. Larry was renting David Crosby's Beverly Glen house and offered to share it with me. Amanda could only shake her head in amazement as Jeanne and Larry were back together again, but just friends. And next door, was Leslie Morris, Larry's ex and her friend Calli. It was Canyon living in the '70s.

Craig had threatened to put all my stuff on the curb so I got a truck and a few friends and drove over to pick up my life. Most of the furnishings had been mine so the place took on that empty, temporary feeling and our voices became boomy as we carried it all out. I couldn't find my photography darkroom equipment and Craig admitted a temporary renter had probably taken it. I couldn't believe that he so cavalierly laid this on me. You let someone walk away with my stuff? He could only shrug. Maybe he sold it to maintain his coke habit which was beginning to get out of hand. Later for him and all that jazz.

Mr. D'z - Kingman, AZ

Chapter Fifteen

Thirty-six Guys and Me

Crosby's house was up a very steep little street in the middle of Beverly Glen. It had brown shingled exterior walls and was three stories high with a nice patio on the lower level where my bedroom was and another one off the third level where Larry had his office and bedroom. Each had it's own bathroom. The second floor was a living room and kitchen with a deck around it, very woodsy, simple living and it gave us enough space and privacy. Larry spent most of his time editing on the ranch with Amanda and working with Neil who was getting ready to release a new album, "Comes A Time".

The word on the street was that this album was going to be big and a tour was talked about. Neil had a brainstorm about this, wanting to create a live theatrical story about a young kid dreaming he was on stage surrounded by Brobdingagian guitar amps and road cases. The crew would be dressed like Star Wars' Jawas in red robes, scurrying around the stage, doing their jobs but part of the show. The Roadeyes! The second act would feature music as a scientific experiment with white-coated lab men, the guitar and instrument techies, conducting it, all overseen by a cone-headed wizard. "Rust Never Sleeps" was born and it had nothing to do with the country feel of the new album, typically Neil, never riding on the laurels, always stretching himself and everyone around him.

This was a huge undertaking and it was set to go in mid-September. Neil, Larry and R.D. came to town, Neil doing interviews for the record release. We went to lunch at Barney's Beanery and the conversation began to include the new tour. It was getting huge and R.D was wondering how it was going to be managed. Steve Cohen, who I knew from the altercation on the

Woodstock stage, was the stage manager, Tim Foster and his brother John would handle Neil's guitars, piano, organ. Mixers Briggs and Mulligan, on stage monitors and house speakers. Riggers, drivers, lighting crew, all needed to be hired.

As they talked crew, I looked Neil straight in the face and said, "You can't leave me behind".

The three of them looked at me. It was well-known that women were not allowed on the road. It had been tried before with "old ladies" but I had become integral to the team and I wasn't a girl friend, I was a professional. They said, of course I was going, although Larry once again took the opportunity to talk about how pushy I was. My only retort was that sometimes you don't get something unless you ask for it. I surprised myself that I had no shyness around these guys at all.

I said I'd handle the Roadeye costumes and make-up and do all the travel. Although the tour had been booked, there were always uncertainties caused by weather, mistakes, accidents as three dozen people, Neil's bus, three semi-trucks went on the road to twenty-four cities in six weeks, visiting the big arenas where basketball and hockey games were held, New York's Madison Square Garden, Boston Gardens, the Philadelphia Spectrum, huge venues in Chicago, Atlanta, Washington, Denver. Even the Coliseum in Madison, Wisconsin! John Thompson was hired to be Crazy Horse's roadie, making sure they got to the airport on time in good humor and John's morning Sports report turned the trick each day. Half way through the tour, John would become a slick huckster on stage during the intermission demanding that the entire audience put on their special glasses (cheap 3-D paper things we found) which they got as they entered the arena. The glasses would allow the audience to see the band rust before their very eyes!

Several weeks later, we were all in San Francisco at a production designer's warehouse looking at the set, huge road cases

Roadeyes Raise the Mike

that were built to cover the stage set amps. Roadeyes would raise a large single RCA microphone at the beginning of the show, one so large it took several of them to carry it on stage and get it placed in the right spot, while Jimi Hendrix' guitar wailed "The Star Spangled Banner". This sequed into the Beatles' song "A Day In a Life".

An organ would fly down on wings, a chariot would carry the Conehead Wizard onto the stage at the beginning of the Second Act. A huge tuning fork, wielded by the Littlest Roadeye, me, would make sure the band stayed on key. Bill, a rigger who hung lights at the top of the arenas, tied a long rope that I could grab and swing out over the crowd in my Jawa outfit, careful to not get my mucklucks stuck in the loop.

The show, ragged at first and plagued by small venues that didn't accommodate the set, began to click outside Washington D.C., at Capital Center in Maryland. The new songs, "Thrasher", "Hey Hey, My My", "Sedan Delivery", "Welfare Mothers",

"Powderfinger" were killers and yes, "Cortez the Killer" was in the set too. At the start of each show, everyone gathered backstage in a huddle, our Roadeye red-light headsets shining as we all embraced, shared a joint, and then Neil climbed up a ladder to the top of one of the amps. Three Roadeyes, led by Larry, working with fervor and purpose, hauled the big mic out on stage as the recorded music blared. When it was set, the large road case began to rise, hauled up by more Roadeyes. As the case cleared the amp, there was the sleeping musician on top, wearing T-shirt and white jeans, hair cropped short, another one of my jobs. He picked up his guitar and began "Sugar Mountain" – "Oh to live on Sugar Mountain, with the barkers and the colored balloons", then on to "I Am A Child" as Neil came down a ladder to the stage. It was thrilling, mesmerizing, the crowd was with us and it rolled through to "Needle and the Damage Done" and "Lotta Love". Second Act, the audience with their rust glasses on, opened with a parade of scientists in white coats, checking the equipment, overseen by Steve Cohen in his wizard array. They took their places on the side of the stage, making sure all was well and Crazy Horse rocked into "Sedan Delivery", then "Powderfinger", one of Neil's greatest songs. By the time he got to "Cinnamon Girl", two of the Roadeyes, Larry and me, couldn't contain themselves and we danced across the front of the stage, "You see your baby loves to dance, Yeah, Yeah Yeah."

The tour gave us some downtime, well-deserved and much needed. We usually did four shows a week. We threw a great party at the Rusty Scupper in Boston Harbor, toured Cambridge, walked along the Charles River. In New York, we had two shows then one more on Long Island. In Madison, Mom and Dad came out early for the sound check, stayed for dinner then the concert. Dad sat on one of the audience amps, Tim Mulligan gave him a beer, and he nodded his head in time with the music. He did always love to dance. But, mainly, he saw how hard all of us worked. He was amazed, as Neil and Briggs, checked the sound of the hall, Neil ran through a few songs, each of the crew attended to their jobs. I gave them ear plugs which they appreciated as by this time, the word was out. This was the loudest show anyone had ever seen and

Larry shows Cameron Crowe how to become a Roadeye

heard. Brian Higgins, now married to Janice Pober, was at the show in Los Angeles at the Forum and summed it up this way, "Let's face it, the acoustic set was too loud."

In San Francisco, we filmed the show. The Cow Palace was Neil's home turf and he wanted it done there. We were all beyond exhaustion at this time, many of the guys were sick with colds or a flu. I was doing fine but I also didn't inhale the variety of drugs that were available. I swear that made a difference in the long haul. We'd hired our film crew, Jon Else, Robbie Greenberg, Hiro Narita, Dick Pearce and Paul Goldsmith was D.P. Neil didn't want us to adjust the lighting for the film stock so they pre-flashed it which made the emulsion more forgiving for low light. It wasn't our best show, but the film captured all the characters and energy, the great songs and Neil at the top of his game.

I went back to the ranch to relax and recuperate. Along with Amanda, we started the long process of synching the footage so that Neil and Larry could edit the film. David Briggs and Tim Mulligan got into listening to the twenty-one shows that had been recorded for an album. All of us lived in The Big White House on the ranch, a sprawling one story structure built above the large creek that cut through the land. We'd work long hours, then go back to the house where I'd cook dinner. Then, more work and around 10:30, we'd say, "Let's go party" and off we'd drive, up the long, winding road to Skyline Blvd. and the bars and restaurants where friends who lived on this stretch of the mountains got together. We'd close the joints then the least drunk of us would make sure we got home, usually very slowly.

Briggs and I shared a room until the fateful day that his longtime love, Connie, showed up while I was preparing a huge Italian feast, and dragged him out to get an earful. I moved up to The Little Red house by myself and worked to make it homey. I never liked the idea of sleeping with another woman's man and I didn't need a conquest to make me feel sexy. Briggs and I remained friends, worked side by side, knew it was all for the best and enjoyed the bittersweet, there-but-for-the-grace-of-god-go-I aspect. It's very powerful to love someone that you shouldn't.

With the film finished, we were back in L.A. for the mix at Goldwyn Studios. Taking a break one day, Neil and I were outside on the landing getting some air. I broached the subject of "Human Highway", was it time to get back into it? He didn't know, didn't think it was working, wished he hadn't chosen to be a musician, didn't know what the next part would be. That got me thinking. What if all the San Francisco, Taos material was a dream. A working guy's dream. Neil was such a car buff, owned a lot of them all stored in the car barn and a Redwood City warehouse. What if he was a mechanic, a fool, a simpleton? He has an accident at work, gets hit on the head and has this dream that he's a rock 'n roller. I wrote up a treatment and sent it to him. It worked but it would be a little while before we got started on Human Highway Part 2. Neil was paying for all of this so I worked with his business managers, Segal Goldman, to keep everything budgeted and accounted for. There was no studio, producer, overseer to question a cost.

While Part 2 was being pulled together, Elliot came to Larry and me and asked if we could produce a video shoot with Joni Mitchell who was going on tour with a great fusion band following the release of a new album, "Mingus". Mingus, of course, was the famous jazz musician Charles Mingus who had asked Joni to write some lyrics for some of his songs. It was a great flowering for Joni as a follow-up to "Don Juan's Restless Daughter" which she had done two years before, confounding everyone because they couldn't find a chorus to sing along to. It was a natural path for her, one of the best musical explorers of our generation.

Joni's boyfriend, Don Alias, was a drummer who had introduced her to Pat Metheny, Lyle Mays and the Brecker Brothers. Along with Jaco Pastorius on bass, they were a kick-ass band that brought new life to some of the older songs and put spit and polish on the new jazz recordings. Along with the Persuasions singing back up on two songs, it was a wonderful concert.

We all thought that the Santa Barbara Bowl would be a perfect place for the video. Smaller than either the Greek Theater or the Hollywood Bowl, the stage faced west which in the summer light would give us a sunset at the beginning of the show then going into a dark night. This became "Shadows and Light", which was also one of her songs. "Every picture has its shadow, And it has some source of light. Blindness blindness and sight." The production would be shot in video, a new adventure in music production for Larry, Dave Myers and me. We brought in three more cameras, using Hiro Narita again, along with Daniel Pearl and Eric Saarinen. Bruce Cannon, Myers' nephew who lived in L.A.,

Michael Brecker, Joni Mitchell, Jaco Pastorius, Elliot Roberts

worked as our PA. He'd caught the film bug and eventually became a successful Hollywood editor.

This was a streamlined job, made easy by the video and recording trucks. Amanda coordinated everything and Myers brought in an L.A. crew to do all the electrical and grip. And, I got another dog out of the deal. The generator operator was one of those guys who drinks blackberry brandy starting around noon. He'd brought a little black dog that looked just like Tas from a distance. I went up to play with it and he said, "She's going to the pound tomorrow. I travel too much." Maybe he saw a soft touch when it was standing in front of him, but I left Santa Barbara with

Amanda, Hannah the Aussie and Jeanne

the dog who would be named Snafu, which indeed she was, a troubled little girl with bad skin and not very bright. But, Tas and I loved her and we were a trio.

Calli Cerami and Joni edited the show. We shot additional material and they illustrated some of the songs with it and with additional licensed footage. The video started out with a scene from "Rebel Without A Cause" with James Dean fighting with his father, kicking the TV screen out and that rebellion was just a beginning. The video came out on Laser Disk, VHS, a Two-CD album and played on PBS. Joni was and is an artist for the ages and will be heard, and hopefully seen, for many years to come. She's also a fun girlfriend, loving to hang out for hours, talking about political structures, people's addictions and affinities, using the Navaho Medicine Wheel divisions in her descriptions. As a night owl, work happened following an afternoon breakfast, then on through the midnight hours until dawn.

The Man In Black - Hollywood

Chapter Sixteen

My Way and the Highway

Director Jim Frawley, invited me to a dinner party. He was now engaged to a dynamic blond, B.J., who worked as a producer in town. They were each inviting a few friends and B.J. had placed me next to a friend of hers she'd worked with in Mexico. He was Steve Peck, son of Gregory, who had made a behind-the-scenes film when his father played "The Old Gringo". He was blond and good-looking, taking after his Finnish mother, and it was easy and fun to talk with him. He called a week later and asked me out. We took it slowly as I was maxxed out with work and he was on his way to another job.

John Binder had written a film script, "Escape", which was a riff based on a true story he'd read in the newspaper about two hucksters, Bo and Peep. These two had come up with a plan to fleece naïve people of all their worldly possessions by convincing them that a spaceship was going to land and they would get on it and leave the planet never to return, ending up in another planetary paradise. You can't make this stuff up. John, of course, being the sensitive humanitarian, found a nice version of this story and when I read it, I loved it. Susan Spinks, a friend of mine who lived down Beverly Glen, was a development executive at a production company. I told her about it, she read it and she loved it. She got it to the big guy with the money and they loved it. Wow, it looked like this could happen and John had promised me a production credit if I helped.

In his version, there's a nice girl, "Arlene", who believes in everything and a man, "Sheldon", who believes he'll have another drink. They fall in love and she starts getting otherworldly messages that a spacecraft is coming and she's going to be on it. He tells a crooked tent evangelist, Brother Bud, about this and he's the one who sets up the scam. Cindy Williams, Fred Ward and Harry Dean Stanton were cast and we were making a movie.

John always liked Gary Burden's artistic sensibility and his eye for arresting California images. Gary and I went out to the Antelope Valley to scout locations and found great places: a trailer park, a big box store, little houses, a bowling alley. It was still in Los Angeles County, very blue collar, but very hot in the summer which is when we did this, May to July. The film company had hired a Line Producer, production manager and as Associate Producer, there wasn't much I was responsible for. Susan and I got a house in Palmdale and Steve visited on the weekends, our romance becoming a nice comfortable thing, not exciting really, but easy.

There was a Spiritual Fair in the script, really, a congregation of oddballs, where "Arlene" and "Sheldon" come to pitch their mission. I had free reign to design this scene and brought in as many friends playing wacky people as I could. Magicians, gymnasts, dancers, witches, inventors, healers, all gathered to represent the far out California fruits and nuts. David Myers was the D.P., Betsy Heimann did costumes and other friends, Hudson Marquez and Kirk Frances were the sound crew. It was a good shoot and we all weathered the 100 F.+ temperatures together.

It was a big break for John who had been in the trenches with Robert Altman and we were all working to make this a good film for him. The movie turned out great but became an orphan, caught in the failure of a business deal between the production company, Mel Simon Productions, and 20th Century Fox, which was going to distribute the film. Mel Simon was a big developer, a shopping center mogul from Indianapolis, a decent guy who had not interfered with the making of the film but somebody else in the mixture, probably someone at Fox, nixed the release of the film which was now called "UFOria".

The film got picked up by Universal which did a test screening with a random audience in Peoria, Illinois. It didn't get the numbers they thought they needed to put the film out. So, it sat there, and sat there and sat there. Finally, in 1984, it was allowed to be shown at FilmEx, the Los Angeles Film Festival and got a rave from Kevin Thomas in the L.A. Times. From there it went to the Bleeker St. Cinema on 8th St. in the Village. It got a good review in the New York Times. Likewise in Boston and the Orson Welles Theater, and in Chicago where Roger Ebert loved it. It played some more art house cinemas, then that was it. John was bereft but kept going, getting good jobs one of which was writing "Honeysuckle Rose", produced by Sidney Pollack. Through this film, he met Chris, who worked for Mr. Pollack, and they became a couple and married.

Steve and I were dating exclusively by now but would not see each other for a few months as he was going off to India with his father who was starring in "The Sea Wolves". Again, Steve would make a behind-the-scenes, making-of-the-movie, movie. I figured this was a good time to see if we were real. Would I miss him or would he miss me? Would he write me letters or would it just be an occasional post card?

"Human Highway" was again Neil's focus and began moving through pre-production. A 360 degree set was designed and built by Ernst van der Bovenkamp. In it, there was a road that led to a gas station and adjoining diner all surrounded by a model train track, with a large model of a nuclear plant glowing in the background. Huge muslin backgrounds surrounded everything and Myers would light this in a flat light or with color depending on the time of day. This was the last day on Earth, so it went from early morning as "Lionel", Neil's character, and his best friend "Fred", played by Russ Tamblyn went to work at the gas station and

Dean, Neil & Russ

ended with a nuclear explosion, our Linear Valley residents climbing a stairway to Heaven.

Dean Stockwell and Russ had met each other on a movie set years ago, "The Boy With The Green Hair", when they were 10 and 12 years old. They were still great friends, both living in Topanga. They knew lots of good actors and the casting was left to them to

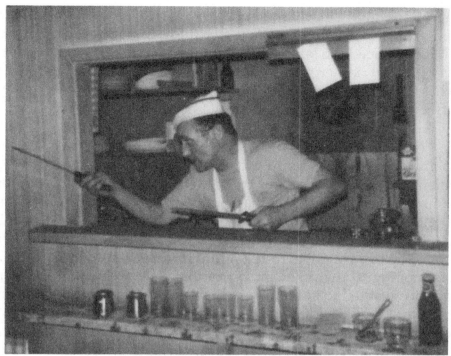

Dennis Hopper as Cracker

populate the diner with an overflow crowd, a cross section of working people, an Arab sheik with his harem, the milkman, the waitresses and the cook. We brought in all the actors we'd used in Taos and added some. Dean would play "Young Otto" who inherited the roadhouse from his father "Old Otto", who had just died. One of the waitresses, Sally Kirkland again, had loved Old Otto and another one, Geraldine Baron, was out to land Young Otto, who had no intention of keeping this run-down, out-of-the-way spot. Charlotte was the blond bombshell Lionel liked but was too shy to date and anyhow, she thought the "Milkman", played by David Blue in a crisp white uniform, was too handsome for words.

Behind the short-order window, "Cracker", played by Dennis Hopper, cooked up a storm, fed the raccoons who would crawl into his kitchen and cracked his knife against the wall as he preached about the end of days. This drove Sally crazy and during a break in filming to re-set lights, he was running his mouth and she insisted,

"Stop." He didn't. He was playing with his big kitchen knife, cutting the serving window wooden frame with it. Sally reached over and grabbed the knife, poor thinking on her part, which caused a very bad cut on her hand. We rushed her to Cedars Sinai ER for stitches. She was back the next day, ready for her close up, with a huge bandage on her hand. So much for continuity.

Dennis apologized profusely and tried to be more sober, not easy in his case. He came to me and admitted that part of his problem was dental pain and so what's a good producer to do but take him to her dentist. He made me a promise that he'd just stay straight until we could finish and he mostly kept it. Years later, he told John and me the story of when he did get sober, when he went wild in Mexico. He got arrested and put in jail but he was so crazy and annoying to the other prisoners that they wanted to kill him. The police wanted to kill him, too, but someone said he was rich and famous and they decided against it. Instead, they transferred him to a second jail with the same results, cops and criminals wanting to put him out of their misery. Fortunately, his lawyer showed up before anyone could do him in and he was escorted back to the U.S.A. Admitting that he needed help, he was introduced to a huge ex-con addict who had devoted his life to helping extreme cases, like Dennis, get clean and sober. When the guy took the job he told Dennis that he would absolutely not let him take one drug or one drink no matter what. Dennis agreed and was locked in a room and forced to go cold turkey except for some food to eat when he was able to keep it down. Dennis acted out his story for us, demonstrating how he writhed and screamed and pitched a fit for many days until he had no strength left to fight. Only then, did his keeper let him out of the room but never out of his sight for months until Dennis was clean and sober. He never did alter his consciousness again. Dennis loved the big guy for the hell he'd put him through, he said. But at the time of our movie shoot Dennis had not yet sobered up.

Bernard Shakey

Back on set, a "Hollywood Businessman", played by Dennis, pulls into this iconic crossroads followed by a big black limo carrying "Frankie Fontaine", a famous musician, played by Neil.Frankie's engine had a whine in it and needed a mechanic and Lionel was thrilled to be up close and personal with his idol. Devo played the "Nuclear Garbagemen", and sang "Worried Man" which was reprised by the whole cast as the nuclear plant starts to blow up, bringing a too-short demise to our cast, except for the mutant Boogi Boy. That's all, folks!

I had moved up to the Line Producer spot on the crew sheet and John Thompson took over as the First Assistant Director. Larry oversaw all of it, staying near the camera with Neil and Dave Myers. Dean was the Co-Director working with the actors. We had top

Joel Bernstein, Tim Mulligan, Sal Trentino & Hudson Marquez

Electric, Grip, Sound, Costume, etc. crews, and, as we were working on a stage at Raleigh Studios, it was all under control. The Studio Equipment Manager was Kevin Costner, a nice young man, who kept hoping he'd get an acting job on the shoot, but didn't hold it against us when it didn't happen. He was helpful at all times bringing whatever Myers needed. Dennis came to me and said he needed an assistant so I hired Leo MacKota, the big, tough roadie, who had worked with us for years and he made sure Dennis got to the set on time and was able to walk and talk.

My life was further complicated by the monsoon conditions of the '79-'80 winter storms that blew in during all of this. At home on the weekend, trying to catch up on sleep, but bothered by the thunder and lightning, I thought I should check around the house. I walked down our little street to Beverly Glen Blvd. and it was a river, moving cars that were parked along the curb into the center of the road. I'd never seen flooding like this and it was mesmerizing. The water that flowed down Lisbon Lane had been clear when

Mark Mothersbaugh as Boogi Boy

started out and it slowly dawned on me that the water flowing past me was now muddy. I turned around and ran up to the house where mud was flowing through the outdoor patio. The hillside had sponged up all the water it could hold and was now collapsing into the house on two sides. It was a scary moment as I watched from a distance to see if it all would give way. It didn't but the house was damaged and would need to be dug out to be inhabitable again. Larry and I had to find other places to live. I moved in with Charlotte and her husband Jordan, bringing Tas and Snaffy with me. She had bought a house in Beachwood Canyon which was very close to Raleigh Studios, just a short drive down Gower.

We stayed on schedule for the film, wrapping it up before the end of the year. It's always hard to know what you've got in the can when you film. There can be moments of brilliance, ones of complete mediocrity, but until you get into the editing room and start to live with it, you just don't have a clue. I did know that we had fun, kept the budget in line, though to an outside eye, Neil plunking down a few million was just another rock star ego trip. The finished film was, once again, too indie and unconventional for most audiences, Fellini-esque with the mysterious dream, the staged reality of Linear Valley like a sit com. As I write this, there has actually been a new version cut, mixed and screened at the Toronto

Film Festival and at South By Southwest and it will hopefully be available soon on everyone's smart tv or cell phone. It's a funny musical and I think it's great. But, don't just take my word for it:

Neil Young's 1982 film *Human Highway* is a comedy, a hallucination, an environmental statement, and a few hundred other things that don't have names. Evie Nagy @ Fastcompany.com

In *Human Highway*, glowing red flies, an owl, radioactive garbagemen, Booji Boy, a dream sequence, a singing waitress, sausage disputes and more, figure into a tale about a group of small-town oddballs in Linear Valley who work at a gas station/diner not far from a nuclear power plant. The one-day adventure is surreal, absurd, slapstick, musical and cryptically ominous. Billboard.com

In *Human Highway*, Neil Young takes a giant step toward becoming the first popular music artist to successfully cross over into film and use cinema as another mode of self-expression.
Mike Thomas, San Diego Union

Chapter Seventeen

Love and Marriage

The '70s were coming to an end and it already was a controversial decade with pundits declaring that the music was terrible, the promises of the '60s dead, the Viet Nam War, a disgrace, national politics, mundane, with ineffectual leaders like Jerry Ford and Jimmy Carter at the helm. Where was everyone? There were things to protest and the streets were empty. Well, look to the "Me Generation", which had to be one of the least understood and most criticized times of our lives. Here's what it was and it all started with one sentence: If I can't change the world, I can at least change myself.

A war was stopped, not on the battlefield but in the streets of cities across the country, at great cost to the people who put themselves in jeopardy, plus the huge number of casualties in Viet Nam. Millions!

People here were burned out, needed a breather, time to step back and think about what they'd been doing. They knew that the world was better for all that shouting and demonstrating, that there had been a hand-off of the power from a patriarchal old guard to a new generation. But, then what? Now that we had what we wanted, what do we do with it? The answer, my friend, is blowing in the wind but it's also waiting in your psyche to be discovered. You just needed to be quiet, sit on a mountain top or by the side of a quiet stream, and think or better yet, don't think. Your brain works better when you give it a rest.

I'd taken the time in the early '70s to read, learn, listen to the gurus or spiritual leaders, philosophers, poets, songwriters, anyone who was seeking. Krishnamurti was the main one I read and listened to but I did a workshop with Pir Vilayat Khan, a sufi master, went to Manly P. Hall's Philosophical Research Society for lectures, to Spiritual Fairs that touted New Age discoveries and presented Elisabeth Kubler-Ross or Buckminster Fuller, who talked to us from their vast worldly experience and perspective. I didn't think it was a silk purse out of a pig's ear attitude, I took it seriously. How can you make a shift? John Lennon had some answers and it only took Imagination. If you can think of it, it will be. Maya.

Politically, philosophically, the aura of the '60s and it's residue in the '70s, came to a gasping, throat-clenching finish with the election in 1980 of Ronald Reagan. The Liberal left had not lived up to it's promise or we figured there was better stuff to do outside of politics. Many of the best and brightest went back to the land, to clear the fields as much as their heads. The aspect of working small, in the neighborhood, the town or school, made sense. It was hard to get everyone on the same page, so why not settle for a few sentences at a time.

The Republicans came storming in with tons of money and a man who had been a middling Hollywood star, who appealed to a whole class of people who were mad as hell and weren't gonna take it from us anymore. In L.A., we knew the back story, how Ronnie had been President of the leftist Screen Actors Guild then switched horses and testified against other Guild members before the House Un-American Activities Committee. The joke about Ronnie had been that he was never the lead, he was the lead actor's best friend. Now, he was the right wing's best friend and he got rewarded for it. He got Nancy scratched from the list of suspected communists in Hollywood. He was rescued from the graveyard of his movie career and made a TV spokesman for General Electric. He gave patriotic speeches, acquired a Kitchen Cabinet of rich industrialist friends, built a crack political team and became Governor of California. It took him a while to get to the White House but the first thing

Reagan did as President was fire all the air traffic controllers gutting their union negotiations, a turncoat all the way. The voters who elected Reagan supported him against the strikers and loved how decisive he was as opposed to President Carter. Obviously, they had forgotten about Carter's Camp David Accord which brought a kind of peace to the Middle East with Anwar Sadat and Menachem Begin agreeing to cooperate. Middle East peace? Hey, no big deal.

The new decade started and I was making another change. I had found a house in the hills of Sherman Oaks that overlooked the San Fernando Valley. It was above the street on two lots, with many mature eucalyptus and evergreen trees, places for gardens and a lawn. Steve had been in India with his father and arrived home just in time to vote for his brother, Cary, who was running for Congress against Bob Dornan, a rabid conservative who unfortunately won. We left the late-night post-election party once Cary had conceded defeat and I asked Steve if he wanted to drive up and see this place. We looked through the windows with a flashlight and he liked it, our love-nest-to-be.

The rent was reasonable, $800 a month, for this two bedroom cozy cottage. We took the place and once I was finished with the film production, we moved in. Larry thought I was nuts as did several other friends who never got Steve, but he was a gentle man and a gentleman. I liked getting domestic again, putting in a garden, cooking, hanging out at home or having nice dinners out at neighborhood spots. I had banked my production money and sharing expenses with Steve bought me time to figure out what was next.

I had an idea for a script and it was based on the story I'd heard in Mission, Texas about the crazy brothers running drugs and I spent some weeks banging out a treatment then a screenplay. I found I liked the work, being solitary, smoking a joint and letting myself become the different characters in the story.

Ben Johnson, Jeanne & Steve

Steve and I had a standing tennis and lunch date with his dad on Sunday at the family house that sat on several acres in Holmby Hills. Veronique, Gregory's wife, was a beautiful, sophisticated French woman with whom he'd had two kids. They were going to college, living elsewhere so we were welcomed there which was good for Steve who was the son of Greta, Gregory's first wife. The Pecks had a circle of friends that included all the greats from his era of working in Hollywood. We played tennis with them, had lunch, swam in the very large pool, all casual and easy. Family was, in the end, all that really counted even for one of filmdom's biggest stars.
Greta also welcomed us in her home at the top Summit Drive in Beverly Hills. Cary and his wife, Cathy, would join us and Greta's friends would drop in for cocktails and dinner. Her Christmas party was an event of the season and again, it was a Hollywood night out.

Steve had made some inroads at Alan Landsburg Productions which had a reality show on television called "In Search Of". They sent him down to Mexico to do a show about Cortez conquering the Aztecs, who thought the Spaniard was the return of Quetzalcoatl, the Plumed Serpent who they deified. Steve called the cameraman he'd worked with on "The Old Gringo" film and the project came together quickly. Guillermo (Memo) Navarro was an up-and-coming D.P. and had a good Mexico City film crew who would do the production. He even offered up his home and so Steve asked if I'd like to come along.

We were there for almost a month and it was the perfect way to get to know Mexico City and all the great archeological and historical sites. We had access to the Tenochtitlan Pyramids, the Archeological Museum, the Plaza Mayor dig, on the days they were closed to the public. We spent a day at the Pyramids when the park was closed, all alone in that huge plaza with the Sun Pyramid at one end facing the Moon Pyramid on the other. Great stone carvings of Quetzalcoatl's head were on the buildings to the side that led down into chambers.

They wanted to shoot in Xochimilco, the floating gardens near the Pyramids, so we rented a small boat, paddled out to meet with the señor whose property they wanted to use. It was a journey through time, back to the 16th century when the floating gardens produced all the fresh food for Moctezuma and his people. It felt like we were traveling in circles but after an hour or so we came to an island and were hailed by the man and his family. We pulled the boat ashore and they had laid out a lunch for us, fresh tortillas, salsas, cold chicken and salads. Memo made the deal and we got back in the boat and paddled back to the car.

I was not working on the film so when production went into high gear I had time to wander around the City, visiting the Tamayo Museum in Chapultepec Park, the centuries-old buildings surrounding the Plaza Mayor where the seat of government is. It

Guillermo Navarro at Teotihuacan

was great to be immersed in this culture that had first captivated me when I started college.

My major at the University of Wisconsin was Political Science with a Latin American Studies minor. I took Spanish and Portuguese, studied the literature, anthropology and history of the countries, but had never been there until my trip in 1967. I had written papers, read books but here I was living in it.

Why Spanish? My advisor was Professor Jim McCamy, whose son, Colin, had been a cut-up in my 5th and 6th grade ballroom dancing class, suggested that my interest in Russian language and history, which I'd studied in high school and was continuing in college, was not politically advantageous in 1960. I was taking Russian lit courses and reading Dostoevsky, Tolstoy, Gogol, Chekhov in their native language. I'd studied Russian history in high school and seen the Eisenstein films, "Potemkin" and the "Ivans 1 & 2". But, he argued, with Mexico our neighbor to the south and Latin America coming into it's own after years of isolation dominated by dictators, maybe that's where I should put my attention.

Indeed, the question really should have been, why study anything that's foreign? But, that's who I was and had been for years, having decided at the early age of seven that I was going to leave Madison. I'm not exactly sure what prompted this brainstorm, but Mom had probably made me leave the skating rink when I was having fun with my friends, tearing around the ice at breakneck speed, playing crack the whip which sent the end person careening into the deep snow bank on the edge. I was mad at her and had that moment of "aha" in the mud room off the kitchen as I was pulling off the many layers we wore during wintertime. I thought, "I don't have to always be here, I can be somewhere else careening to the edge."

When my fifteenth birthday approached, my dad asked me what I wanted and I replied, a foreign intrigue coat, the iconic Burberry raincoat worn by all the clandestine spies in movies like "Casablanca". We were riding in his car, him on the way to work, me to school. He wasn't sure what I was saying and reported to Mom that I wanted a "fortitrigue coat". So, obviously I was caught up in some romantic notion about my future being borderless, exciting, European, Global.

In fact, I did spend time in Spain in 1964, quitting a grand tour of Europe, when I got bored of just traveling and decided to stay in Madrid. This enabled me to get my Spanish up to a fluency which I thought would be important when I got a job in New York City, where I was headed once I returned to the U.S. I stayed in

Madrid for two months, taking a room in an unmarried woman's apartment. A college friend, Sandy Aanes, had done her junior year abroad there and a friend of hers, Carol, was living in Madrid and she connected me with everything I needed. The soltera also rented rooms to two Dutch girls and a French girl so the common language for all of us was Spanish. The rhythm of the day in Madrid was very different from what I was used to, with a late morning start, a large meal at 2pm, followed by siesta or leisure activity. At 5pm, work began again or in my case, it was time to hit the bars with the wonderful tapas, then on to clubs until it was time for the 10:30pm supper. That was followed by more partying, closing the jazz clubs in the middle of the night. I went to the Prado Museum a lot which I loved and out of Madrid to El Escorial, the huge royal residency and La Valle de los Caidos, a memorial to the dictator Franco and the millions of people who died in their 1930's Civil War.

After a few weeks, I figured that if I was going to stay in Spain a while I should get a job. Carol gave me the name of the head of C.E.A., the movie studios outside the city. I went out for an interview and he said an English film was coming in to do production and he'd call me. Winter was coming on and I was really tired of the clothes that I had been carrying around with me since I'd arrived in Europe in September, and they weren't warm enough. I found a tailor and had a red wool coat and some other clothes made, beautifully done, fitting perfectly.

I got into that European casual lifestyle, no pressure, enjoying long conversations with people I met, tasting all the delicious new food. My mom called me, expecting to see me at Christmas time, two weeks away. I was torn. My life was my own for the first time in my life, yet that sentimental side was also telling me I should be there for the holidays. I knew I couldn't count on the film studio job and indeed, my money was running low. I reluctantly said I'd fly home the next week. On that day, the cab was at the curb, my suitcase was packed and the phone rang. The head man at C.E.A. asked if I could come out the next day. The English director, David

Steve in Diego Rivera's studio

Lean, had finally arrived and they were going to begin production on "Dr. Zhivago". I told the man I couldn't, I was going back to Wisconsin. Just think, I would have gotten into the film business that way, working on what became one of my favorite all-time movies. Later in life, this moment made me so aware of the choices we make, many of them everyday, but some become monumental, determining everything else that comes after it.

Steve and I finished our stay in Mexico with a side trip to San Miguel de Allende, north of the City, about four hours. In the mountains, it's a beautiful place, old with windy streets, great restaurants, and popular with world travelers who come to the language and arts institute there. But, all was not well with us. We were now in the second year of our relationship and had yet to find a rhythm that suited both of us. But, we were determined and kept trying.

Back home, my work continued with a music film shoot with Devo and their songs, "Freedom of Choice" "Girl You Want" and "Whip It". This was a new format, way before MTV, the forerunners to music videos. Paul Goldsmith shot them and I produced them. It appealed to me that Devo, is short for "Devolution".

David Cline, "R.D.", showed up at our place with Larry who had moved into the neighborhood with Leslie Morris. This time Leslie and he were pledged to each other and in time they welcomed their kids, Ben and Hannah. R.D. was carrying little black plastic cases and he gave me one. I opened it and it had a keyboard and a screen. At the time, I thought I was very hip because I had an IBM Selectric typewriter that could self-correct with a white ribbon and was really responsive and quick. But this thing in front of me was the next big thing, a laptop computer. RD took out a phone line, connected it to the computer then into my phone jack. He opened a program, the screen came to life, he wrote a message then typed in a number. The computer screeched as it connected, then with a flick of the wrist, he sent the message to Larry who would get it when he got home. We were sending email in 1982. Gee whiz. R.D. had promoted a dozen or so of these machines for all of Neil's people and this was how we could communicate about all the jobs we would have. Cool.

I interviewed for and was hired for a production job on a Rick Springfield full-length film, "The Beat of the Live Drum". The film was to be directed by a new young filmmaker, David Fincher, who'd been working at I.L.M., George Lucas' film studio in Marin County. It was a huge undertaking because the concept included a live in-concert film plus theatrical music videos using plate footage shot with several Mitchell cameras that were used for visual effects. The music videos would punctuate the live performances in the final version of the film and brought the budget up to $1.5 million, an astronomical amount for a music special. I hired cameramen Bob

Elfstrom, David Myers, Hiro Narita, Fred Elmes, Jon Else, Walt Lloyd and Marty Pitts.

As it was Fincher's first film and Springfield was acting the star, it was a clumsy shoot. Fincher hadn't planned for the cameramen to meet with the star to discuss the show so they could get good coverage. All of his attention went to tech stuff like the plates he needed from the Mitchell cameras. We shot in Tempe, AZ in an arena and I kept wondering what I was doing there.

The antidote to this was to do something I really cared about and that would be another shoot with Neil, "Solo Trans", in Dayton, Ohio, that beloved indie director Hal Ashby was going to direct. But this also became a tough shoot for me as lines were being drawn and snorted. Larry had promised the tour lighting designer that he could be the gaffer on the shoot but D.P. Bobby Byrne, who we had worked with on "The Last Waltz", had already hired his usual gaffer. I stuck my foot in it and told the roadie he could work alongside our film crew but he wasn't the boss. He cried all the way to Larry who came screaming into the backstage area and got in my face. He was so over the top and crazy in a way I had never seen before. I stood my ground and he ended up slamming me into the lockers. I couldn't believe it. He was taking out the frustration of a long tour on me and I had made a decision that overrode his. Then, at a pre-production meeting with Neil, I asked if he wanted the people in the audience to be able to be at the edge of the stage hanging on to it like rabid fans, and he said he did. That meant a lower stage than usual. I passed this on to the tour manager but the crew either didn't get this message or ignored it and put up a six-foot stage which then had to be struck to put in the lower one. Again, Johnson was apoplectic, haranguing about women on the road. Hell, I was just doing my f-ing job. And, I thought this was going to be fun.

"Solo Trans", the show, had mutated from a typical Neil Young tour highlighting new songs along with a retrospective of favorites, into another costumed event in the Second Act. It featured the Shocking Pinks, complete with Neil dressed as a '50s rocker in a white suit and his wife Pegi and a few other women on stage singing back up and dancing. Newell Alexander, our friend from the movie "Junior High", was brought on the tour to be a TV commentator breaking into the show at various times to bring newsy backstage updates and an interview with a fictional manager, Vito Toledo, who asks the crowd if they really want to rock and roll. It was a fun show. Hal Ashby arrived in a limo, stood around watching the show, then got back in the limo and that was all she wrote. "Solo Trans" would be released on LaserDisk which everyone thought was going to be the next big thing. You can find bits and pieces on YouTube.

I was beginning to feel like music films were a thing of the past for me. MTV, in it's infancy, was taking the culture by storm. A younger group of filmmakers were cutting their teeth on rock and roll and punk. I really wasn't that interested in these quickies and was wondering whether I'd already done it with "Woodstock", "The Last Waltz", "Rust Never Sleeps" and "Shadows and Light".

I had a Ticking Clock, in my professional life and personal life. Here I was in my late 30's and I wasn't getting pregnant which was the base line of my relationship with Steve. Larry and Leslie had welcomed their firstborn, son Ben, and Larry and I had put our differences to rest. I enjoyed hanging out with them or going to a golf driving range with Larry to hit balls while Ben watched from his bassinet.

I sat down with my gynecologist and discussed my baby-making possibilities. This was in the early days of reproductive surgery and my age was against me, both personally and vis-a-vis the medical field, which wanted to be able to show high success rates. Amy Goodman was my doctor and was personable and professional and, reportedly, at the top of her game. My interest in pursuing a surgical answer to my problem led Amy to suggest the other rhythm efforts used for many years. Count the days from your last period, take your temperature which tells when you're ovulating, then have sex. Steve was game and we tried that for a few months with no luck.

I scheduled a surgical procedure, a laparoscopy, to see what was going on. The results were not promising as she could see that there was a lot of damage from P.I.D., pelvic inflammatory disease, caused by the Dalkon shield I'd had in the early '70s. This IUD had been touted as the best contraceptive device to date. It even looked like the Lunar Landing Module. Unfortunately, it slipped around while inside the wearer and caused infections. The only hope was a very invasive operation with a hip-bone-to-hip-bone incision, during which she would open my fallopian tubes, remove any tumors or cysts and see what shape my ovaries were in. This was a big commitment and Steve and I discussed it thoroughly. He was very intent on having a baby and I was too, but I had to admit that I wished my maternal urge had hit me earlier in life. My eggs were old and not as reliable. The realization that carrying on the genes of my family, procreating and giving my parents grandchildren, was a huge part of my responsibilities to them was only just occurring to me.

It also dawned on me that if I was going to put myself at risk and go to all this trouble, shouldn't I be married to Steve? I broached the subject and he agreed. My mother was ecstatic that I was finally getting married and that Gregory Peck was going to be my father-in-law. She bragged about it all over town.

The operation went off without a hitch and Amy declared that I should be able to get pregnant within a year. The recovery was not too bad. I was slow to move around for about 3 weeks, then was fine and into planning our wedding. We wanted to get out of town for the ceremony and settled on Ojai. The Ranch House Restaurant had a beautiful garden where we said our vows. There were about 75 of us and it was simple but lovely. We honeymooned at the Santa Inez Ranch in Montecito in the same suite Jack and Jackie Kennedy had years ago. And then it was back home and back to work.

Steve and I went to the Banff TV Festival which was honoring his father, flying up with Greg and Veronique. The Canadian Rockies were beautiful, Lake Louise and the historic Banff Springs Hotel a great spot. But, something was wrong. Steve became very distant, shut down, not interested in talking. Back at home, we would go our own ways during the day, have dinner, then find ourselves in bed with not much interest in sex. I wondered what I was doing wrong. I asked him. No answer. Was he bothered by something he could talk about? No, he wasn't. But, in the end, it turned out he was.

Steve had been drafted for the Viet Nam war and had been a lieutenant in an artillery company. They were stationed behind enemy lines, operating the big 105mm guns that would blow apart the jungle, the villages, the enemy wherever they were hiding. In retaliation, the Viet Cong would get them in their sites and out of nowhere a barrage would rain down on them, wounding or killing soldiers in his company. Steve's wounds were invisible but as he crawled further into his shell, it did not bode well for our marriage.

I threw myself into more work, another music film. David Myers had been approached by two young producers from Oakland, Fred Ritzenberg and David Leivick, who wanted to put on a Gospel show at the historic Paramount Theater. They had contacted the top names in that world and it was a rush to get it done. Myers suggested me so I flew up to meet them. We went to the Paramount which was a beautiful old movie palace, restored to it's previous wonder. We didn't need to add much but when they said they wanted to hang a black curtain and shoot the black groups in front of it, I had to put my foot down. I asked Myers if he wouldn't prefer a nice sculpted muslin screen that he could light with rotating colors to get some separation between background and subject. He agreed and I called Ernst van der Bovenkamp who could do it in a week, using a stretch cream colored fabric that could be attached to a metal structure.

I hired Amanda to work with me on the production and Myers brought in Chuck Minsky, John Toll and several more operators. Amanda and I stayed at her house in San Francisco and one night Chuck was tagging along. I offered to drive and the two of them climbed into the back seat and necked all the way home. They married a few years later and had three kids proving that some location romances work!

The shoot was a good day's work as James Cleveland, Shirley Caesar, The Mighty Clouds of Joy came onto the stage, one after the other, hours of great music, captured like it never had been before. Ernst's scrim was shaped like a cathedral, sweeping across the back of the stage up to a peak then down to the other side. Myers worked with the same gaffer we'd used on "Human Highway" and "Uforia", Mel Maxwell, and got great colors that coordinated with the suits and dresses of the performers, James Cleveland in a dark red suit, the Clark Sisters, huge women in chiffon. These people dressed up when they performed not like the rockers I was used to.

Joni Mitchell was returning home from a six month world tour with her band, led by Larry Klein, who was also her boyfriend. He'd put together a rocking sound and they wanted to do a video for "Refuge of the Roads." L.A. Johnson was busy with Neil so I was asked to produce it. I was thrilled to get this one. We rented a stage at Culver Studios, brought in the backdrop from the show, a San Francisco video truck, couches for a small audience and shot the show over two days. Jordan Cronenweth was our Director of Photography and at the time was one of the hottest cinematographers in town. As we were loading in, Jordan and Joni's lighting designer began to discuss how to set the lights and they were of two different opinions. For the show, they used front lights. For the video, Jordan wanted to backlight Joni, with fill from the front. It was war. Joni's crew was exhausted from the tour and didn't want a bunch of filmies telling them how to do their job. I had to step in and tell them they were no longer in charge. Joni's manager, Elliot, would disappear at these tense times only to bark at me later when he'd hear the grumbling. I had two roadies I'd worked with as my crew and they were helpful in leveling the playing field.

We had another problem. The synching device on the truck was unreliable, causing the audio to waver in relation to the picture. The techies worked to get the 60 cycle pulse, the SMPTE code, laid down on both tracks. Ultimately, it would fall to the post-production team to make it right and we ended up jam-synching everything, a costly mistake for the video company.

Norm Levy of San Francisco was hired to edit the show with Joni and lived at her house for months working with her. As a song would be cut, Joni would ask for images to illustrate the piece. I worked with them and enjoyed the creative input I had. For a song called "Beggar's Banquet", I remembered Luis Bunuel's film "Viridiana" which had a great scene of beggars breaking into a rich man's house, ravaging the laden table of all it's food then striking a "Last Supper" pose. For another song, "Wild Things Run Fast", I brought in a French short, "Dream of Wild Horses" that was shot in the seaside area of the Camargue in southern France which had been set afire. It's dramatic, almost violent imagery as the white horse race through the flames. The one-hour video turned out beautifully with Joni closing the show with an acoustic version of her song "Woodstock".

"The Horse Dealer's Daughter" was a D.H. Lawrence short story about the responsibility a person has if he saves someone's life. I loved Lawrence's work, had been to his mausoleum in Taos, and at one point had tried to get the rights to one of his novels only to learn that one man in England had tied them all up. Kathryn Butterfield told me about a friend of hers, Bob Burgos, who was getting his degree in directing at the American Film Institute and had gotten the rights to the Lawrence short story for a film adaptation. He was having trouble raising money, didn't have a producer and time was running out. I met with Bob, read his script and signed on.

We had just a few months to get $17,000 together which would be matched by AFI for a total budget of $34,000. Ours was a period piece which also posed a location problem, not to mention costumes, animals and the right cast. I made some calls to people I knew who cared about film and one of these was Dale Djerassi, who I had first met when I lived on Neil's ranch in 1972. I would see him on The Hill when we'd all venture off the ranch to hit the bars and restaurants. Dale's father, Carl, was a Stanford chemistry professor and researcher and he and a few of his colleagues had done all of us a huge favor by inventing the birth control pill. Of course, it also made them wealthy, with an income stream that would continue as long as women took the pill. Can you say the phrase "ad infinitum"? The Djerassis had the SMIP Ranch above Neil's property, the initials for "Sic Manebimus In Pace", which is "Thus we shall remain in peace." It was a good thought and we all embraced it as we drove down the road to the ranch which had views forever, winding through the dramatic barren hillsides, draped with clouds blown in from the Pacific.

I described what I needed and a week later, a large check arrived from Dale and his mother, Norma. With that in hand, Bob and I were able to parlay small increments from friends. Film director, Robert Wise, was the AFI Senior Advisor and had insulted us at an early meeting, challenging that we were the only ones who probably would not get our budget. It was with real pride that Bob and I announced we were in pre-production. I was able to get the Disney Ranch out in Santa Clarita again defying the predictions of the AFI staff. It had turned out that an earlier AFI student had left a gate open, which allowed the vicious dogs that protected the property to get out and run havoc all over the area. I kept talking to the man at Disney and told him I wasn't a student, I had experience, etc. We shot out there for two weeks and the film went on to win prizes at film festivals. It played on A&E for three years, becoming one of the most financially successful AFI short films.

It was now almost a year since my surgery and I was failing at my attempts to conceive. My doctor gave me the names of a few lawyers who helped with adoptions and I brought the list home to talk with Steve. On Valentine's Day, we joined another couple for a romantic dinner at a restaurant. The next morning, waking up, I wrapped my arms around my husband and felt him draw away. I asked what was wrong. His reply was that he wanted a divorce. "Can we discuss this?", I asked. "No." No couple's therapy, no "let's take some time and think about this." He was gone in 3 weeks, taking a friend's small apartment while she was on location.

I immersed myself in finishing up Joni's video. It was beautiful and I was really proud of it. Maybe this was the time to make the change, move out of music films and videos and into films with stories, documentaries or features, for television or film. But, try as I might, my lack of self-confidence, my sadness, my failure, didn't allow me to get traction on anything. Here I was, in a house I couldn't afford by myself, running through the money I'd made producing with Joni, miserable, unloved, and even blamed by my own mother for the break up of my marriage. When she said that, I realized she'd lost face with her country club friends who would never ever meet Gregory Peck.

I wallowed, I ran miles and miles trying to race ahead of the misery. It literally was the worst time of my life. You can't pitch a project if you don't have the confidence, walking into the office of the money guy who's going to say "Yes." How was I going to keep my house, maintain a lifestyle, regain any composure that made me feel worthwhile? Friends helped but we all know that it has to come from within.

Chapter Eighteen

And So It Goes

Strength and renewal can also come from a change of scenery and that was provided by Dale Djerassi who had an idea for a film and would I be interested. It was another music film but also had a great story. Flora Purim was a Brazilian jazz artist with a six-octave range who had come to New York with her husband Airto, a brilliant percussionist. She had tremendous success in the clubs there then was busted for being a drug mule, did time in jail, got out and was rebuilding her career in Los Angeles. There was a book about Flora written by an ex-con writer, Edward Bunker, but Dale and his partner, Isabel Maxwell, wanted to start from scratch and get Flora's story from her. We would all stay at Dale's house and tape record everything, then get a script and shoot the movie. I was in.

I drove back up to Woodside and breathed a sigh of relief. There was always an embrace that I felt from this land. We all worked hard, getting up early, Flora would tell her stories, Airto would punctuate with his, and within a week we had a good idea of what we wanted to do and how to tell the story. We were celebrating this when Dale and Isabel said they were pregnant and getting married. What a great thing for both of them. It would also mean a delay in moving ahead with writing a script or hiring a writer to do it. I headed back home to contemplate the immediate future.

Dale called a few weeks later and said they were married. They'd just done it the easy way but we're now indebted to go back to England and have a big party. They were also going to honeymoon in France and did I want to come. I accepted and made plans to get to England. Betsy Heimann had married an English bloke, a special effects guy she'd met on a film, and was living outside of London. I spent a nice time with her, walking through rhododendron forests which were in their springtime prime. Betsy had helped me in Ojai as I dressed for my wedding to Steve and I shared my pain with her. I was trying to keep my grief in check but in truth, I was very depressed. I was now in my forties, newly separated, no children, and looking at these English flowering plants with huge colorful blossoms, dripping with dew, I felt incredibly barren. I knew I would never have a son or daughter to raise and love, know the challenges, defeats and triumphs of parenthood. I was a single woman living a singular life. And, I was trying to make the best of it.

I took the train up to Oxford where the Maxwells lived at Headington Hill Hall and where I'd be staying. It was a huge mansion, historic, sitting on a hill overlooking the towers of Oxford University. Oscar Wilde had partied there. Isabel's father was well-known in England, a publisher, journalist, raconteur, member of Parliament, with a questionable past which possibly changed depending on who he was talking to. Was he the "bouncing Czech" tycoon, a spy for the Mossad, the Gregory Peck of England? Depends. He'd met Carl Djerassi through his company, Pergamon Press, which published scientific papers from all corners of the earth, his attempt to make sure friends, enemies and frenemies kept talking through crises rather than go to war. He had lost all of his family in the Nazi camps and it had scarred him and his large family. The Peck connection came from the fact that he had married a pretty French woman, Betty, so all the kids were bi-lingual and had many relatives in France. He had thick black hair and eyebrows and was tall. Betty was refined and devoted to her many children, and welcomed me to their home, a refugee from the American Pecks.

In no time, many friends from California were with us for dinners around town, a day trip to Stonehenge and the near-by

Avebury, punting on the Cherwell River, then the big party in a tent on the lawn. Champagne for all, including leaders of the Labor Party, an ex-Prime Minister, Harold Wilson, Isabel's brothers, including the handsome Ian, who despite our age differences, seemed interested. He mentioned that he was driving Dale and Isabel on their honeymoon and heard I'd be along for the ride. Yes? That was the plan.

The honeymoon trip was going to be a meandering journey from aunts to friends to cousins to artists, staying in great places, seeing a few sites. We'd be leaving in a week as Isabel needed some time to recover, her pregnancy being a little difficult.

I didn't feel right just hanging around Oxford and mentioned that to a tablemate at the party. He said he had a flat in Chelsea and wouldn't be there, would I like it. That seemed perfect. An old friend was also in London working, Chris Hodenfield, and we could hang out and he would be just what the doctor ordered. The next morning, I hugged Dale and Isabel, made plans to meet up with them in Southampton to catch the boat to France, and took the train back to London. The Chelsea digs were an old stable that had been converted into living quarters and were on a quiet street but near everything, Hyde Park, the Tate, the Thames, Natural History Museum, the V & A. I walked everywhere, caught up with Chris and spent a great day in Hyde Park, rowing on the Serpentine. We still liked each other a lot and he made me feel like my old self again.

The regeneration continued in France, where we stayed with Betty's sister who had a small hospital in Maison Lafitte, near Versailles. Ian and I ducked out of there one night to go into Paris where his father had an apartment near the Sorbonne. We partied at a Cuban night club closing it near dawn then fell into bed to catch a little sleep before we met up with Dale and Isabel. They said we needed to be at their cousins for dinner. Where was that, I asked. It's in the Rhone valley, five hundred miles south. And that's for dinner? It was now noon. No problem, said Ian and I swear he went 130mph the whole way. We arrived as the sun was setting over the apricot orchards the cousins owned and their table was set and dinner was served.

The itinerary continued and included several days in Grasse, known for the perfumes they produce, where we stayed with two artist friends of Betty's who'd also been at the party in Oxford. From there, we hit the casinos in Monaco and a visit to a yacht in Cannes that Mr. Maxwell wanted to buy for $7million. Lunch followed at the Hotel du Cap and a visit to the Picasso Museum. On the road again, we saw Avignon then the walled city of Carcassonne where we stayed at a beautiful little hotel near by. We walked up to the old town at night, much quieter now as the tourist hordes had moved on. Being in an ancient town, one that was first fortified in 100 B.C., gave a perspective on my life and how insignificant our short time on earth really is. Steve Peck didn't think I was worth his time on earth. So be it. I was on my way to neutral on my emotional gauge, not so raw, bruised and used.

We drove on to Biarritz to a cousin's place in the country, a peaceful compound around a gravel courtyard where we played Petanque, the French version of Bocce ball, for hours with our hosts. Then we were served the best foie gras I'd ever had. Isabel's cousin lived near a farm where the geese were forced fed and humanely killed. She knew these birds and believed that this was the reason her pate was so excellent.

On that note, I flew back to Paris, then on to New York where I stayed with Beverly Ross who had been John Binder's girlfriend a few years before. It was a nice prelude to the first movement of returning to Los Angeles and an undetermined life.

Home again, I faced the fact that I had to take a job, but where? Jane Zingale, who I'd known from freshman year college, was working with a successful catering company, Ambrosia, and they needed someone in the kitchen. Really, go back to the food business? At the moment, it seemed like my only choice and it would be a place to go everyday, get out of the house, bury myself in pots and pans and other people's parties.

I also did some volunteer work with an NGO called Office of the Americas. Blaise Bonpaine and his wife, Teresa, were liberation theologists who worked in Central America to squelch the power of the right-wing dictatorships. On the days I wasn't slamming food together, the salmon mousses, guacamole tortes, chocolate-covered strawberries, or turkey and kale salad, I'd go and do some good for the campasinos in Guatemala and El Salvador.

Another friend however, was in worse shape than I. Charlotte was in the hospital, a malnourished alcoholic who had nearly been done in by her own hand. Here we were, golden girls of the '70s and at the bottom of the pit. Char had a business manager, Sid, who was flamboyantly gay, handsome, southern and brilliant. A lot of us had him do our tax returns but he ran Char's business. She'd made good money over the years on "Little House on the Prairie" and other TV shows, commercials, and had bought a house in Beachwood. Now, her marriage to Jordan had recently collapsed and she'd grown out of the starlet age in Hollywood. Sid had come upon hard times or hard living and had been dipping into the accounts of his clients. He ruined her, lost her house and did real damage to several other friends of ours, including John Binder, who had tried to buy some land only to realize $60,000 wasn't available because Sid had spent it.

I went to visit Char in the hospital where she'd been for two months. That seemed a little long for rehab but it turned out her doctor wouldn't let her leave just to go back to the little cottage where the drinking had done her in. I had an answer for that. She would move in with me. Once again, we were roomies. It brought back all those memories: Char giving Larry and me her apartment in 1970 before we moved to Jim Morrison's house; me moving into Observation Drive after I left Everybody's Mother; me living with Char in Hollywood on Gower while I found my Beachwood place;

now I could be there for her. I called Steve and asked that he get all his stuff out to make room for Charlotte's belongings.

One day I walked into the Ambrosia kitchen which was on Ocean Avenue in Santa Monica. It was a horrible place that used to be a small restaurant. The walk-in was down some narrow stairs in a smelly basement and it was not conducive to creative cooking. The proof of that was the chef sitting on the floor crying. I asked if I could help and she looked at me and said, "Yeah, take over," and walked out. There was another cook there and he quit too which left me in charge. I could barely handle the cooking load, when I learned that the owners, Carl Bendix and David Corwin, had found a new kitchen and we had to pack up and move.

This turned out to be a great change because we were moving to a huge industrial kitchen at the former Hughes Aircraft Company on Washington Blvd., just east of Lincoln. With this big step up came a new head chef, Roland Stephens, an Englishman, trained to cook for huge events and the personality to handle anyone from the dishwasher to the wealthy client. The work took on a very different tone, professional, clean, inventive and fun. Our kitchen crew, all Mexican, really got in step and they were the ones who really did a lot of the work, whether it was the tried and true recipes that were Ambrosia's calling cards or the new ones we came up with.

In the mid-'80s, Los Angeles was going through a culinary renaissance, kicked off by Wolfgang Puck, who became an industry once he left Ma Maison. This brought in more chefs from around the globe and fusion was the name of the game, using touches of French, Japanese, Thai, Italian, Spanish, etc. in everything. There was also a ton of money around which could support expensive restaurants. We heard that at Harvard, professors told their M.B.A. students that there were two places they could earn a lot of money. One was Wall Street, the other was Hollywood. The influx of these business guys, who knew bottom line but nothing about story is, well, another story. But, the resulting restaurants, hotels, resorts and clubs turned parochial Los Angeles into a world class dining destination.

My cooking skills, which had gotten stronger as I became more domestic with Steve, took off and ascended to another level. I was working with Culinary Institute-trained chefs and keeping up with them. I learned it's all about your palette. You can have the greatest technique, a book full of recipes, but if your taste buds are dull or have a proclivity to one taste over the complex blend, your food will not inspire. It's all about timing too, how long to cook, how long to let it rest and meld. The finer points were entering my repertoire. But, I think one of the chief reasons I kept my job there was my approach to kitchen psychology, keeping the vibe on an even keel as we did huge events or small intimate dinner parties. Running a crew is basically the same regardless of product, dinner or video or film. Making sure egos aren't bruised or personality conflicts don't take center stage became a big part of my job. I also helped Roland with the ordering, getting to know our suppliers for the staples but also for the special items that make a meal a fine memory.

Remember when Dennis Hopper cut Sally Kirkland? I got a call from Elliot Roberts that she was suing Neil and his company. It was a day or so before the statute of limitations ran out. I said I'd handle the insurance broker and her lawyers and keep Neil out of it. Besides, there was one person on our crew who would tell the wrong story and I wanted to be sure they were not on the witness list. As usual, the haggling dragged on longer than necessary and eventually the case was thrown out of court.

Bruce Springsteen came to town. I had loved him and his music, in fact the whole band, ever since Bill Murray and I had caught him at the Santa Monica Civic. He was playing five nights at the Sports Arena at USC, a terrible place for music acoustically, but it packed everyone in close for a dynamic show. I had to go. The tickets were sold out. I called a friend, Debby, who was a film account, and she had a friend at Ticketmaster. She would work something out. She scored two cheap tickets and when we got there we knew why. They were in the last row, the worst seats in the house. But Bruce's four hour concert was worth it and we loved every minute.

The next day, I got a call from Tim Mulligan who was in town doing some Neil business and had a friend on Bruce's crew. He knew I loved Bruce and asked if I'd like to go with him and a few friends, gratis with the roadie comps. We had great seats, in the loge, on the side. Another fabulous Bruce evening.

The next day, Elliot called. Neil and Pegi were in town and had never seen Bruce. Did I want to join them? Of course, I didn't admit that I'd seen the show and of course, I went. I met them at the very exclusive hotel they stayed in when visiting LA. We rode in a limo to the Arena, driving into it down the ramp, into the bowels of the place, and walked to our perfect seats. At intermission, Bruce's guy came up to Neil and asked us to follow him backstage. He showed Neil, Pegi and me into the dressing room and the three of us spent the whole time alone with Bruce. He and Neil discussed how they treated their vocal chords doing back-to-back shows in drafty arenas. In fact, Bruce sat over a steam inhaler while we talked. His roadie gave us notice that time was up and we got up to go, hugs all around. As we left through the door, we had to go past a well-dressed woman who obviously had been waiting all the while we talked. It was Elizabeth Taylor. Oh, Hi Liz, sorry to keep you waiting.

Dale and Isabel called. Their son, Alexander, had been born and they were in town to see Flora and Airto who were going to be playing at the Long Beach Jazz Festival which was held at the Queen Mary pier. We all had to get together to continue our work on the Flora story. Isabel was all jazzed out with a bright blue aluminum wig and very sexy clothes, quite a change from the vedy English lady she usually was. Dale was his usual high-energy self and we drove down to Long Beach. Flora and Airto did a great show, with her amazing vocals and his percussion adventures, and the crowd loved them. We got great energy from seeing them. Miles Davis was next. Impulsively, I got out of my seat and went backstage, courtesy of the pass that Flora had given each of us. I had remembered that Miles, known as the "Human Question Mark", didn't always play to the audience. It was empty behind the stage and I chose a spot stage left of the drummer. The band walked out, took their places, and Miles turned to me, or to the spot I was standing, and started to play. He was in his own creative world and I, aware of an artist's sightline, knowing that it can be disturbed by movement or intensity, stayed cool and so did Miles.

It was moments like these that got me out of myself and my complete disappointment that I had not gotten everything in life that I wanted and expected. I had been humiliated and being disposed of in such a perfunctory manner was a hard one to overcome.

I stayed on top of the Flora project, wanting to go to the next step, hoping that Dale would be willing to pay for a writer to get a first draft screenplay. His life with Isabel and a new baby was complicated and as he didn't have an economic imperative to keep it moving, it was pushed to the side. Eventually, he called and said he had found a script called "68" about an immigrant coming to America during that tumultuous time. I read it and wasn't that crazy about it, at least to the point that I wanted to be part of the production team. I elected to stay where I was and kept working at Ambrosia.

I heard through the grapevine that John Binder's marriage was breaking up. Chris had wanted to get pregnant and didn't take John's vasectomy that seriously, thinking she could convince him to have it reversed. That was one issue, the other being that she did not really get along with his two sons, Joshua and John Henry, who had moved to California to live with their dad. There were lots of stories about the arguments, the fights, the thrown kitchen pots that I'll leave up to John to retell if he ever cares to. What interested me most was that she had gotten a new job and was in New York buying clothes for it. We all know from reading Henry David Thoreau's quote on the box of Celestial Seasonings tea, "Beware of all enterprises that require new clothes" that this did not bode well for her. I've always hated dishing the dirt, but Chris was one of those women who corralled their man once they'd caught him, pushing away old friends, especially female ones, so they could have him all to themselves, and control their social life. John was an old friend of mine, we'd worked together since the late '60s. I knew his kids from the time they were very young. During the last two years, I'd called him and never heard back. I missed my friend.

This time, I picked up the phone and he answered. I gave my sympathies for his present situation then asked if he had plans for Saturday. He didn't. Good, I said, I'm picking you up at 8am and we're driving up to Ojai to hear Krishnamurti at the Oak Grove.

John was exhausted from the months-long battles with his wife and the final decision that they would divorce. We had a leisurely drive up the coast, into the Ojai valley, parked and found our places on the ground amongst the crowd. We were both quiet, took in the lecture, then drove into town for lunch. We hung out at a café, talking up a storm about our lives, our marriages, our work. It was so good to have my friend back.

My life had settled into a pattern of work in the Ambrosia kitchen, life at home with Charlotte, our pets, my gardening, all a struggle on a reduced level due to the low pay I was earning, $9 an hour. Char worked for a couple who were very wealthy Hollywood producers doing office work for them. They were nice to her but didn't pay her much either. But we got by and didn't feel the need to party, go out that much, which helped our slow healing. Larry and Leslie were near by, other friends too, but we were captured by our own little lives, making ends meet. And, this was okay.

The film business seemed very far away. The closest I got to it was catering parties for people in the business. A friend worked for a successful executive who wanted to do a July 4th party but have it be low key, like it wasn't catered. Could I do it at his beach house in Malibu? I could and suggested that I would arrive with help and we'd just be part of the party, no uniforms or tray-passed hors d'oeuvres, just make the food, put it out for people to eat casually. I'd just come up with a way to do a whole salmon which I stuffed with onions, herbs, tomatoes, lemon juice, then wrapped in banana leaves and chicken wire and threw on the grill. We had lots of side dishes and it was a huge hit. The problem was that I knew more people at the party than the host did and they kept asking how was I and what was I doing. Thank god, I wasn't in chef's attire so I could bullshit them about all the fabulous projects I had going. Once the food was on the table I left the clean-up to my proficient assistants and fled. I never went back to a party again, always preferring to do the cooking at our kitchen and sending it out. I couldn't admit I was washed up and out of the film business.

Well, not quite. John called and said that there was interest in "UFOria" and he was talking with Universal about distribution and I said I'd help in any way. He seemed glad to have a sounding board especially as he was in the throes of moving, settling into a new place, keeping the boys busy, writing a script, ending a marriage. He would call on occasion to give me updates and we could commiserate on the entanglements of love gone bad. In my case, Steve and his wife, the mother of his child. Surprising, yes??! Steve had met and married already and only fifteen months had gone by since our split. She was an artist and maybe having postpartum problems, because she called me several times to tell me to stop calling them. Why on earth would I call them? It certainly wasn't my style. She barely believed me but that was her problem.

In August, the Los Angeles County Fair opened in Pomona and I thought it would be fun to go. I called John and said I was going with my friend Amanda who was now living with Chuck in L.A. Did he want to join us? The three of us headed out in the early afternoon to take in the animal barn and all the Crafts displays. We ate the usual junk food then hit a few rides before we were going to drive back to town. We got on one ride that was a round frame with benches hung off it. The operator was a sleazy-looking skinny guy with long hair, tattoos and an evil smile. The three of us sat down, John at the end, then me, then Amanda. The ride started slow then picked up speed and the bench flew up in the air sideways. I slid into John and Amanda slid into me, which it was probably designed for. The ride went on forever. Just when I thought we were slowing down, the evil-looking carny goosed it. Yow! I was getting nauseous. Excuse the graphic description but snot was flying out of my nose, saliva out of my mouth. Amanda and John were leaking too so when we finally stopped and fell off the bench we were a mess. We looked at each other and broke down further, laughing so hard we couldn't breathe. We'd been had and it was hilarious.

A few weeks later, Phoebe Larmore called and said she was having a dinner party and would I like to bring someone and come. She was thrilled when I suggested John. She was an old friend of his as well and had also been cut off during his marriage. She was more than surprised when she realized that there was something going on between us which hadn't quite defined itself but was surprising us as well. After dinner, we stayed at the table talking, telling stories and John began to relate how he'd had a dream of me years ago, sometime in the early '70s, and that I was his companion. Phoebe and I looked at each other, questioning.

Later, I took her aside and added that we had spent the night together one time when I was living at the Rodeo Grounds, separated from Larry. John would come over to wash his car, a hot Chevy that he roared around in collecting speeding tickets, and we'd have a beer or smoke a joint, maybe go to dinner. He was still seeing Sarah Kernochan and probably a few other babes as well. I was on the loose and miserable and one thing, alcohol, led to another, marijuana, and we fell into bed. I was very interested at the time but didn't think I could keep him, hold him, make him true to me. So, it was a one-night stand, something that wouldn't compromise our friendship which I cherished. This was always a dilemma when we're attracted to someone. Should we take a chance to kiss, to explore what else a friendship can be, risking failure and the friendship? One question I've often asked single friends who are lonely and looking, was "Who's your friend?" Will you, could you see them as a romantic partner? Do you dare?

I dared! And on July 4th, Independence Day, we had that kiss. When two old friends, look deeply at each other, and lean forward, not for a peck on the cheek, but a real liplock, it's like a rolling earthquake roaring over the mountain. Fireworks for real. But, we both still held things close, not wanting to get carried away like a couple of twenty-somethings.

Sliding into this new relationship, every Wednesday and Saturday, I'd leave Ambrosia and drive up to 26th Street and Montana Avenue where there was a pay phone on the corner next to the Brentwood Art Center. I'd put in my dime and call Binder. We'd talk a bit and I'd say I was down the street, what was going on? He'd say, "Come up." And, I did. Josh and John Henry were now grown boys, Josh ready to start at UCLA, John Henry would be in his first year at Palisades High. Dennis Hill, good friend and an editor for Altman, lived in the downstairs room and his teenage kids, Erin, Devon and Jimmy, were also there and occupied guest bedrooms in the house. It was summer camp, with a pool table in the dining room, bar-b-ques by Dennis who'd been a cook and then a warrior in Viet Nam. The house was a magnet for friends and family. It was overwhelming at times and hard to find the quiet room to figure out what exactly John and I were doing. Or, maybe it was just as well that we didn't over-think our growing attraction to each other and just let it take its course.

In late August, John invited me to go on a rafting trip on the American River, I knew we were reaching a destiny. We were both wounded from difficult marriages, ones we had put so much faith in. Would it be possible to create a new ideal that involved love, respect, space, inclusion in Los Angeles, home of the non-stop parade of gorgeous, available people? Was it even desirable? I have always had lots of single friends who live lovely lives, who aren't partner people, preferring to not have to ask permission, adapt to the baggage everyone carries, sleeping alone most of the time, having casual relationships on occasion, friendships with benefits. I was just beginning to feel normal again which takes a while after you split up with your significant, or less-so, other. All the little shifts to the left or right, the slowing down, speeding up alterations I had made over the past five years to adjust to Steve were now in the past. At age forty-two, perhaps I was just the person I was always meant to be and should take more time to explore her, find out what she really wanted and needed. I could ask my mother, as she was still sick at heart about my divorce. It had taken me forty years to get married and it was eleven months and out. So, don't ask my mother. At my age, it was my decision. Or, John's.

John had a house at the top of Mandeville Canyon. When his marriage ended, he drove to the top of every canyon in west L.A., looking for another place to hide. He had previously lived on the beach in Malibu when he'd first come to Los Angeles in the early '70s. It was cheap, with one large living/kitchen, two bedrooms, bath and a nice big deck facing the ocean, a perfect place to write and just big enough to accommodate Josh and John Henry who would come for the summers.

The boys were eight and five when they first came out from New York where Sharon was still living. John Henry was full of beans and couldn't understand why John would sit there typing all the time when they should be out on the beach having fun, playing ball or splashing in the waves. John Henry was a persistent little fellow. His dad ignored him as long as possible but finally reaching his boiling point one day, he jumped off his stool and threatened to throw the kid off the deck if he didn't shut up and go read a book. John Henry was terrified, of course, as any child would be. Josh immediately jumped in to console his little brother, explaining that his dad was kidding and wouldn't really do such a terrible thing. Josh, a kid who'd been forced into a father's role by John's absence, then turned to his dad like an adult and explained that John Henry hardly knew him and that it would take some time for the five year old to know when his father was kidding. John was mortified at his own stupidity and knew that it would take him some time to get up to speed on this fatherhood thing. Then they went on to have a phenomenal summer.

When John first arrived in southern California, he had gotten in touch with a woman he'd known in Ohio, a friend of Sharon's, who was now working with filmmaker Robert Altman. Scotty was a tough girl, no nonsense, who started out in costuming and casting then became Bob's producer and lioness at the gate of Lions Gate, Bob's company. Very few got past her. John had written a script on George Washington that Scotty admired and felt he had the credentials and creativity to become part of their team. Bob hired John to write an adaptation of "North Dallas Forty" and he cracked the code of the book, finding the threads that made a great movie. True to Hollywood Snakes and Ladders, Bob was kicked off the project, the script was cut and pasted with the work of subsequent writers by a producer who took John's name off the title page and put his own on it along with the novel writer's, Peter Gent.

Before "North Dallas" was to be made, Bob was in pre-production on an Alan Rudolph script, "Buffalo Bill or Sitting Bull's History Lesson". Bob offered John the job of Script Clerk on the film, saying this would be the worst job he would ever have and he'd hate him for it. But, John would learn more about making a movie than he'd ever learned in his life. This job entailed "holding script" for the director, keeping him informed of details as he needed them, doing continuity noting of the actor's movements and gestures for matching in the cutting process, logging and describing each camera take for the film editors, noting the director's opinion of the best takes, keeping track as well as possible of all the improvisation that is the meat of an Altman project, and selecting which takes to show for the screening of the "rushes" or "dailies" from the previous day's shoot so Bob and the actors could evaluate their work in progress. It was, as promised the worse job of his life, and one of the best, reading lines with Burt Lancaster and Paul Newman in the morning, laughing on set with Newman and his endless pranks.

The job opened doors in Hollywood. With the "North Dallas Forty" script and others he'd written, John landed one of the big agents in town, Jeff Berg at ICM. Jeff got him a job writing the shooting version of the Willie Nelson feature "Honeysuckle Rose". John's own film "UFOria" got made but not distributed, locked up by Universal for a few years. John turned to television, getting big meetings and jobs, working with many top bosses and producers. He worked with Alan Rudolph on several films including "Endangered Species" and "Trixie" and a TV series that Alan backed out of. Other things got made but he was also in the turmoil of development hell. The compensating thing about Hollywood, even as you endure the purgatory of waiting for a project to get green-lit, is that you make money, sometimes a lot of it. There are writers in town you've never heard of who live the high life paid for by re-write jobs, script doctor passes, first-look deals that never come to fruition. It's the R&D of Hollywood. And, it afforded John a good living and another place to hide.

There had been a succession of women in John's life, some of whom I knew and befriended, but secretly thought they weren't worthy of him. They all had beauty, inside and out, but they didn't seem to get the whole package that was John Binder. Not that I had given it any thought during previous years, but I certainly was at a point now that I did.

After Malibu, John rented a house in Pacific Palisades, tucked away down a driveway, overlooking a canyon. It was painted red and was a typical California ranch house, with a nice eat-in kitchen, rooms with lots of windows, a swimming pool, and a nice office in what had been the detached garage. A basketball hoop was outside the office in the driveway for pick up games and breaks from writing while he worked out a scene in his head.

In summer months, the boys had come to stay with John. Sharon had never attempted to turn the boys against their father as she might have, and she now thought they needed the steady

John

influence of a man. The boys had enjoyed their summers in California and they were content not to go back to the east coast. Josh could play football and baseball at Pali High and John Henry loved baseball. Sharon was also considering a change, a move from Greenwich Village and her teaching in New York to Richmond, Virginia to teach dance at Virginia Commonwealth University, VCU.

Mandeville Canyon was the longest dead end road in town. Five miles up a winding two lane road, you came to a narrow driveway that wound up the hill, made a sharp right turn that led up to a house on a granite ridge, overlooking the canyon to the mountains across the way. You didn't see the city with its spectacular lighting grid of millions of homes nor the ocean. It was a peaceful view which removed you from the city; you could be anywhere. It was like Malibu or Topanga but better because when you needed to get to a meeting, you were that much closer to the studios and production companies. It was sprawling post and beam house with six bedrooms, four bathrooms and a large downstairs room, poolside. There was no lawn as the steep sides of the ridge didn't offer any flat space, but it was a lush wooded acre surrounded by hundreds of acres of open land. Peace and solitude, your name was Mandeville.

Back in Madison, my brother Charles was getting married. He'd known Mary Seffrood for quite a while and they wanted a family so it was time to make the commitment. We all liked her as they were a good match and she even came from the area where Dad had grown up. Her family owned a hilltop farm in South Wayne, a small town near Monroe, but Mary didn't see herself as a farmer's wife and left after high school. She worked for several very successful dentists, running their office and assisting at their sides. She was smart, liked to have fun and was salt of the earth, just right for my brother who could be shy sometimes. Other times, he was funny and surprising, like the time at Venice Beach when we were watching a street performer. The guy had lots of dance moves and that was his gimmick. Bring the tourists into the circle and have them imitate his hip hop style. Charles was chosen and to the amazement of all, kept up with the music and added pizzazz to the moves.

I arrived in Madison with a full-blown case of poison oak caused by my unfortunate choice of some colorful leaves to go in a fall bouquet. I should have known better as I'd had run-ins with the weed in the past, one time having blisters for close to a year as it traveled by my inability to not scratch an itch. I had to get a shot of cortisone and was basically miserable for the celebrations, a ceremony in Mary's home church conducted by an old friend, Father Mike, then back to Madison for the party at The Top Hat restaurant.

The next day, I took a walk to the campus as school was in it's first weeks of the fall semester. Our house was nearby and it was always a beautiful hike, out of the village, along the shore of Lake

Mendota, through the woods then climbing the hill to the flagship building, Bascom Hall. It was still such familiar territory as I stood in front of the Lincoln statue, the one about which was said that if a virgin walked in front of him, Abe would stand up. I walked down the hill to the Student Union and into the hallway where there was a refreshment stand. This was where I stood when we all learned that JFK had been assassinated. Down the hall was the small movie theater where I'd first seen Bergman's "Wild Strawberries" that opened my eyes to what a film could be. Upstairs was the Union Theater where I'd performed in my high school cheerleading uniform as part of a modern take on "Two Gentleman From Verona" along with Ann Haberman Armstrong; where I'd seen Merce Cunningham and company; heard Ayn Rand lecture; Julian Bream play his lute. The Theater Committee office was there too where we met and chose all the theatrical and music programs we wanted to bring to the campus during the coming year. Above that, were the banquet rooms where I met Gov. George Wallace, Barry Goldwater, Dwight McDonald, speakers chosen by the Symposium Committee. Across the street was the Memorial Library where I studied and also worked. For two years, I catalogued all the Russian books that were sent from that country as reference materials. Ann Armstrong and I worked in a lone room with four weird women one summer revising the Dewey decimal library system, working with the card catalogue, manually writing down new numbers, probably the most boring job ever. Across the street from the Library was my first dorm, Langdon Hall, where I was a 5th Floor Virgin for two years before moving up to the Kappa Kappa Gamma house for my junior and senior years.

In little old Madison (as Mom would call it), the world did come to us and gave us opportunities and a good education which at the time cost my Dad $180 a semester. When I started college at the age of seventeen, I basically never quit as I took summer school courses to get some of the boring or difficult requirements out of the way. I'd live at home, work at the library or at Dad's company, play golf, tool around in the TR-3, waterski, go on some dates.

The two men in my life at that time were Bill Weiss from Wauwautosa, a good swimmer who dropped out of school a lot and Michael Mann. They were so different from each other and I would date them off and on for several years, going to the Milwaukee area to visit Bill and his family or to Chicago to stay with the Manns. A permanent relationship wasn't to be with either one of them.

Although getting engaged was very popular with my friends, I really was not ready to settle down. During my sophomore and junior years, I'd gone to visit a girl I knew from the dorm, Sue Frank. She lived in New Jersey and her family loved to go to the city, New York, that is, to see shows and visit museums. The visit changed my life as we toured Fifth Avenue, Central Park, went to the theater. That old adage about New York, "It's a great place to visit, but I wouldn't want to live there." did not apply to me. I knew then and there, I had to live there. This became my goal. Get my degree in Political Science with my Latin American Studies minor, get a job at a company in NYC that specialized in international relations. Marriage wasn't even a factor in my mind. When I'd go shopping, I'd buy clothes for a professional lifestyle, conservative dresses and pumps.

Madison was then and still is a magnet for progressive people, a small city situated on four lakes, with four beautiful seasons, academically advanced, with good sports teams I would support all my life. I used to say that Madison was a good place to be from, yet part of me never left.

Chapter Nineteen

Love At Last

In Los Angeles, Charlotte threw a birthday party for me and John came. The next day, I packed a few things and left. Sitting at the breakfast table the next morning with Josh, John told him he wanted me to move in, what did he think. Josh replied that he had always loved me and it was fine with him. October 10, 1985, the first day of the rest of my life. Having failed to bring children into the world, here I was getting two sons. Instant family, just add water. And love, understanding, good cooking, and dogs. Oops, that became our first fight. What about Tas and Snaffy? I'd left them with Char but of course, that was just temporary. I had to have my furry friends around. John had Bandit, a German shorthair pointer, who ruled the house and was very attached to John Henry. John put his foot down. I accused him of wanting someone to move in with nothing, no baggage, just a smile and a willingness. I won my case eventually, because as an old farm boy, there was no way John would let the dogs be left behind.

John called to tell Sharon, who now used her maiden name, Kinney. She said she was very happy for both of us and would see us soon. I was very relieved and glad that John and I had found our way to be together in a way that didn't hurt another person. Whenever Sharon came out, I would disappear for a few hours so that she and John could be with their sons and deal with any family matters that needed discussion. It was good for everyone. In turn, I appreciated that Sharon let me into the circle.

On occasion she has thought I have overstepped my place when I've gotten mad at one or the other boy and have let them have it, but we all have been able to congratulate ourselves that

One DNA - Josh, John, John Henry

we've kept an elevated attitude about each other and the family. We've celebrated Mother's Days, graduations, birthdays, marriages, grandkids, all with genuine respect and caring. We all think it's a monumental accomplishment, true to the ideals we expressed decades ago, love, freedom, forgiveness for mistakes. I'll add to that one of my personal mottos, "Always keep moving."

I continued my work at Ambrosia but had also started a new project, this time for the theater. Darrell Larson had acted in "UFOria" which was how we met. He was a friend of Sam Shepard's and made his mark with some of Sam's plays, as performer and director. He asked me to produce a play, or rather a musical, based on Bob Dylan's book "Tarantula". This was a collection of stream of consciousness poems written in the mid-sixties and, as interpreted by us, about two people driving across the country, expressing their fears of powerlessness, death, sex, and their own images.

We incorporated as The Tarantula Society and I made some inroads with both Bob's manager and lawyers and was in the process of closing a long-negotiated deal for the rights to do this. Now all we needed was the money. At work, whenever I needed to talk with Carl or David about a menu or party, I walked from the kitchen, across a huge room that had been the Hughes Aircraft cafeteria, to the company's offices. We used the cafeteria for setting out food that was going to be picked up or sent to a client but otherwise it was wasted space. I showed the space to Darrell suggesting that maybe we could use it, have a fund-raiser, put on a show! Carl and David didn't care if I did something with it, so we created "Theateria". We planned a fund-raiser, catered by me, dressing up the huge room and dividing it with vast yards of fabric supplied by Darrell's friend, Jamie. Other talent, Susan Krebs and John Acorn, Mitch Greenhill, Peter Kors and Leon Martell, would pitch in to make it a fun evening.

At home, I was getting ready to go down to oversee the set-up for the party, when I heard a terrible yelp from one of the dogs. I didn't think anything of it until Dennis Hill came up and said I needed to go down to the driveway. Josh had backed his truck over Snaffy. I ran down to my little pet and when I put my arms under her to lift her up, she raised her head and died. Josh felt horrible, apologizing, explaining he hadn't seen Snaffy in the driveway. Snaffy was not in good shape, old, deaf, nearly blind and hadn't done her part to get out of the way of a vehicle. She was gone and there was nothing to be done except bury her which would have to wait. I had to get to "Theateria".

The show and party went into full swing and lots of people showed up, paying the cover and then some to help us launch our play. But, something was up with Darrell. He wasn't helping out, disappearing to talk with one friend, Dennis Hicks, then another, ignoring me when I needed him to help run the party. Was he on drugs? What the hell was going on? I would learn later that he had just learned that he was HIV-positive, which at that point in time, 1986, was disastrous. But, the party and show had to go on and we were a success clearing $4,000.

I was amazed. We kept the ball rolling with some other investors, wonderful John Densmore of the Doors for one, and we were able to book The Powerhouse Theater in Santa Monica. Darrell did the adaptation of Dylan's poems, set to original music, performed by our cast of eleven actors which included Susan Krebs, Peter Kors, James Morrison, Keith Kreger with music by Mitch Greenhill. Betsy Heimann did the costumes and Catherine Hardwicke, our set. Ed Harris showed up one day with a truck full of lumber and built our raked stage. We had some artful slides that played on the back scrim, four video screens showing images that included burning tenements, nuclear tests, napalm explosions, civil strife. The music, played by a six-man live band was great.

The first number was "Having a Weird Drink with the Long Tall Stranger": "black betty black bready blam de lam! bloody had a baby blam de lam! hire the handicapped blam de lam! put him on the wheel blam de lam! burn him in the coffee blam de lam! cut with a fish knife blam de lam."

This was Dylan's riff on an old African-American work song as he hit the high points of growing up. Each piece introduced another character or wove in more story line. The play ran for two months, got reviewed in the L.A. Times, which for an avant-garde exploration of life among Dylan's hipsters, was more than we expected. Daily Variety said: "Dylan's wit and wisdom at The Powerhouse comes off as a high-tech, multimedia experience that is a cross between joyful and thoughtful." They concluded that it was a first-rate evening with a group of talented players.

Despite the seriousness of Darrell's diagnosis, he was able to combat the virus, have two kids, and live on into the 21st century. But, in our world this illness brought a huge sadness. It had hit hard and it moved quickly, devastating friends and others in all walks of life, primarily men who were actors, musicians, dancers. Young and old, it struck with a vengeance and there was no cure in sight. The carefree lifestyle of gay men in Hollywood, San Francisco, New York was ripped apart as we all started to learn about the sexually-transmitted virus. And then, the judgments came down from the straight world, reminding everyone that sex kills. Sick men were belligerently turned away from clinics and hospitals, sometimes turning away from their own children out of fear. President Reagan did nothing; neither did Gov. Wilson. The only answer any of them came up with was stop having homosexual sex. But, women and children became victims as well as it was learned that blood and needles carried the disease. No one was safe and wouldn't be for a few decades to come.

I went on to produce another play at The Powerhouse with Lucinda Zeising called "Neon" which was written and directed by Shirley Kaplan, who was in the Theatre department at Sarah Lawrence. Again, it was a musical so my creative juices were beginning to flow after a long, dry spell.

Living with a writer, who needed both the physical space and head space to create, was a new one for me. I'd spent a few months working on the Texas script a few years before and during that time would shut my self up in a room with no interference, so understood this and gave John all the room he needed. We fell into an easy daily routine which was appreciated by both of us. Josh was living on campus at UCLA, John Henry was driven to school each morning, I went to work or did the household duties of cleaning, gardening, laundry.

We did have help once a week from Rosa who had worked for John for several years. Indeed, he had gone the extra mile for her and her family, helping her get a green card. This meant that he put an ad in a small newspaper, The Palisades Post, asking for housekeeping help. When it wasn't answered by a legal citizen, he could hire Rosa and pay her on the books. She could then apply for legal immigration. She was a lovely person, raising two kids, and he was happy to help her. Even after she moved on to a better job, she would come to our house at Christmas time with a present for him.

John's nephew, Peter Reynolds, lived with us for a few months during this time. He had just graduated from high school in Pittsburgh and was interested in cooking. He got a job working in a pizza place, learning to make the new California style pizza and eventually left for Florida where he trained more cooks in his boss's restaurant chain. Peter's brothers Dan, a hopeful writer, and John, a musician/sound editor were also around. They were all big, strong guys, the sons of John's sister Betsy and husband Reamer. John's other sister, Barb Jones, lived in Orange County, and still had two of her eight children at home. She'd lost her husband Bill the year before to cancer and was glad her little brother was nearby. The older children were married and having their families so she would visit them in Connecticut, Michigan, Illinois and the San Francisco Bay area. She would eventually have thirty-two grandchildren and all her kids did very well in business and life.

John was writing a television project, "Assault and Matrimony", an NBC movie of the week about a warring couple. Both of us having been in at least a few difficult relationships, I found it fun to listen to his bits and pieces as his characters started to define themselves. This was a comedy, unusual for TV at the time as most MOWs were dramas, "disease of the week" stories. He had been writing it for several weeks and the end wasn't coming. One night I dreamed a final scene. I woke him up and told him and it worked. That was a revelation for me, how your brain can work on its own and send the message to your dream world. I began editing John's scripts and helping him when he needed it. It was becoming easier for me to put words on a page.

I had always been a reader, favoring the well-written novels to the typical best-sellers, so intrinsically, I had a story sense. It was late in coming to me, as I had a terrible time in college English classes, defining all the references, metaphors, similes that creative criticism demanded. I made a decision. I'd look for stories or books for adaptation to the screen, concentrate on this rather than falling back on my past credits in rock and roll.

This was easier said than done. Just because I had producer credits, knew how to put a production together, I soon learned that "creative" execs and producers looked down on crew people. And, if a woman friend had a big job at a company, she wasn't about to bring in another woman who might take her place at the table. Hollywood was still a man's business and, although they relied on women to read screenplays and offer advice, they were in charge. Women I'd known over the years who worked in the studio or network systems were showing no interest in my going from producing music specials to putting together a feature film. It was a rude awakening.

I did manage to set up one project based on a novel I optioned intitled "Abra", at Hearst Entertainment but after several pitch meetings at the networks, the fire went out. It was a difficult piece, a character study, of a woman who walked away from her husband and two children, without letting them know where she'd gone, which was to an isolated cabin she'd inherited. She lived a Spartan life, off the grid, sustaining herself from her garden and infrequent trips to the nearest town. It was obviously a feminist slant and probably before it's time. Was it Abra's mental illness or her search for mental wellness? I found it fascinating and with the right cast, it would have been a strong look at a woman's place in society. But, it was viewed as being too much of a downer.

A movie for television John wrote, "Houston, Gone To Texas" about Sam Houston's war with the Mexican general, Santa Ana, and his winning that huge state for the U.S. of A., had played on CBS and John won an award for the script. We were invited to Oklahoma City to attend a ceremony and banquet at the Cowboy Hall of Fame which was the presenter of his "Best Teleplay" statue, a bronze cowboy seated on a horse. This was a great acknowledgement for John who had been influenced by western movies and television shows from his earliest beginnings.

His dad had always owned horses and John grew up riding, first ponies then well-bred horses. When John came to Los Angeles, he came with a horse, Jake, a beautiful bay quarter horse and this animal had become a symbol of John's efforts to make it in Hollywood. Jake was boarded in Topanga for years then moved to a ranch in Mandeville that had been owned by Robert Taylor and Barbara Stanwyck. The current owner of the ranch had another horse in the stable and Jake was a good companion for her. The fee was nil because we took care of both horses, feeding them, mucking out the stalls, keeping them company. We'd also go down and work Jake on a lunge line. On a quiet Saturday, as we tended to the horses, we saw a good-sized mountain lion sauntering down the middle of the road, our own king of the jungle.

So, life was good. John and I had floated into a rhythm that was a quiet life on the Westside of Los Angeles, money coming in from his prodigious efforts in the television business. He had made it possible for me to quit my kitchen work at Ambrosia, something I was ready to do. I loved it but now I made good food at home. I walked away from that huge industrial kitchen with its wall of ovens, wall-mounted soup vats, yards of shiny stainless tables, Roland, Susan Sullivan, Jose and the boys, Carl and David. I had learned more about the food business than I cared to but would take it. The big downside of catering is the clientele, many of them wealthy beyond anyone's wildest dreams who pinched pennies when it came to "the help", very demanding because they could be. The upside was learning new menus, seeing that I was a good cook with discerning taste, with good skills, knowledge of all the equipment that was available. I'd learned the nuances of sautéing, roasting, braising, grilling and had been in the business when cooking in Los Angeles took a big leap forward. "Fresh" was in, the best ingredients money could buy were readily available, whether they were steaks, chickens, greens, vegetables, herbs.

I still loved being in the kitchen, going in at the end of the day to rattle those pots and pans and coming up with something delicious to eat. We ate a lot of pasta with turkey bolonaise, or alfredo with vegetables, fish or shrimp, stir fries, roasted or bar-b-qued chicken, large salads, Mexican, Chinese, all healthy food, a result of the Los Angeles melting pot. The joke on John had always been that he could do a grocery shopping in ten minutes because he would cook the same few meals every week for the boys then go out for sushi on Fridays. My repertoire put a crimp in his in-and-out style but he enjoyed the payoff.

I enjoyed my comfortable relationship with the boys. Josh was enjoying UCLA. He had been granted the "Alumni Scholarship" for his academic achievement at Pali Hi. He pledged Zeta Beta Tau, the only gentile in a Jewish fraternity. He signed up for a special EMT class and became an escort for women who needed to go from the library or a late class to their dorms. John Henry starred at second base on the baseball team at Pali High, where Josh had also excelled, and was a Leader of the Pack of his teenage friends. On the phone at night, we'd hear "Hey, Vargas. It's me Vargas. Yeah, Vargas." and on and on, ten phone calls to determine who was driving, where they were going. He had a boa constrictor in a terrarium in his bedroom, feeding it "pinkies" on a weekly basis. If you have never been a snake lover, a pinkie is a baby white mouse. I couldn't complain much, as I had Bob, a Mexican Red-Leg tarantula, left over from the play, in a terrarium in the dining room.

John Henry's boa wasn't the only snake around. We also had a lot of rattle snakes, sometimes in the house. My favorite sighting was one morning, arising and getting ready for the day, we were dressing for a hike in the hills. We had left our bedroom screen door open during the night.

John was bent over, retrieving his running shoes and heard me say quietly, "Don't move. Look at your cowboy boot."

There was a rattlesnake wrapped around the boot top with its head near the heel. A perfect iconic western image, but one that had to be dispatched with immediately. I credit myself with calmly commanding "Don't move", and John for obeying my orders. Never shout "SNAKE!" in a such a situation for fear of the panicked reaction you might get. John moved carefully away to get his .22 rifle, then gun in hand, naked, he crept toward the snake.

"You're not going to destroy that boot, are you?", I asked.

It was a beautiful Tony Lama. John reached for the top of the boot and carefully slid it out of the snake's coil, gun ready. Once the boot was freed, John sighted and pulled the trigger. Good-bye snake. John swears he's a crack shot but I learned that the reason all the snakes John killed had their heads blown off was that they, as heat-seeking vipers, strike the bullet. That's how fast they are.

We were spooked by the large number of snakes we were encountering until we learned we were living on top of a rattlesnake den. We were doing some remodeling which included replacing a cement slab outside the house and as the crew jack-hammered away, removing one section of the deck, they uncovered a nest of rattlers and there were lots of them. The Mexican crew destroyed the snakes and had fun scaring each other, tossing the carcasses at unsuspecting crew members before they filled in the snake pit and covered it with a new cement and terracotta tile patio. We still would have snakes coming round as they're territorial, but also figured that if you take away their prey, meaning rats and mice, they will go elsewhere. We didn't want to use poison because of the other hunters at the top of the canyon, the red-tail hawks, peregrine falcons, coyotes, bobcats, raccoons, possums, etc. that also depended on the animals toward the bottom of the food chain. Traps were set out and it was always surprising how many critters we had. It took years, but eventually, we were rodent-free.

We continued to make the house our own once we bought it in 1987. Tearing fencing out, planting new gardens, adhering to the Fire Department rules that mandated 200' clearance of vegetation, pruning trees, all demanding and hard work we did ourselves but incredibly rewarding. I became active in the local busybody group, as John always referred to the Upper Mandeville Canyon Association, and we had some real issues to learn about and in some cases, make a stand.

The property ringing the top of the canyon was owned by a Mission Canyon development company that wanted to put houses on every ridge, extending the already large community, Mountaingate. It would be one thing if there would be a house here or there, but their plans required vast amounts of bulldozing, clearing, dirt removal, making way for hundreds of homes. I started making trips down to City Hall with Betsey Landis of UMCA and Nita Rosenberg of the lower canyon association, MCA. Nita had been instrumental in the creation of the Santa Monica Mountains Conservancy which saved 69,000 acres of parkland across the swath of mountains that divide the Los Angeles basin from the San Fernando Valley then continue west to Malibu. This connected to the Topanga State Park and was called The Big Wild, one of the largest urban parks in the world. Through my work with these two warrior women, I learned about the real powers in the city, the Sanitation District which owned most of the canyons to the east and west of Mandeville; the Department of Water and Power, the Oil Companies that had pipelines running from the Santa Barbara Pacific Ocean derricks down through the Valley, over the mountains, down Mandeville Canyon and on to the refineries in south Los Angeles; and of course, the wealthy development companies for whom the City Council members rolled over. But, in this particular fight, we came out the winners. Betsey, a civil engineer, spent the time to go through the written security logs that counted every truck that came up to Mission Canyon when it was a city dump and what their load consisted of. She found that one trash removal company came in with low-grade x-rays from dental offices all across the city and that was enough to put a stop to the excavation. To date, those ridges are clear of any further development, and we all will forever fight to keep them that way.

There was life after rock and roll and movies, but I kept hanging on, thinking I could crack the studio system and get a film done. Then, I wrote one myself that was based on Larry Johnson's parents' experiences in Japan and Korea during the war there in the early 1950s. His mother, Margaret, had written a recollection of those times and I optioned it from her for my adaptation. I knew I'd have to expand on the story, perhaps dramatize aspects of it, but it had the bare bones of an exciting tale. It was called "Ichi For The Michi" which came from a G.I. toast saying "One for the road." In 1949, Dale Johnson was stationed in Beppu, Japan after WWII. Margaret lived at an army base in Georgia, near where she'd grown up. In 1950, she got her port call, the right to join her husband overseas. Three weeks after she got to Japan, the North Koreans crossed the 38th Parallel and the Korean War was on. The story had it all, fish out of water, action, romance, slam dunk.

It was then I realized I was a nobody. People in Hollywood talk about the script that came over the transom and how they discovered the next hot thing, but it didn't happen to me. So now what?

Chapter Twenty

All Business

John's agent, Marty Hurwitz, called one day and told John he was leaving his company which was merging with another mid-sized agency to form UTA. Marty didn't want to work for a large corporation and was starting his own boutique company. Would John follow him? Yes, he would. On another call, I asked Marty who was setting up his business. He hadn't gotten that far. I offered to help and was hired on the spot. Marty had taken offices in a nice, small building in Beverly Hills, the Courtyard Building and needed everything done: furniture, artwork, business license, agency license, computers, software. Instead of "Let's put on a show" it was "Let's start a company." All the same, really.

Darrell and Susanna had some furniture designed and built for their home and I loved it and thought it would be perfect for the office. I introduced Marty to Tom Colgrove who proved to be the right guy to make a custom semi-circular desk and shelf unit. I found a beautiful antique Korean credenza, had some leather chairs made for a corner, brought in my dear friend Barry Michlin who had beautiful photos of Rome and we had art for the walls. We had two more rooms to furnish, one for the assistant, another for all the scripts, copy machine, etc. By the time, I'd finished, I was also answering the phone, keeping Marty's schedule, and we both decided I would stay on. I had to learn a very complicated computer agency booking system that was also our accounting system because basically, I was it.

Our day started at 9:30 and ended at 7:30. We'd roll calls to clients and buyers, some names I knew, some I didn't. Marty was a great negotiator and I'd be on an extension as he went through all the deal points of a contract, hear the give and take, where to press and when to give. We represented a few actors but mostly writers: Delta Burke, at the height of her fame with Designing Women; Joseph Wambaugh, the ex-L.A. cop who had become a famous crime writer; Arthur Kopit, famed on Broadway and in Hollywood; young writers on the way up, earning their stripes running half-hour sitcoms; and John who continued to get good jobs creating series, re-writing scripts, all for TV. Which still was a problem for John. He craved the chance to follow up "UFOria" with another feature film but this wasn't Marty's department. Marty's self-interest was television. He pretended to try advancing John's career in film but it was easier to get him jobs in TV. Marty was shrewd. John was naive, not realizing how much agents tend to specialize. Big agencies had an agent that only dealt with each studio, Paramount, etc.; another agent would handle Universal, film, television, new media, plays, books, all different departments. Everything was compartmentalized and don't you dare step outside your assignment.

In my case, considering those initial dreams I had as a teenager, buying my business dresses, seeing myself making a deal, I realized I had finally reached that goal as an agent. The hippie days, the smoky haze, had given way to serious buy and sell. Quite a new direction, but I was happy, or at least, fulfilled, making money, seeing a new path.

After about a year, Marty suggested that I think about bringing in my own clients and I went for it. I wondered if I should begin with "Below the Line", the crew people I knew. It was called that because when you look at a production budget, the first items are the power positions: Producer, Director, Writer, Stars. All these highly-paid people are on the first page and their salaries are entered in one after another and then totaled at the bottom. Then, there's a line. Below that line are listed the Cast, secondary characters and day players, Camera Department, Production

Design, Sound, Editor, etc. I put the word out and started signing a few people.

Another friend called to say there was a book that needed representation, a deal was at hand. I talked to the writer whose name was David Schneider. He was a Buddhist priest who'd written an oral history, "Street Zen" about a fascinating character, Issan Dorsey. I did a contract for him.

Susanna Styron, who was married to Darrell, asked if I'd host a party for her parents, William and Rose. Her dad had gone through a difficult time with depression and it was the first time he'd traveled to L.A. in a while and there were some friends he wanted to see. Susanna and Darrell's house, as nice as it was, would be too small for the gathering. I was happy to do it. That night, I met Edward Bunker and his wife, Jennifer. She and I hit it off and when we discovered we had offices near-by in Beverly Hills, made a plan for lunch. I knew Eddie had written a successful book, "No Beast So Fierce" that had become the movie, "Straight Time" with Dustin Hoffman. When she learned I was an agent, she asked if I'd consider representing Eddie. He had other books and a new manuscript.

I remembered the last time Eddie's name had come up when I was working with Dale Djerassi on the Flora Purim project. Eddie had written "Freedom Song", with and about Flora growing up in Brazil, coming to America, her success as a jazz singer, her downfall and bust and the prison sentence. They'd met at Terminal Island Prison. Dale had said at the time, he certainly didn't want anything to do with a book written by a known felon like Edward Bunker.

Eddie didn't like the agent he had and wanted someone else doing his business. I was definitely interested. Eddie and I talked on the phone and he came in with a manuscript which he called "Dog Eat Dog", an L.A.-based story about a kid he'd met in prison. I sent it to Ed Pressman's company which optioned it and on the basis of that, Ed's New York book agent got a deal at St. Martin's Press which would continue to publish all of Bunker's books thereafter. Eddie wrote a letter to his agent saying thanks but he was moving on to an agent who wasn't afraid of him.

Working in Beverly Hills, driving in every day, going to lunch, meeting development people at all the companies and networks made one thing clear to me. I was a lot older than most of my peers. When I first started working with Marty, I became aware of several women in New York who had spent decades representing playwrights whose names were famous. I figured if they could do it, why couldn't I? And, I was proving I could, dressing well, having good energy, cultivating a phone voice that defied age. But then my body began to give me away. I became menopausal with full-blown red-faced hot flashes which caused sweat to literally drip off the end of my nose. Try sitting in an office with a bunch of thirty-somethings and be cool under those conditions. I really didn't want to start a regimen of hormonal replacement therapy, but if I wanted to take those meetings I had no choice.

On top of these early warning signals that my body was changing, I also began to put on weight and I was noticing that my waist was disappearing. Trying on clothes at a store, I looked in the mirror and a frog looked back. And, I wasn't eating any differently! The stress of my work didn't help, with the ten-hour days, arriving home at 8:00pm, eating a late dinner and not turning away a helping of carrot cake. I know, I know. I still hiked several miles everyday before heading into work. John and I took a yoga class every Saturday morning then would hit the Farmer's Market to stock up for the week, emphasizing good, fresh food.

Finally, I just accepted that middle-age spread came with the territory of office life. I'd avoided office culture for years and now, this new chapter had begun. I was plugging back into the film business, not as a creative person but their agent. I thought I could bring something to agenting that was fresh, that the clients would appreciate that I'd done production. Marty didn't agree and said they really didn't care what I'd done as long as I got them their next job. That was the bottom line, work and money. It was a different side of life but I acceded to the demands and got to know the buyers.

As with any business, it's not always how good you are, it's who you know. This depressing fact got pounded into me time and time again. I'd read good books or scripts, go out with them to good producers and it would be a pass. Then I'd read in the trades what these companies were doing and usually it was the same old, same old with producers they'd just worked with.

Elaine Markson, a New York-based book agent and good friend of Phoebe's, wanted an L.A. presence. She arrived in town one day with a young cohort, Lisa Callamaro, who would run the office out here. Elaine's office was in the Village and I told Phoebe our little Courtyard Building would be the perfect place. They came, they saw and they rented, right across the way from my office. Sue Berger, who had worked for Penguin Books for a long time and had taken over the books-to-movies department, also moved in. We had a great time, working, sharing contacts, lunching, complaining.

Whatever Marty's aproach was, I found that because I had worked in production with such varied personalities in situations where you must get the job done at any cost, I had the ability to work through difficult deals, get the parties talking, convincing them that, egos aside, they were very much in synch with each other. Almost like therapy sessions and I enjoyed the new rhythm of quiet conversations done with patience. If tempers flared, emotions on the sleeve - we are in a dramatic business, after all - I could help my clients use their anger as a helpful energy, not one that blows a deal.

One night, John and I had finished dinner which we usually did in front of the TV set. Somehow the news didn't cause indigestion and it was a good way to catch up on the world and with each other. He looked at me with a sly grin on his face and he proposed. He actually asked if I would marry him. I didn't hesitate to say "Yes." I was thrilled. We'd been together for eight years, this was in the fall of 1993, and were happy, enjoying our combined lives. Josh was working with John on a TV project, "Return To Lonesome Dove"; John Henry had graduated from UC Santa Barbara and was working in Los Angeles as a bartender and taking acting classes. I was comfortable with our status and hadn't even dropped any big hints. John had come up with this all on his own and it was surprising how it deepened our relationship and resonated in looks and conversations. Or so I thought. Later, John admitted that Josh and John Henry had come to him and asked what it was we were doing. Was I a girlfriend or was there more to our relationship after eight years? Shouldn't we be engaged or....legal somehow?

We started planning the celebration. My parents were thrilled having been bruised by the failure of my first marriage and our friends greeted the news with compliments and delight. Once again, I would be married in a restaurant and with my foodie connection, I guess that was just perfect. We chose the Saddle Peak Lodge in Malibu Canyon and decided on a noon wedding on Saturday, December 11. We booked the whole place and planned a lunch buffet for a hundred people. The Lodge was a one-hundred-year-old place that had been a roadhouse, pony express stop and hunting lodge. It had a large dining area with a beautiful stone fireplace, intimate upstairs chambers and a rustic patio where we could have the ceremony. We went shopping, Savannah for me on Montana where I found a long green velvet dress and coat; John bought a beautiful walnut-colored suit.

Mom, Dad, Charles, Mary and son Alex arrived from Madison. John's brother Pete came from Florida to join Barb and Betsy. Josh and John Henry would stand up with us. Friday, Dec. 10, was a gorgeous day, sunny and warm and it boded well for the

John, Jeanne, John Henry, Dad

wedding. We talked to the Lodge and they'd set up everything on the patio which looked out on the beautiful Santa Monica Mountains. Charlotte and husband David Banks, would oversee all of that for us.

Saturday, we woke up to rain. Not just any rain, but torrential rain. By the time we got out to Saddle Peak, it was being driven sideways. The ceremony had to be indoors and with the help from the staff, the tables in the main dining room were set up to allow standing room. It all looked beautiful to me with a large fire going, the Victorian lamps set low, lighting the evergreen garlands and dozens of poinsettia plants in the rustic room with it's assortment of hunters' trophies. Liz Barron, a friend and county court judge, officiated and guests participated. Mom read a poem she wrote, Joe Romano played an aria on the trumpet, Susanna Styron and Rob Sullivan read poems, Susan Krebs sang, James Lee Stanley did too.

We all sang "Amazing Grace", not your typical wedding song but everyone knew it. After lunch, the sun broke out from behind the rain clouds and everyone joined us outside for cake and photos. We honeymooned in Santa Fe and Taos for a week, relaxed, shopped and ate great food, the cold weather making it just perfect to curl up together and be thankful for our good luck.

Darrell came to me with another theater idea. It started with a book called "Dreams Die Hard", written by David Harris, who had been a draft card burner, had married Joan Baez, then gone to prison for the crime of protesting the Viet Nam war. David had also been active in civil rights, going down to Mississippi to register voters, recruited at Stanford University by Allard Lowenstein who was a brilliant political thinker, a protégé of Eleanor Roosevelt. A third character was another student, Dennis Sweeney, who was a dedicated civil rights worker, and had been present in McComb, Mississippi when bombings and shootings were the norm. Dennis hung on to the attentions he got from Allard and it's probable that the two men were involved in an intimate relationship. David admitted in his book that Allard had made a pass at him when he was driving him around to California college campuses. Dennis also had done this.

After Mississippi Summer, David went back to Stanford and was subsequently arrested and convicted for defying the draft. Dennis continued to fight for civil rights but life never came together for him and he descended into madness caused by schizophrenia. In 1980, he went to Allard's office in New York City and murdered him. The timing of this crime with the election of Ronald Reagan as President, became an iconic symbol of the death of the '60s liberal movement.

We talked to John about the book and he loved the idea as much as we did. Darrell was very involved with The Met Theater in East Hollywood and we could do the play there. First, we needed to get the rights and we needed a script. This time around, all of that happened fast. I got an option deal for the book and John began writing the adaptation. He would co-direct with Darrell and Darrell would also be involved in the script.

The story just jumped off the book page and John quickly had a first draft. It was strong, scary, a composite picture of the times. There was so much at stake in the mid-'60s, with the heightening of the Viet Nam War, the draft with its lottery. President Johnson got caught in the web. He really didn't want the war, but he was damned he'd be the only president to lose one. He had won a huge fight when he signed the Voting Rights Act that brought voter registration to all the states in the South. People were putting their lives on the lines for the right to vote, for the right to not go to war. Men fighting in Viet Nam, came home to anti-war demonstrators who hated they'd gone there. When Martin Luther King connected civil rights and anti-war, he was assassinated.

The story was multi-faceted, with the romance between David and Joan, David and Dennis' friendship, the hero worship of activists like Allard and Bob Moses, a leader in SNCC, the Student Nonviolent Coordinating Committee. Scenes were set in the Stanford commune, on the road with Allard, in Mississippi homes, where white kids learned how to be nonviolent as they registered voters, homes which were sometimes bombed. It was a big undertaking and I welcomed it. I liked being an agent but I had missed the creative juices you get from doing a project.

I set to raising money and realized the Internet, a new financing avenue, could be helpful to us. In fact, I had $10,000 in no time from an investor who loved the book. We held a fundraiser at The Met with James Ellroy and Eddie Bunker reading from their books. Darrell brought in another producer, Veronica Brady, who had much more theater experience than I, and she opened more

Poster and Cast/Crew painted on The Met Wall

doors. Faster than I thought possible, we had enough money to rent The Met for several months, hire a crew and cast our actors, all sixteen of them.   Darrell would play Dennis; the other main characters, David, Joan and Allard took a talent search. We got three great actors for these roles, Matt Salinger, (J.D.'s son) for David, Barbara Williams, (married to Tom Hayden) for Joan and Gerrit Graham as Allard. Other parts included Palo Alto commune members, SNCC black activists, Fanny Lou Hamer, Stokely Carmichael and Bob Moses, Pres. Lyndon Johnson, Dean Rusk, Hubert Humphrey, Robert Kennedy.

John Henry had dedicated himself to acting and he played two roles and it was so great to have him be a part of this project. We included songs that were meaningful during the protests and marches: "Ain't Gonna Let Nobody Turn Me Around", "HardRain's

A-Gonna Fall" "We Shall Overcome", "Freedom Got a Shotgun", "I Ain't Marching Anymore", "Joshua Gone Barbados", the haunting song, "Strange Fruit".

I loved the play and the actors and musicians were great. We got killed by the critics. We had tech problems with a new light board on opening night, sometimes the theater had six people in the audience. But we had captured something. Tom Hayden put the word out. Robert Sheer, a political columnist for the Los Angeles Times, wrote a piece saying it was dynamic theater and the critic who had panned the play didn't get it. Warren Beatty showed up and gave our cast a standing ovation. The word got out and by the time we closed two months later, we had become one of the most successful plays in The Met history. George Firth, who had written "Company" with Stephen Sondheim loved the play and worked with me to get it to other cities. But, it was not to be. David Harris thought that the play was going to be all about him and pulled the option. No one ever said that the political players and founding fathers of the '60s generation, then the next "Me Generation", were not self-centered and then some. Perhaps they had to stand up to all the fury and hatred aimed at them from police, government, and their own demons. Still, we were disappointed.

Marty was in trouble. A secretary at his former company was suing him for sexual harassment, claiming proof of late-night phone calls, prurient language. Meanwhile, Marty was getting married a second time, paying a hefty alimony to his first wife, which meant that the coffers were drained. This also effected his moods and the amount of time he had to be productive.

It occurred to me that I should move on. I put the word out and a friend introduced me to a successful agent who had her own business representing below-the-line talent, good people, as she referred to them "the crème de la crème". And they were.

Sandra Marsh had married Terry Marsh who I would have met had I stayed in Spain and worked on "Dr. Zhivago". He was a production designer and still worked on big Hollywood films. Sandra was also English and a dynamo, working both sides of the pond. She thought I would be a good match for the company, bringing in my below-the-line people and being attentive to her clients who were interested in taking a step toward doing their own projects. I would also bring my writers and directors. We made a deal which required me to rent office space, pay for an assistant and parking, but gave me a beautiful office on Wilshire Blvd.

Now, I had to tell Marty. I was advised that when I left the job, I'd better be prepared to speak my piece then get the hell out. That meant that I had to take a lot of books, scripts, files beforehand without causing alarm. I had my own office which Marty didn't spend that much time in, but our secretary noticed. She kept her peace. Friday came, the day I'd chosen to sit down and deliver the news. It almost made me sick to my stomach, but I marched in, said I needed a moment and told him I was leaving. I didn't ask for any severance and I thanked him for giving me the opportunity to learn another side of our business. He was shocked but perhaps relieved, as tension had definitely built between us. I felt I'd done a good job quitting, but the spectre of Marty loomed over me for a long time. I'd avoid going to restaurants I knew he liked or even visiting my friends in the building, just so I wouldn't run into him. And, I never did.

The good news was that all my clients followed me to the new office. Besides Sandra, there were two other agents, Linda Koulisis and Paul Sessum, who were terrific people, and once we got past the idea I was competition, new friends. Michael Vasquez worked with me, sending out scripts, reels, fielding phone calls. There were lots of invitations to premieres, parties, all done for business. But, there was also a lot of running in circles: breakfasts, lunches, drinks meetings, building contacts, selling clients, either their original work or pushing to get them hired on someone else's project. And, on occasion, I'd get that call, an offer, with no hustle required.

New clients were signed. I worked with Sandra's clients on scripts they were writing, or had found and which they wanted to direct. There was so much energy put out for any return, and the ratio favors the disappointment. Hollywood is driven by "No". Everyone gets turned down a thousand times more than they get hired and if you couldn't deal with that, get a 9 to 5 job. Talent had little to do with it. Luck, perseverance, sexual favors, who you knew, who you'd kick back to, was the fodder for the machine. We tried to believe that because people were called artists, and some did have great talent, that it was different than the construction business or real estate, but was it really? The Hollywood egos were huge, as were the financial gains. Producers made millions on projects that were not worth the celluloid they were printed on, the TV time that was paid for. But, that's just sour grapes, isn't it, the way of the world. It was so easy to be dismissive of a film or an actor, but the truth was everyone was just doing the best they could, trying to meet the people who could greenlight their film or TV show. At the end of a day, if a film got made, you had to congratulate the makers for just achieving that.

I had to face the fact I was in a rat race. I drove forty-five minutes to work, through rush hour traffic, down Sunset Blvd. into Beverly Hills, parked in the expensive garage. Then I'd sit at the desk and make phone calls, set up meetings, go to lunch, come back, read a script, roll calls at the end of the day, then head home, back down Wilshire through rush hour traffic, forty-five minutes up to the top of Mandeville. Day in, day out. It occurred to me I could do this at home. The computer was becoming more and more a partner in the game, with emails, tracking lists, accounting. I could do contracts via a fax machine; meetings could take place in a restaurant. I did myself a huge favor and moved into my office home. And, I could spend a lot more time with John and our dog, Brando. I breathed a sigh of relief, put on some casual clothes and never looked back. Or, as a Bruce Willis' character was heard to say, "Adios, Motherfucker!" Windfall Management was born.

I did lose one client with this move, W. Blake Herron, a writer who also directed. I'd set up his film, "A Texas Funeral" with Tim Daly's company at Paramount where a friend, Julie Kirkham, worked. They'd gotten it made and it enjoyed a nice indie run. I'd done a deal for him at Fox for a Patricia Highsmith novel, a follow-up to the very successful, "The Talented Mr. Ripley", entitled "Ripley Under Ground", directed by Roger Spottiswoode, starring Barry Pepper, Alan Cumming, Tom Wilkinson and Willem Dafoe. He subsequently wrote "The Bourne Identity" which he got based on the Ripley script, but I didn't commission that deal as he'd departed for CAA, not trusting that my management company would have the clout he now needed. Truth be told, CAA did bupkis for him and he landed at another management company.

John had given Blake a job writing on a television series he was a showrunner on, "The Lazarus Man", which was on TNT. John was brought in by Norman Powell, son of the famous actor and producer, Dick Powell. They had formerly worked together on a trio of TV movies, westerns at CBS called "Black Fox", starring Christopher Reeves. "Lazarus Man" had Robert Urich in the lead and was the story of a man, James "Lazarus" Cathcart, who, in the fall of 1865, woke up buried in a shallow grave outside the town of San Sebastian, Texas, not remembering who he was, or why someone would want to bury him. He set out on a journey to find these answers, met people who still wanted to kill him, and had fragments of memory about the night President Lincoln was killed, not knowing if he was in on the plot.

John brought Josh in on the show as the story editor, which was great for them personally, and also good for the show. John directed three episodes that he had written and went on location in Santa Fe, having a great time renewing his directorial chops. But, the good times didn't last long. Urich announced toward the end of the first season that he had a rare form of cancer that attacks the joints of the body. We were all devastated by Bob's bad news. At first it was thought he would recover. They cast a second lead and planned to continue the show, giving Bob a lighter load to carry. A second season's scripts were begun. Bob was sure he could do the work and go on, but TNT after deep and sensitive consideration, decided to collect on their insurance and canceled the show anyway. Bob Urich lived for seven years after that. Rest in Peace, Bob. Just when John was making his mark as a director again, the businessmen pulled the plug.

Susan Krebs was planning a trip to Jackson Hole, Wyoming to see her good pal August Spier whom I'd also known when he ran DC-3, a great restaurant at the Santa Monica Airport. She had spent a few months working at his restaurant, The Snake River Grill, during a summer when things got hard for her, when she'd lost sight of why she was banging her head against the wall called Hollywood. Suze had a good run in the business, with lots of television work, plays, improv sketches, but the work was getting spotty. Music, singing jazz tunes, was pulling her in a different direction and she needed a time out to think about things. Jackson Hole and the Tetons had rejuvenated her and her singing career had coalesced.

Suze asked if I'd like to ride along and it sounded like a perfect break. I hadn't been back to Wyoming since a family trip in 1954 when Dad visited his Hirsig cousins. Two of Grandma Rose's brothers, Fred and Charles Hirsig had decamped from Wisconsin in 1897 and settled in southern Wyoming, starting sheep and cattle ranches which gave them the money to help develop Laramie and Cheyenne into good-sized towns. Their younger brother, Otto, also spent some time with them as a cook and we heard tell, he liked to ride a donkey named "Hambone". Charles had also started a small airline he called Summit Airways which became Challenger Airways and eventually Frontier Airlines. Fred and Charles' sons, Beanie and Willis, were Dad's cousins and welcomed us warmly.

Frontier Days Rodeo was a big event and the Hirsig boys had been founders of it too. Pretty Miss Margy Hirsig was Miss Frontier so I was real proud that my cousin, a few times removed, was a

Susan Krebs performs

rodeo queen. She took me shopping one day to a western-wear store and I bought some gabardine ranch pants and a silver belt to go with them. They were my favorites as long as I could fit into them but being twelve years old, that wasn't as long as I would have liked. I also got to ride in the parade on a covered wagon.

Suze was planning to drive to August's and that sounded like a fun trip to me. We would make it an easy four-day ride, then I would hang out for a few days then fly back home, while she stayed a few more weeks. We stopped east of Vegas to tour Hoover Dam which is really interesting and overpowering, supplying all that electricity that brings millions of people to that city. The next day was Zion and Bryce National Parks, truly beautiful colors, huge rock formations, edifices, that had to have been the inspiration for the dam. Our third night out was in northern Utah at Heber City, settled by Swiss people, so both Suze and I enjoyed our heritage connection to it. Near by was the Homestead resort which had a caldera, a geothermal hot pot, that you could swim in. That definitely called to us and it was a truly unique experience to be floating in this rocky mineral dome which had a small opening on the top, in 90 degree water. The next day we stopped at the Bear River Migratory Bird Refuge near Brigham City, an amazing spot on the north shore of the Great Salt Lake, thousands of acres of marshland habitat for water birds, surrounded by mountains.

Then on to Jackson Hole, a prosperous place which probably rivals Aspen for it's median income. A favorite of the Rockefeller family which helped to preserve Teton National Park, it's long been a watering hole for the rich and famous. Which is why August was up there, having started and now managing, the town's best restaurant. He had a charming house on a hilltop overlooking land that produced huge wheels of wheat. The sun set behind the mountains across the way and it was an idyllic spot. Suze and I hiked around Jenny Lake, which had to be re-christened Jeanne Lake, walked along the famed Snake River and hung out in town.

John called. My mom was trying to reach me which was puzzling. Two days before, I had called Dad on his eighy-third birthday and Suze and I sang to him. That next day, he had gone out to the country house and he didn't come home. 8:30pm, it was dark and no Chuck. Mom called Charles who called the Barneveld police who went out there to check on him. When Mom and Charles arrived, the car was there but he wasn't. The police called in a K-9 unit and they spent the night searching the woods for Dad. Very early in the morning, someone heard something and they found him, dazed, confused, covered with dirt and leaves. He'd had a stroke and had probably lost consciousness, then revived and wandered around in the dark. He was rushed to a Madison hospital and was in critical condition.

I flew back to L.A. the next day then caught a flight to Madison. When I walked into his hospital room, he was sitting on the bed, his bruised legs hanging out of his gown.

"They're poisoning me," he said.
His hair was all askew and his eyes were frightened.
"I don't know what's happening."

I told him that they were moving him that day to a care facility near by. He wanted to go home but they wouldn't let him. He needed more surveillance. Mom was a wreck. She blamed herself for letting him go out to the country alone, even though he'd been doing it for years. All during the night he was missing, she was frantic. And in fact, after Dad's incident, she never went back out to The Shack.

That night at the nursing home, Dad tried to escape out a back door three times, setting off the alarms and requiring the Supervisor to call us. All that did was give the nurses cause to pump him full of more drugs. Early the next morning, I grabbed some snacks and reading material and went there. I found Dad and he dug in his pocket and showed me the little pills that he'd taken out of his mouth instead of swallowing. They'd had him on Ativan and another depressant. I told him fine, don't take the medication today, I'll be here, let's see how you are at the end of the day. By 5pm he was a different person. Mom had arrived and we asked to sit down with the Supervisor. She agreed that Dad's temperament had changed a lot. I told her we were taking him home. She said we couldn't unless Mom signed him out. I talked her into it and we had him home in time for dinner and a Packer game on TV.

He was very relieved but he wasn't well. He had T.I.A.s, transient ischemic attacks, mini strokes that began to take their toll. Within two weeks, he had fallen several times and his legs were beginning to be paralyzed. Mom couldn't take care of him and chose a care facility near the house. Middleton Village was a one-story building surrounded by a wide yard and lots of trees, but it was still an old folks home. John and I went back for Thanksgiving and brought him home in a wheelchair for turkey dinner. He sometimes was responsive and bright, but also would have a dim day, not knowing who or what. Mom visited every day, sometimes twice a day, bringing clean laundry or special treats for him.

Within seven months, he was done. I flew home when he was rushed to the hospital, his organs shutting down. "His numbers aren't good", I was told.

Charles, Mom and I stayed by his side for a week but there was really no hope. He would know that one of us was there but only spoke in unintelligible mono-syllables. The positive side to all of this was the agreement and closeness that I had with Mom and Charles. We took care of each other and when the tough decisions had to be made, we were in agreement. Do we withhold food? Yes. When Dad rallied, that moment late at night when it looked like he was going to get better and we called for an emergency meeting with one of his doctors, again, we all decided to not intervene.

Insurance timed out and we had to move him back to Middleton Village in an ambulance. He was put in the hospice unit where he was the only patient. He was skin and bones, still muttering gibberish, and it was clear the end was near. He was smacking his lips, a sign he was thirsty so I went to get some juice for him. I also found a Dixie cup of ice cream and brought that back too. What could it hurt? At this point, he hadn't had any food for over a week. Mom took the little wooden spoon and started feeding him the ice cream, which had always been a favorite of his.

I said, "Dad, isn't that good?"
Surprisingly, he looked at us and said, "It's delightful."

After a week of not talking, this amazed us. It was the last thing we ever heard him say and I'd like to think it captured his view on life and his place in it. After the last bite, he slipped into a sleep.

Mom was exhausted and asked to go home for lunch. We had just finished eating and were putting on our coats to go back when the phone rang. He was gone. One of the nurses who had known him from the other unit, had heard he was back and had come to see him, bringing a radio. She had just tuned in a song when he breathed his last. I was glad he hadn't been completely alone and that maybe had even heard a few bars of the music, a country song, she said.

We stayed with him until the mortuary workers arrived to cart him off. Hugging that cool body, I realized what life really is, that force of energy that defines us. This physical temple we have that protects us, carries us around, gets strained, sprained and broken when we abuse it, is not us. The real Dad had gone on, his work done, a full life accomplished with it's successes and losses, having fulfilled his task of giving a lot of love to us and to friends, earfuls of complaint and criticism to those who deserved it, his pact with his spirit completed. It was March 5, 1998.

A month later, we had a memorial for family and a few friends at home then a large life celebration at Blackhawk Country Club. We played some of Dad's favorite songs including Louis Armstrong's version of "Wonderful World". My eulogy included a description of Dad, resplendent in plaid with shirt, pants and jacket all different clans, being way ahead of Ralph Lauren. We were surrounded by the cousins we see mostly at funerals and that made it just right. At the large gathering we were joined by people Dad had touched with his work and attention to details, his long public service in the Village, as a volunteer fireman for fifty-seven years, a leading force in the construction of the swimming pool and community center, and just being a good neighbor.

John and I flew back home and another difficult subject was in front of me. We were broke. John hadn't worked in a year. I had money coming in but everything went to pay our nut. We struggled to buy the necessities, ran up a lot on our credit cards, missed two payments on John's life insurance and it was cancelled, $90,000 down the drain. We got some help refinancing and went for an interest-only loan, which helped. The only thing we could do was to whittle down our cost of living. Keep it simple. Spend a lot of time at home. Not such a depressing thought, actually. John was habitually a homebody, spending his days at his desk, writing a script or ideas for other ones in an ever-growing stack of notebooks. And, truth be told, I was ready to hunker down, quietly grieving the toll of time and the loss of my dear dad.

I worked at home and liked being there, waking up after a night's sleep to my own natural rhythm, taking a hike, having breakfast, sitting down at my desk by 9:30am. John had moved his office downstairs so he wouldn't be bothered by the phone calls, so I had the nice upstairs office he had been using. Fireplace, large desk, couch, a comfortable chair. Perfect. The day went by quickly and by 6:00pm, I was in the kitchen making our dinner, relaxing after a full day of work and my car hadn't moved. This could work.

Home maintenance also figured into the day, all DIY tasks which I saw as the Zen of Housework. Weekly cleaning inside and out, painting, refurbishing, re-planting, sweeping, the all-important job that is meditation at its best. On the westside of the city, so many women have housekeepers, gardeners, nannies, poolmen which gives them time to go to the gym. My regimen gave me the same workout and also a nice reward.

Kalanchoe in the patio garden

Chapter Twenty-one

Life's A Smorgasbord

Mom called and she was in good spirits because she had an idea. We would go to Norway. Friends of hers from Madison, a professor and his wife, led two-week tours that included seeing the country by bus, train and boat. She had never been to the home of her parents and now was the time. She and Dad had been to Europe several times before, but it always included Switzerland, not Norway. I was thrilled she asked me to go as her guest and we made the plans. I'd fly to Minneapolis and she'd join me there for a flight to Reykjavik then onto Oslo. We would be gone from August 3rd to the 17th, 1999.

After the long flight across the topmost part of the globe, flying over icebergs, we arrived in Oslo around noon. Our tour group assembled and what a mixed bag. Twenty-seven ill-assorted people from all over the states. Sun Prairie farmers, Minneapolis travelers, Florida snowbirds. I couldn't think of another event that would have brought us all together in one bus heading for fun.

We got to our hotel in Oslo, in the center of town, showered, changed and Mom and I headed out. No naps for us. We were going to the Munch Museum, devoted to the life and paintings of one of Norway's most famous artists. We took the subway, walked through a beautiful park then into the building. One of the first paintings we saw was a large canvas of friends gathered at the beach, many of them nude. I pulled out my video camera and asked Mom to stand in front of the painting and tell one of her "Ole and Lena" jokes. She chose the one where Lena gets a phone call and the man on the other end asks her if they'd ever had sex. She asks who's calling. This was the beginning of "Norway, Our Way", a video of Mom who was never a prime candidate for any sort of interview. She hated to reveal anything about herself preferring to hide behind her "feminine mystique".

We stayed in Oslo another day visiting the Viking Museum, with the dragon-headed boats, Frogner Park, with the Vigeland bronze or granite statues and his famous marble monolith of bodies. I was surrounded by healthy blond casual people, many of them so handsome or beautiful in their Nordic way. There was a pervasive spirit of well-being, maybe due to a society that gives free education, money to new mothers for the first year following the birth of their child, and other safety-net allowances, paid for by the country's discovery of a huge oil patch in the North Sea.

We left Oslo and headed south through Telemark where Mom's family emigrated from. It was beautiful country, mountainous and green, but what had motivated my grandmother and her sisters and brother to all leave and come to the U.S.? Mom didn't know or didn't want to recall. She was always very private about her family and just as I had left Madison, only returning a few times a year, so was she when it came to her aunts and cousins. We, my grandmother, my mother and I had all left our homes. I'd always thought that the short distance my mom had traveled after high school to begin her adult life in Madison, was a generational equivalent to the miles I'd gone when I set out for New York. All three of us were determined to find our own way.

In southern Norway, in Lillesand, we boarded a small yacht which traveled slowly through an inter-coastal waterway. On the shore, in small sheltered coves or on the islands, were brightly-painted small cabins, weekend getaways for city people. After two hours we came to a small port east of Kristiansand, our next stop. After dinner, Mom and I walked through the town, then sat down in a waterside park and were amazed it was 10:30pm and it was still very light. Land of the midnight sun. We both felt a wave of emotion, like we'd come home.

The tour continued north through the mountains following a river which I swam in during a light rainfall, to a railroad trip to Flam, past huge waterfalls, the Kjosfossen, which were absolutely mind-blowing. The power of the water and the speed and volume of it was astonishing. I was captivated by the thunderous falls and then an actress dressed as a legendary forest creature danced and sang in front of the waterfall. Another woman appeared in a rock hut and lit a candle and they continued the song. It was an art moment, magical and haunting.

In Bergen we went to Grieg's home where he wrote the music which I grew up loving. "Peer Gynt" was always a favorite and I'd play it on the 78rpm record player we had. I went swimming in Bergen fjord then we boarded a boat to go north through the Sognefjord, one of the most beautiful places in the world, the combination of water, land and sky in perfect balance with each other.

When we'd first boarded our tour bus, the man in front of us was coughing. I'd offered him a homeopathic throat medication but he got worse. By the time we were heading back to Oslo, the whole bus was sick. We caught a flight the next day and were glad we'd made a hotel reservation in Minneapolis for that night. The next day, Mom flew back to Madison and I to L.A.

I made Mom a book with my diary as text and lots of pictures I'd taken. The video was an hour long and caught the woman on tape who was the real Vi Field, fun to be with, curious about the places and people in front of her, energetic and vivacious. I was so relieved that she was making her own way after losing Dad and thankful she took me on the adventure back to a homeland. Our Viking beginnings gave us a strong spine, a love of nature, our bright faces, an acceptance of what is. The Norwegians we met and the lives we glimpsed seemed to have enough. Homes were

Mom with a Norwegian Troll

comfortable but not huge, restaurants weren't gaudy or pricey but warm and good, clothing was comfortable and attractive without demanding attention, values I still embrace.

A recurring dream I had over many years was of a green landscape with farm meadows flowing down to a wide expansive sea. It was a calming dream and having been to Norway, I wondered if it was my subconscious way of touching my beginnings, my DNA, a place that was part of me and always would be.

I was home for a week then flew out to Philadelphia to visit the set of "Animal Factory", a film based on Eddie Bunker's book. Eddie had been there from the first day as a technical advisor and played a small part. Steve Buscemi was the director, Willem Dafoe played the Eddie role, Edward Furlong, the "fish", a young man incarcerated before his time and easy game for any perverted con. The flight in was a nightmare caused by summer storms and we were diverted to JFK, then back in to Philly at 3am. My seat mate was a nice local woman who worked for Campbell Soups and she drove me in to my hotel near Rittenhouse Square.

Eddie was bored stiff and complained the whole time I was there. I didn't blame him as there really wasn't much to do and how fun was it for him to be back in a prison. The only set was an ancient prison, now closed, the Eastern State Penitentiary, a wagon-wheeled shaped building that once held Al Capone. The upside was that he had a few friends, Danny Trejo and Mark Boone, who were in the cast and who had apartments near his.

Buscemi took a very low key approach to the story, keeping it real and the resulting film was good, not necessarily in Hollywood terms which goes more for "Shawshank Redemption" or "The Longest Yard". Eddie wrote about what he knew, the day-to-day life of serving time, the boredom, the cruelty, the bad food, the threats, when to stand down and when to never back down. He could be very hyper and one day, I asked if he would be interested in learning to meditate. He said, "Jeanne, I spent three years in the hole. What do you think?"

It was this deep understanding of his own nature that brought Bill Styron to him when he was suffering from depression. Eddie was one of the few people he would talk to about his darkness. Eddie was very impressive that way, how he affected men. They knew what Eddie had been through, that he had done real hard time and had come out of it an artist. Michael Mann hired him as a technical advisor on "Heat" and he served in that capacity on Jeff Bridges' movie "American Heart". He had read every notable book ever written, all of it done in prison. He met the infamous "Red Light Bandit", Caryl Chessman who talked to him about writing the stories only men like them know. Eddie was in prison when Chessman was a victim of the Iron Lady, the San Quentin gas chamber, a call from the judge coming seconds too late.

I optioned Eddie's books several times and continue to do so. Everything he wrote came from his life. "Little Boy Blue" told of the spiral into crime of a ten-year-old boy, Alex, whose mother abandoned him to a drunken father who placed him in a state home. "Dog Eat Dog" was based on a true story of three criminals Eddie knew. Twenty-two years after Eddie brought me that manuscript, the movie was made with Paul Schrader directing, Nic Cage and Willem Dafoe, starring. "Education of a Felon" also entitled "Mr. Blue" was his memoir. Eddie had played Mr. Blue in Quentin Tarantino's first knock out film, "Reservoir Dogs".

Windfall Management continued to thrive with my clients getting their projects optioned and some even got made. John Binder, Maryedith Burrell, Stephanie Waxman, Randall Sullivan, David Schneider, Leon Martell, Mark Waxman, Terry Frei, Robit Hairman, Beaty Reynolds, Tony Abatemarco, Billy Field, Benjie Aerenson, Elizabeth Whitehead, Barry Michlin, Judy Howard, Rance Howard, Kathrine Bates, Dave Pomes, Clark Carlton, Tom Huckabee, Audrey Lewis, all very creative people, dedicated to exploring how to bring a great story to the screen or stage.

The Binder family grew by a new generation. In mid-September, 1999, Kathryn Binder was born to Josh and Patti. They'd been together for ten years having met while both were working as paramedics. They were in their mid-thirties, had sampled L.A. life and the time came to start the family. Laura Rose followed thirteen months later. Three years later, John Henry and Stephanie, an elementary school teacher from Providence, Rhode Island, brought Sophia into the world, then Gianna. Four granddaughters to carry on the Binder name and spirit. All were healthy and beautiful girls, each one with her own discoveries, sports, ballet, art, music, good friends, the world as described by their teachers at Ocean Charter School. And now, both of Josh's girls are enrolled at Palisades High which their father and John Henry attended.

Top Row: Alex, Charles, John, Gianna, Stephanie, Patti
Middle: Jeanne, Kathryn, Mary; Laura, Sophia,
Front: Josh, John Henry, Waylon & Amy

Thanksgiving celebrations were the time we all gathered and the table was sometimes set for twenty people, extended family and friends. I'd roast a twenty-two pound turkey and barbeque some pork or turkey legs and all the sides were covered. John led off with a greeting and grace and you could always count on one of the boys to chime in. The girls and their cousins would move in a flock, hiding away to gossip and giggle, the dogs lay under the table waiting for scraps, the rest of us traded stories, jokes, recent events in our lives. Football games blared from the TV and either John Henry would be yelling at his Cowboys, the Reynolds boys for the Steelers or I'd be cheering for my Green Bay Packers.

Mom would join us until it was too tough to travel. Hers was a slow slide into the small life centered around her house. We hired some help, a woman who would arrive in the morning to drive her to the library, grocery store, hairdresser. Her food consumption dwindled to Boost, soup and sandwiches and ready-made entrees from the deli section. I went out to visit frequently, especially when she broke an ankle on the basement stairs then followed that with a somewhat debilitating stroke. A short stay at a nursing facility made her more determined than ever to die at home. And, that's what she did, due to an abdominal aortic aneurysm.

We had learned that it was there, threatening, but both of the procedures that could fix it were too invasive. Six weeks after that discovery, she got up on April 4th, spit up something in the sink, went into the sunroom with the Wisconsin State Journal crossword puzzle and drifted away, the blood seeping into her body cavity. She didn't have a helper that day; the woman arrived the next morning and there was no answer at the door. Charles was called and came running and could see her through the windows, lying on the couch, peacefully contemplating the next word in the great crossword puzzle in the sky. She was eighty-nine and had lived her life in service to us, her family. Once Charles and I were out of the house, she looked out for herself and told Dad a thing or two which always made him laugh and call her sweetheart.

So, now I was an orphan, an old one, among the last lines of defense. With this came the responsibility of settling the family affairs, selling the Field Family home. America was skidding to a halt and in a few months, was in the greatest recession since the Crash of '29. Thanks, Bush and Cheney for all the good decisions that led us into a war no one would ever win. 9/11 eviscerated everyone's psyche and we haven't been the same since. During my lifetime, there's been World War II, Korea, the Cold War, Vietnam, and lots of undeclared Police Actions that kept the Defense Department Number One on the Budget Hit Parade. I still don't have a real answer why people have to make war on each other rather than choose to live in peace. Domination on a personal, societal, political level is temporary and so much is lost in its application.

As I grow old, I've learned to take it moment by moment. I have a few mottos: "A girl's best friend is her wheels." "Nothink" and "SNAFU but don't let it ruin your day" Corruption seems to be at every level of our lives; people lie about their accomplishments, aggrandize their opinions, polarize the political landscape. I always loved John Lennon's line: "Life is what happens when you're making other plans." I have also believed, truly, that everyone is just doing the best they can. We all fail and succeed a lot and every failure is just a nanosecond away from being a success and probably teaches us the big lessons. Whoever said, "Follow your bliss" captured it well.

Charles and I took stock of what needed to be done and took the path of least resistance. The house was going to be sold and that was going to be emotionally wrenching. The housing market was beginning to weaken and we needed to polish the house up after fifty-five years of our habitation. I went back to Madison for several weeks. We worked with a good crew and tore out all the carpeting which revealed the beautiful old oak floors. The house had been built in the early '30s by a contractor for himself so the attention to details was there in the construction of the walls, moldings, windows, etc. After a good sanding, the floors were a golden oak color and a fresh coat of paint brightened the house considerably. It still took months to sell and we got several hundred thousand dollars less than if we had sold it in the early 2000s. So be it. Mom and Dad had left us in good shape and we were both thankful.

While I was away, John decided to go cold turkey on getting high. No more white wine or tequila shots and beer. Good-bye marijuana. A few years later, I followed the same path. I never thought I'd give up pot, but there I was, stone sober. John's excuse was that he'd perfected it and I think I had too. One thing I gained was a long evening. Rather than crashing at 9:30pm, I now stayed awake for hours more, reading in bed before sleep.

Both John and I have film projects we'd love to see done. We worked very hard on several and one got close. Maybe one day they'll catch the attention of a young filmmaker and our dream will come true. Meanwhile, we made several short films because no one said we couldn't. They were real life situations with good dialogue, actors who really deliver and simple cinematography. John Henry and Alex worked on them and so did Susan Krebs, Charlotte Stewart and Rance Howard. They got a distribution deal with Direct TV so they're out in the world. Look for them: "New Listing", "Where's My Sandwich?" and "Fatal Femme".

Hiking our Mandeville trails is a morning ritual several times a week. Being part of the natural life is a touchstone of my well-being, integral to my over-all health and moment-to-moment energy. Waylon loves to be on these walks that we take with friends Bruce Cannon and Nancy Cipes and their dog, Cody. We work out physically, climbing the vertical trails at a good pace, also working out the kinks in business relationships, the knots in family muscles, stretching our understanding of love and life.

For all the hiking I do, it was amazing to me that I could make a really stupid decision on a Good Friday in the early '90s. I was doing the Loop, the 6.5 mile trek that circles the end of Mandeville, with Sam Shepherd, a foundling dog - a shepherd, of course - that we had taken in. I was on dirt Mulholland looking down into what I called Hollyhock Canyon, as it was just over the ridge from the Hollyhock Trail. It appeared very steep at the beginning but then it looked like it would be an easy hike and tempting as I'd never done it before.

We started down the steep grade, came to an almost new motorcycle that had probably been stolen and dumped off the road. I realized then that there was no going back as the climb up would be impossible. On we went. I had thought there would be a path at some point but I was lucky to find deer trails. Then, we came to a cliff that had been obscured by the heavy vegetation. It was about 20 feet down to the next level and I knew I could do it, but could Sam? We had no choice and she was amazing to watch as she picked her way down the rocky wall.

At the bottom of this we found a stream bed and that was a lucky thing because in front of us was nothing but poison oak. We followed the narrow waterway, mucky and smelly, as it took us under the vegetation. No mice, no snakes, no other critters shared our way. At one point, we had to hunker down, crawling along the rocky bottom. I found a beautiful rock, emblazoned with scallop fossils and couldn't leave it behind, so now I was hauling a six pound stone.

Finally, the stream bed opened up on a meadow with trees and grasses and we neared the road. I was covered in mud, twigs in my hair and burrs stuck to my clothes. I was exhausted and, trying to clean myself up, stopped at the first house. A neighbor answered his door and looked at me askance as if I was a homeless scary person. I asked if he could call John to come get me. John wasn't home so he actually drove Sam and me up the hill to the house. I realized that I could have died out there, a half mile from home, and never did another off-trail hike alone. My Good Friday.

On a less adventurous early morning hike, alone on the trail just before the sun rose, I saw two amazing things. A Pacific fogbank had rolled into the canyon and covered everything except for the very tops of the mountain where I was walking. The first image was a white rainbow that slowly evaporated when the sun rose over the hill and caught it. As I was standing on the edge of the trail watching this, I looked down and the sun, low on the horizon threw my shadow onto the top of the fogbank. This too, disappeared slowly as the fog shifted and a cloud covered the sun.

A magical moment like that can only be followed by another one and it happened in the 2008 election. Barack Obama was chosen to be the Leader of the Free World. How many people said, "I never thought I'd see this in my lifetime."? His campaign was ridiculed, "Hope" and "Change" mocked by the opposition. He ran a strong campaign, then learned the hard facts during those early days in the Oval Office, as the Pentagon, CIA, FBI, NSA, Trilateral Commission fed him the reality sandwich of what really happens in the center of the universe. Congressional leaders vowed to make him a one-term president. He fooled 'em, though, and continued to create a legacy that could go down as one of the greatest in modern times.

Like many people, I read the obituary pages in the newspaper, and lately it's apparent that most of the people in them are my age. I had a dream once where a man was saying to me, "It will be nothing. You'll close your eyes and go to sleep. You just won't wake up." I shot out of that dream and woke up. No, I thought, I don't want to do that. I don't want to leave this planet, although it's inevitable. When I hear or read about suicides I can't fathom that either. I honestly think that we learn something really important while we die a natural death and won't even speculate on what it may be. Perhaps it's because my Dad said "It's delightful", an hour before he died, having endured the pain and suffering of his body shutting down. Maybe it's my eternal optimism, my lucky star. Right now I feel like I could live for years more and hope I do as long as I can do it on my own.

Larry died a few hours after I talked to him on the phone. It had been raining like mad that winter, January, 2010, and Larry

Larry on the Gabrielle

loved weather, so we compared storm systems, San Francisco Bay area, where he lived, to Los Angeles. His weight had become a problem and at sixty-two, was not something to ignore. He was at an In-an-Out Burger and he was working too hard, on Neil's project, an electric car video, "Linc-Volt", on a re-edit of "Human Highway" and others. But he was funny and catching his lunch on the run. The last thing he said to me was, "Gotta go, my sandwich is here."

A few hours later, he was running around the parking lot of the marina where his boat, the Gabrielle, was moored, offering tickets to the Sharks hockey game. Mission accomplished, he jumped into Ben Young's van and died in the driver's seat. I learned a few years later that he'd had a terrible tooth ache, or maybe he had a heart attack that transferred the pain to his jaw, in November and hadn't seen anyone about it. I would never get over it. Was he afraid to hear the truth, afraid to change his lifestyle so he could relax, lose weight and enjoy his kids? Once again, he was the Master of the Fast Exit.

From that and all that has been written here, I have learned to not be directed by fear. It is my default position anyhow but I know I have to stand up, face it, get a base line, do what I have to do. When I talk like this, John calls me "Feeny Jield", the tough little girl who grew into a woman and continues to grow. End of story.

"All personal suffering stems from overlooking the truth
Of who you are in favor of the story of who you are.
You are not just a character in a story.
You are the totality of being."

Post Script

As we float into the universe and think back on the real and unreal, the big decisions of what kind of person you want to be, a few things come clear. Are you motivated by money, to be wealthy and live in the best section of town? Or, be revered as a person of character? What is it that defines who you are? Do you need a 9 to 5 job at a company that will employ you for a lifetime or can you be loose, independent, confident the right thing will come your way or even the wrong thing, but it doesn't matter because it's all temporary.

And what of that ghostly presence you felt, the stories of Roswell and conspiracies that government officials whisper on their death beds. What did you think when you saw "The Manchurian Candidate" and did you wonder if Lee Harvey Oswald, Sirhan Sirhan, James Earl Ray acted alone? As a child you were told to believe that Jesus rose from the dead and ascended into heaven to sit on the right hand of God the Father. We can choose to accept that there are no answers and go on faith or you can demand that there be hard and fast evidence.

One Sunday, years ago, I was working in the garden, puttering around and I smoked a small roach. About 1pm, I grew very tired and went into the bedroom to lie down. A voice inside my head said, no, go into the living room. I crashed on the couch and went into a dream that was vivid and real beyond belief. I was being kidnapped by aliens, taken aboard a spaceship and measured, probed, investigated while I lay helpless on a table surrounded by creatures. Once they had what they needed, I was dropped off and had to make my way, Ulysses-like, back home, tested at every turn, walking along paths that were precarious on steep mountainsides. The last thing I remembered, I was a human Caduceus, my body wrapped with two snakes whose heads were next to mine, their eyes penetrating mine. I heard the call of hawks and looked up and they swooped down, took hold of my hands and pulled me up and out of my dream. In reality, hawks were calling outside the front window as they swooped over the house and down the canyon.

The sun had set and John walked into the living room. He was worried, as I'd been lying there for hours. I felt like he only saw part of it - my body was there, but I wasn't. Did I believe that I'd been abducted? Does it really matter? I had a remarkable journey, into the abyss or heaven, into my sub-conscious or alternate reality, it was fraught with symbolism and would keep me wondering for the rest of my life.

"Remembrances take on a luminosity from their repetition in your mind year after year, and in their combinations...and as you work them out and understand them to a greater and greater degree...so that what you remember as having happened and what truly did happen are no less and no more than...visions."

E.L. Doctorow - "The Waterworks"

Photo Credits

Cover - Jeanne - Larry Johnson, May, 1971
p. 4 - Look Magazine, 1966, Thomas R. Koeniges
p. 11 - Curt, etc - Betsy Chase, 1967
p. 19 - Peter/JF- Tim Carter, 1967
p. 22 - Maroon Bells - Jeanne F.
p. 30 - Reefer Services - Jeanne F.
p. 42 - Hotel Balconies - Jeanne F.
p. 56 - LA - Jeanne F, 1969
p. 61 - JF/woodstock - © 1969 bzlevine@WoodstockWitness.com
p. 68 - LA & Jeanne on the beach
p. 70 - David Crosby, etc. - Jeanne F. 1970
p. 72 - LA/Myers - Jeanne F.
p. 73 - Fred & Gary - Jeanne F.
p. 80 - Sharon, Josh, John Henry
p. 87 - Oscar night - © Joel Bernstein
p. 90 - Marjoe shoot - Jeanne F
p. 93 - Marty Andrews- Jeanne F.
p. 94 - Cambridge - Larry Johnson
p. 96 - Liquid butterfly - © Julian Wasser
p. 97 - Harvest - Jeanne F.
p. 98 - JF/Tas/ranch - Larry Johnson
P. 102 - El Corte de Madeira Creek - Jeanne F.
p. 105 - Carrie & neil - Jeanne F.
p. 106 - Neil plays horseshoes - Jeanne F.
p. 111 - Dad's family -
p. 113 - Mom - Jeanne F.
p. 115 - Charles/shack - Jeanne F.
p. 116 - Dad/hospital - Jeanne F.
p. 120 - Maz, Mulligan, Christiani - Jeanne F.
p. 129 - L.A., JF, Johanna
p. 131 - Ranch group photo - David Myers, 1972
p. 134 - Lamp Light - Jeanne F.
p. 145 - Bob & Carl/Topanga - Jeanne F.
p. 153 - Fire - Jeanne F.
p. 155 -- Restaurant poloroids - Charlotte Stewart; Jeanne F.
p. 156 - Thanksgiving - Topanga - Jeanne F.
p. 161 - Carl - Jeanne F.
p. 164 - Flower in the Crannied Wall - Jeanne F.
p. 169 - Skating - Tim Nelson family
p. 174 - Lake Mendota - Jeanne F.
p. 177 - Hollyridge - Jeanne F.
p. 178 - Big bus Set - Jim Frawley

326

CPSIA information can be obtained
at www.ICGtesting.com
Printed in the USA
BVOW07s2104010816

457561BV00012BA/100/P